VIOLENCE AND VENGEANCE

Violence and Vengeance

*Religious Conflict and Its Aftermath
in Eastern Indonesia*

Christopher R. Duncan

Cornell University Press
Ithaca and London

Cornell University Press gratefully acknowledges receipt of a grant from the Faculty of Religious Studies in the School of Historical, Philosophical and Religious Studies at Arizona State University which aided in the publication of this book.

First published 2013 by Cornell University Press
First printing, Cornell Paperbacks, 2013

Printed in the United States of America

Library of Congress Cataloging-in-Publication Data

Duncan, Christopher R., author.
    Violence and vengeance : religious conflict and its aftermath in eastern Indonesia / Christopher R. Duncan.
        pages cm
    Includes bibliographical references and index.
    ISBN 978-0-8014-5158-4 (cloth : alk. paper)—
    ISBN 978-0-8014-7913-7 (pbk. : alk. paper)
    1. Maluku (Indonesia)—Religion.   2. Violence—Indonesia—
Maluku.   3. Social conflict—Indonesia—Maluku.   4. Conflict management—Indonesia—Maluku.   5. Islam—Relations—
Christianity.   6. Christianity and other religions—Islam.   I. Title.
    BL2120.M35D86 2013
    200.9598'5—dc23
                                                            2013010587

Cornell University Press strives to use environmentally responsible suppliers and materials to the fullest extent possible in the publishing of its books. Such materials include vegetable-based, low-VOC inks and acid-free papers that are recycled, totally chlorine-free, or partly composed of nonwood fibers. For further information, visit our website at www.cornellpress.cornell.edu.

Cloth printing   10   9   8   7   6   5   4   3   2   1
Paperback printing   10   9   8   7   6   5   4   3   2   1

CONTENTS

Illustrations

Maps

Photographs

ACKNOWLEDGMENTS

This book draws on several periods of fieldwork spanning 2001–12, so there are numerous organizations and people to thank. Financial support for this research has come from several sources. The Royal Anthropological Institute and the Anthropologists' Fund for Urgent Anthropological Research in conjunction with Goldsmiths College, University of London, funded eighteen months of fieldwork in 2001–2 with an RAI Fellowship in Urgent Anthropology. George Appell, the magnanimous founder of the Urgent Anthropology Fellowship, was very understanding when the outbreak of violence in North Maluku forced me to adjust my research topic away from tropical rain-forest hunter-gatherers. I thank him for his understanding and for helping me pursue an entirely different sort of Urgent Anthropology. I prepared for the 2001–2 fieldwork while I was a Luce Postdoctoral Fellow at the Australian National University (ANU) in 2000–1. ANU is a wonderful place to be if you work on Southeast Asia or the Pacific, and I thank Greg Fealy, Jim Fox, Ben Kerkvliet, Alan Rumsey, Kathryn Robinson, Philipus Tule, and Nicholas Tapp for their intellectual support and hospitality. My visits to North Maluku in 2004 and extended fieldwork in 2005 were funded by a Research and Writing Grant from the John T. and Catherine C. McArthur Foundation that I shared with Pamela McElwee. During this period I was affiliated with the Agrarian Studies Program at Yale University. I thank Kay Marvel Mansfield and James Scott for arranging this affiliation despite my absence from New Haven. Gerry van Klinken from the Royal Netherlands Institute of Southeast Asian and Caribbean Studies (Koninklijk Instituut voor Taal-, Land- en Volkenkunde, KITLV) graciously invited me to spend a semester in Leiden in the fall of 2008 to work on the manuscript as part of the KITLV research project *In Search of Middle Indonesia*. Gerry, along with Henk Schulte Nordholt, Fridus Steijlen, and the rest of the faculty and staff at KITLV were excellent hosts and provided a stimulating intellectual environment in which to think about all things Indonesian. During that semester I had the good fortune to share an office with several luminaries in the world of Southeast Asian studies, including Lene Pederson, Ed Aspinall, Oscar Salemink, and Meredith Weiss. At Arizona State University, a number of units have provided funding. A small grant from the Guillot Endowment in the School of Global Studies enabled a research visit in 2010. An A. T. Steele Travel Grant from the Center for Asian Research funded a trip in October 2012. Finally, the Faculty of Religious Studies provided support for a visit in April 2012, as well as a subvention for this publication.

While in Indonesia, my research has been sponsored, both officially and unofficially, by Universitas Sam Ratulangi in Manado, Universitas Khairun in Ternate, Polyteknik Perdamaian Halmahera in Tobelo, and (for reasons that still remain unclear to me) Universitas Islam Kalimantan in Banjarmasin. I am grateful to all of these organizations for their assistance. In addition to these local sponsors, the Indonesian Institute of Sciences (LIPI) helped process my never-ending requests for research permission, and I thank them for their patience, particularly Aswatini Raharto.

In North Maluku there are far too many people to thank by name, and I know I will anger some by not mentioning them, but I will do my best. My "older brother," the late Fence Boroni, known to friends as Om Ben, accompanied me throughout North Sulawesi and North Maluku over the last decade, helping with interviews and introducing me to a seemingly unending stream of people, almost all of whom he seemed to know. Om Ben, along with his wife, Tante Sin, and their two sons, Acel and Viktor, proved to be gracious and understanding hosts on numerous occasions. Om Ben passed away in November 2009 before this project was completed, but I already know that he would have criticized me for not having at least an entire chapter devoted to his home island of Morotai. I apologize for that lacuna.

In addition to Fence Boroni, I worked with several other research assistants during the course of this fieldwork. Their contributions are much appreciated. Freddy Salama from Dokulamo in Galela gathered accounts of the violence in Galela. Sabir Maidin from the National Islamic Theological School (STAIN, Sekolah Tinggi Agama Islam Negrei) in Manado conducted interviews among Muslim IDPs in Ternate. Muhammad Uhaib As'ad, a professor from Universitas Islam Kalimantan in Banjarmasin, conducted a wide range of interviews across the province. Rizki Farani helped with transcribing some of these interviews in Tempe.

In Tobelo, Jesaya Banari has always taken great interest in my work since we first met in 2001. I am grateful for his friendship and inexhaustible eagerness to help me learn more about Tobelo culture. Ci Mei and Ko Seng have been good friends, always quick to provide assistance, good food, and even better conversation over the course of the last decade. Ci Mei graciously let me use two of her photos in this book as well. The current bupati of North Halmahera, Hein Nemotemo, and his wife, Joice Duan, have been good friends since I began this research. Without Pak Hein's help in obtaining the proper letters, I would have had far more difficulty doing my research in North Maluku in 2001–2. Ever since I first met Lence Soselisa, who was lost with the sinking of the *Cahaya Bahari* in July 2000, the Soselisa family of Ambon and Tobelo has assisted with my research in eastern Indonesia. Whether it was providing me with some of my first Tobelo word lists in 1995, or helping take care of my *anak angkat* in the 2000s, the Soselisa family, particularly the late Ibu Soselisa and her son Pak Jopy, have in many ways become my surrogate family in Tobelo. They are much appreciated. Ruddy Tindage has been a fountain of information on conflict and reconciliation in North Maluku, as well as on the dynamics of church politics in the region, and always ready to help. Other people I thank in Halmahera include Samsul Bahri, Benny Doro, John Pattiasina, Theo Sosebeko, Pak Safrono, Pak Prakas, Seth Name and his family, Pak Mardi from Markati, and Hersen and Ventje Tinangon from Pediwang. I also am grateful to the people of the Modole village of Soamaetek who, since 1994, have been wonderful hosts each time I visit, in particular Jefta Sengo and his family.

In Ternate, Lili Ishak and Pak Suratman at Universitas Khairun and Agus Salim Bujang at Universitas Muhammidiyah Maluku Utara provided help in obtaining various documents and paperwork for my research. During part of my fieldwork in Manado, Jennifer Munger, Patricia Spyer, Rafael Sanchez, and Susie Cassels were also in town doing fieldwork on other topics. Conversations with them were insightful and helped guide my research. Once again Keith and Anita Miles and Bob and Debbie Clark, in Manado due to the violence on Halmahera, provided food, friendship, as well as the benefit of Keith's inexhaustible knowledge of Halmahera.

In Jakarta, Philip, Tinuk, and Arief Yampolsky were kind enough to house and feed me the many times I passed through that city in 2001–2 to arrange permits. However, I would be remiss if I failed to note that they did not fix the electrical short in the shower, which threatened to electrocute me on numerous occasions, until an anthropologist with far more prestige stayed with them and noted the same problem! I am grateful to Federico Visioli who has always been a gracious host and good friend in Jakarta over the last decade.

Despite the never-ending reorganization of the university, colleagues at ASU have provided a supportive intellectual environment that allowed me to pursue this project to its completion. The Faculty of Religious Studies, the Center for Asian Research, the Council for Southeast Asian Studies, the Center for the Study of Religion and Conflict, and the Faculty of Global Studies provided opportunities for me to develop my thinking in one way or another on the complicated issues I explore in this book. Linell Cady, John Carlson, Anne Feldhaus, Abdullahi Gallab, Joel Gereboff, Chad Haines, Alexander Henn, Chris Lundry, James Rush, Yasmin Saikia, Juliane Schober, Shahla Talebi, and Mark Woodward all helped me develop my arguments and thinking over the last six years.

I have presented papers that became part of this book at Goldsmiths College, the Australian National University, KITLV, Sekolah Tinggi Agama Islam Manado, the GMIH Theological Seminary in Tobelo, Universitas Udayana in Bali, Cornell University, Yale University, Arizona State University, the University of Hawaii, the Asian Studies Association, the American Anthropological Association, the European Association of Social Anthropologists, and the Society for the Anthropology of Religion. I thank all those who invited me to present my work and who provided comments and criticisms at these talks. Numerous people knowingly or unknowingly read parts of this manuscript and offered their comments: Lorraine Aragon, Linell Cady, Nils Bubandt, Richard Fox, James Hagen, Gerry van Klinken, Lene Pedersen, James Rush, Juliane Schober, Henk Schulte Nordholt, Shahla Talebi, Mark Woodward, and a host of anonymous reviewers.

Parts of this book have been published in earlier forms as articles in *Bijdragen tot de Taal-, Land- en Volkenkunde* and *Indonesia*. I thank the editors of those journals for their permission to use revised versions of that material here. At Cornell University Press, Roger Haydon shepherded the book manuscript through the review process, and I am thankful for his patience and support. I also thank the two anonymous reviewers for their input on how to improve an earlier version. Jack Rummel did the copyediting and Dave Prout helped with the index.

Friends and family have played a great part in the completion of this project. Rebecca Hardin, Bonnie Adrian, and Denise Brennan have offered constant encouragement and support over the years as the book slowly made its way to the surface. Beatrix Marengko has been a constant source of moral support and inspiration for this book. Although initially reluctant to talk about her own experiences during the violence, and rather dismayed by my apparent obsession with the conflict and its aftermath, she eventually came to help in innumerable ways with my research and has made subsequent visits to Indonesia fruitful. Yeni Takasengserang, my *anak angkat* in Tobelo, whom I met in the first months of research, has made the entire project worthwhile if due only to her own academic success. As one insightful friend in Tobelo pointed out on my last visit, Yeni was able to graduate from junior high, high school, and basically complete her college degree in the same amount of time it took me to finish this book.

My family has been a continuous source of support over the years. My grandparents, Richard Phillips and the late Vera Jean Phillips inculcated in me a desire to travel and see the world from a young age and have always been supportive. My parents, Robert and Susan Duncan, have helped in innumerable ways and always been there with words of encouragement. I am grateful for all they have done.

Finally, my wife, Pamela McElwee, has been my closest friend and staunchest supporter over the years. Although she has never been to North Maluku, Pam has been with me since this project began. She has long tolerated my passion for fieldwork and my frequent absences as I returned once again to Halmahera. From Washington, DC, to New Cross, London, from Hanoi to Tempe, she has always been there and been a source of encouragement. If my scholarship can even approach her level of brilliance, then I have succeeded.

ABBREVIATIONS

DPRD	Provincial/District/City People's Representative Council (Dewan Perwakilan Rakyat Daerah)
FKASWJ	Communication Forum for the Followers of the Sunnah and the Community of the Prophet (Forum Kommunikasi Ahlus Sunnah wal Jama'ah)
GMIH	Evangelical Church of Halmahera (Gereja Masehi Injili Halmahera)
GPM	Protestant Church of Maluku (Gereja Protestan Maluku)
IDP	internally displaced persons
IPOT	Imam's Deliberative Council District (Imam Permoesy-awaratan Onderafdeling)
Ind.	Indonesian
KGBI	The Convention of Baptist Churches in Indonesia (Kerapatan Gereja Baptis Indonesia)
NGO	nongovernmental organization
NHM	Nusa Halmahera Mineral Mining Corporation

NMM   North Moluccan Malay
PPP   United Development Party (Partai Persatuan Pembangunan)
RMS   Republic of South Maluku (Republik Maluku Selatan)
SARA   Tribe, Religion, Race, and Class (Suku, Agama, Ras, dan
          Antar-Golongan)
UZV   Utrecht Missionary Society (Utrechtsche Zendings
          Vereeniging)
VCD   video compact disc
VOC   Dutch East India Company (Vereenigde Oostindische
          Compagnie)

A Note on Translation and Pseudonyms

All translations from Indonesian, North Moluccan Malay, and Tobelo are my own unless otherwise indicated. Indonesian terms in the text are labeled (Ind.), and terms from North Moluccan Malay are labeled (NMM). Terms from other languages, such as Dutch, Tobelo, or Galela, are labeled as such.

I have used pseudonyms for all individuals in the text other than when quoting prominent public figures about issues unrelated to specific instances of violence. In the few instances when I have quoted published reports or media pieces I have left in the published names, unless otherwise indicated. Some of my friends and informants specifically asked me to use their real names in text, but I have refused in order to err on the side of caution should anyone read the book and take issue with a quotation or a story. I realize this will anger some (and I know it has seriously annoyed one person already), and I apologize in advance. Most likely they will be able to recognize themselves in the text, but others will not. I have not changed place names, but in specific instances I have left them out if someone made a reference to a particular instance that could identify them or their actions. None of these omissions of names or place names are of consequence to the arguments based on those particular cases.

VIOLENCE AND VENGEANCE

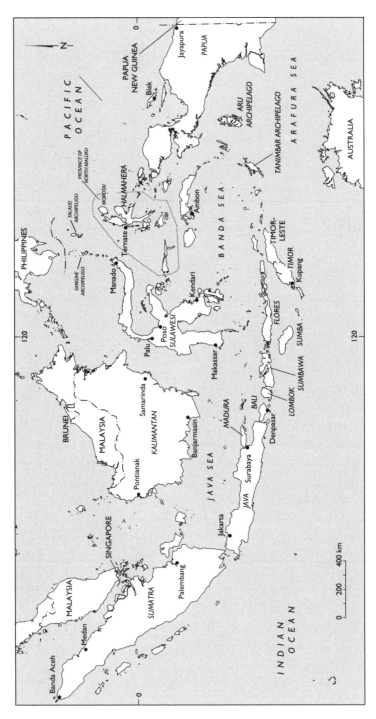

Map 1. Indonesia

Chapter 1

RELIGIOUS VIOLENCE?

In May 2002, I attended another in a long series of meetings about forced migrants in the Indonesian city of Manado. This particular gathering had been arranged by an international NGO to lessen tensions between displaced youth and locals. The hotel conference room was filled with dozens of young Christian men and women who had lived in crowded displacement camps since fleeing the 1999–2000 communal violence in the eastern Indonesian province of North Maluku. A small group of young adults from Manado had also been invited. After explaining the purpose of the meeting, the moderator asked if anyone had any questions. A young Muslim man from Manado promptly stood up and started to deliver a speech that the forced migrants in the room had heard many times before. He began: "As a Muslim, I would like to start by pointing out that Islam does not preach violence. Religions don't preach hate. Islam, like all religions, is a religion of peace and love. The conflict in Maluku is not a religious problem. It is—" Before he could finish a young woman from the island of Halmahera jumped to her feet and interrupted him: "Just sit down! That is nonsense!

You say Islam does not teach hate, but it was Muslims who invaded my village. It was Muslims who wanted to kill me because I was Christian. It was Muslims who chased us through the forest. Don't say Islam does not preach hate. I have tasted it!" (*Kita su rasa*, NMM). Marline, the young woman in question, had fled her home in the provincial capital of Ternate when Muslim rioters expelled that island's Christian population in November 1999. Muslim friends smuggled her back to her natal village on the neighboring island of Halmahera where several days later her family and their Christian neighbors fled into the forest to escape a large Muslim attack on their village. Over the next several weeks her family was hunted through the forest by Muslim militias. Once they emerged on the other side of the island, they were forced to flee from one coastal village to the next, always one step ahead of Muslim militia. They finally made a stand at a village named Fida in southern Halmahera. Marline stood behind the barricades with the women and young girls and sang Christian hymns while the men and teenage boys successfully fought off their attackers. Marline and her immediate family eventually made it to safety in North Sulawesi where they moved into a camp for forced migrants. Over the course of the next eight months of violence, however, fifty-two members of her extended family were killed and many others were displaced from their homes.

Thousands of North Moluccans, both Christian and Muslim, have stories similar to Marline's. They were chased from their homes as attackers shouted "God is great" (*Allahu Akbar*), "Praise the Lord" (*Puji Tuhan*, Ind.), or sang "Onward Christian Soldiers" ("Maju Laskar Kristus," Ind.). Others were in these militias, deciding who they should attack or kill based largely on religious identity. Despite the multiple political, economic, and cultural factors involved, to those caught up in the violence, to those that did the killing and dying, this became a conflict focused primarily on religious differences. Although it started as a dispute between ethnic groups over a redistricting initiative, for the vast majority of people involved, regardless of their motivations, the eventual dividing line in this conflict became and remained religion (*agama*, Ind.). People were not interested in the politics of their victims. Being a member of a one political party or another was irrelevant; not being able to recite the Lord's Prayer on command could be a death sentence.

Despite the importance that participants placed on religion and religious identity in the conflict, outside observers, such as academics, journalists, and NGO workers, have quickly dismissed the religious framing of the violence.[1]

Like the young man shouted down by Marline, they argue the violence was not about religion. They have turned to rather sophisticated, instrumentalist explanations of the conflict and looked at the political and economic issues at stake. Most academics are quick to argue that religion was simply a tool that the North Moluccan elite instrumentalized to achieve political and economic aims. They argue that the religious factor was introduced into the conflict through the manipulation of religious symbols, or carefully placed rumors that manufactured religious-based fears and played on local insecurities. Local communities only perceived this conflict as one about religion because that was the fault line instigators had chosen to utilize. Some argued that the violence was about the aspirations of middle-class civil servants (Klinken 2007a), while the more conspiracy minded saw nefarious efforts by remnants of the recently deposed military dictatorship of General Suharto to sabotage the transition to democracy (Aditjondro 2001; Tomagola 2006). Even those who recognize the religious nature of the violence (Sidel 2006) view religion as a stand-in for larger political and economic interests and ignore other ways that religion influenced people's actions.

In contrast, the people I interviewed who took part in the violence were not interested in issues of political decentralization, democratization, or the rising political ambitions of one group or another. You could try to explain the violence to Marline in political or economic terms, pointing out how the conflict was not "really" about religion. In contrast, she would argue that political and economic issues were actually just camouflage for the true religious goals of the violence, the destruction of a particular religious community. In what follows I explore how North Moluccans experienced the violence as a religious conflict and continue to remember it that way into the present. Whether it is in their narratives of the violence or the way they commemorated it, the focus on religious fault lines overwhelmed, or at least overshadowed, other understandings of the 1999–2000 conflict.[2]

I am not arguing that economic, political, or other differences did not influence the violence or people's decisions to take part. They clearly did, and we can find a wide variety of reasons why different individuals chose to participate, ranging from politics to economics, from settling old quarrels to impressing the neighborhood girls. This multitude of rationales should come as no surprise. However, regardless of the motivating factors for their participation, the violence remained focused on religious differences. Those enacting violence in the name of revenge killed the religious other. Those taking part as thrill seekers, or in an effort to prove their masculinity, killed the religious other. In the aftermath of the conflict, this religious narrative solidified, while the polysemic nature of the violence faded. The way people talked about the conflict in the decade after its conclusion, how they commemorated the violence, and how they structured postconflict interfaith relations all point to the solidification of the view that the violence was about religion. Admittedly there are outliers to this position, as should be evident as my argument develops. The 1999–2000 conflict began as one between indigenous people and migrants over a redistricting issue. Some indigenous communities involved in that initial outbreak of the violence have sought to maintain that narrative of the conflict even as they took part in violence based on religious difference, but as I will show, the nature of violence changed significantly once the focus shifted from ethnicity and land to religious differences. Another exception is the regional elite. They have gone to great lengths, at least in public, to argue that the violence was not about religion but was the work of outside provocateurs or a small number of individuals exploiting the chaos.

Arguments that the violence had nothing to do with religion make the same mistake that decades of theorization about the category of religion have sought to overcome (Asad 1983; Lincoln 2006); they place religion in a distinct sphere of social activity, marking it as something separate and distinct from politics and other aspects of culture and society.[3] Others commit the error of postulating that while something called "religion" can never be an autonomous sphere of social interaction (if indeed it exists at all), something called politics always is (Strenski 2010). The challenge is to explain the role of religion in the violence (which can include beliefs, identities, social networks, material culture, the use of particular texts or imagery), without essentializing it, while at the same time appreciating that local communities were involved in this very process of essentialization. We need to move beyond the tendency to simply dismiss religion as a tool of manipulation. We should, as Peter van der Veer (1994, ix) suggests, "take religious discourse and practice as constitutive of changing social identities, rather than treating them as ideological smoke screens that hide the real clash of material interests and social classes."

Along these lines I find Bruce Lincoln's (2006: 1-18) model of religion helpful in thinking about how religion functioned in the conflict in North Maluku. In response to Talal Asad's (1983) critique of anthropological

conceptions of religion, Lincoln (2006: 1-18) puts forth what he calls a definition of religion, but what may be more appropriately seen as a Weberian
ideal type. He argues that any attempt to define religion must attend to four
domains of varying significance:

> A *discourse* whose concerns transcend the human, temporal, and contingent
> and that claims for itself a similarly transcendent status. . . .
>
> A set of *practices* whose goal is to produce a proper world and/or proper
> human subjects, as defined by a religious discourse to which these practices
> are connected. . . .
>
> A *community* whose members construct their identity with reference to a
> religious discourse and its attendant practices. . . .
>
> An *institution* that regulates religious discourse, practices, and commu-
> nity, reproducing them over time and modifying them as necessary, while
> asserting their eternal validity and transcendent value. (Lincoln 2006, 5–7,
> emphasis added)

Lincoln argues that these four domains are present to one degree or another
in anything we could arguably call a religion. Although some have faulted
this model (Fitzgerald 2006), I find this way of thinking about religion helpful in exploring how North Moluccans conceive of the violence as religious
by looking at how they called on these four domains.

Lincoln's model of religion allows me to take into consideration some of
the concerns expressed by my colleagues whose interests lie in politics and
social movements, by paying heed to identity politics (Lincoln's community)
and religious networks and elites (Lincoln's institutions). It also lets me pay
attention to how religious ideas, symbols, and actions were deployed in the
conflict (Lincoln's discourse and practice), concerns that are too often dismissed or ignored in discussions focused on the political or the sociological.
Thus we can incorporate narratives of divine intervention and performative
acts of violence that call on religious discourse, alongside an analysis of politics in a newly democratizing Indonesia. We can examine why people were
willing to die to protect their places of worship, or to hunt down and kill a
relative who had switched faiths, while also taking into consideration the
economic concerns of different segments of North Moluccan society. This
framework allows me to look at power relations, while also accounting for
the meanings that participants invested in the violence and how those
meanings shaped their actions during and after the conflict.

My discussion of religion in the North Maluku conflict is linked to the particular understanding of "religion" that has developed in Indonesia over the last century.[4] When I say religion, I am referring to the Indonesian term *agama*, which represents a very real category in the lived experience of most Indonesians. Due to a variety of historical and political circumstances that I discuss in the next chapter, religion is a significant aspect of identity in Indonesia.[5] All Indonesians are supposed to affiliate with one of the six religions officially recognized by the government (Islam, Catholicism, Hinduism, Protestantism, Buddhism, and more recently Confucianism). During the regime of Indonesia's second president, General Suharto (1967–98), religion became a required field on national identity cards, which were necessary for voting, registering land, or getting a driver's license. It is a category that Indonesians deal with from an early age; it has been a compulsory subject in school since the 1960s (Kelabora 1976; Mujiburrahman 2006, 227–30). As a result, not having a religion has not been a viable option for most Indonesians. Despite the constructed nature of religion as a category in Indonesia—in this case one constructed by the Indonesian state in reaction to a particular history—it is one that shapes Indonesian's lives and their interactions with their neighbors both political and apolitical (Aritonang 2004; Husein 2005; Mujiburrahman 2006).

The most basic perusal of recent Indonesian history shows that religion and religious identity were highly politicized issues in the last half of the twentieth century under the New Order government of Suharto (Hefner 2000; Bertrand 2004; Husein 2005). This politicization of religion, however, should not remove religious practices and religious discourse from the equation and leave behind only politics for analysis. If we recognize the historical construction of religion as a category in Indonesia and acknowledge the role of power and politics in its construction, we can discuss how people deploy religion in their understandings and discussions of collective violence while at the same time avoiding the charge that we are relying on "the religious version of 'ancient hatreds'" (Bowen 1996, 13n.6). To note that religious identities in Indonesia or elsewhere are constructed, whether through ritual practice or political discourse, does not make those identities any less real for those who lay claim to them. Although there is nothing inherent in ethnic or religious differences that leads to violence, people do call on these differences in the course of conflict and act in their names. Recognizing the former point does not require we ignore the latter. If we want to understand how North Moluccans, or others, made sense of the violence around them we need to pay heed to their identity claims and to the categories and concepts that people actually used.

Moving beyond Causation and Chronology

Most writing on communal violence in Indonesia has focused on two aspects: causation and chronology. The former has been the focus of many political scientists working in Indonesia, some of whom have sought to provide overarching explanations for the numerous outbreaks of violence surrounding the fall of Indonesia's long-reigning military dictator, General Suharto (Bertrand 2004; Sidel 2006; Klinken 2007a). Others have focused on particular instances of communal violence (Davidson 2008; Wilson 2008). In these works, we learn of the machinations of regents, police chiefs, and sultans, or the shifting fortunes of particular politicians or political parties in a changing post-Suharto political landscape. The chronologies often focus on the actions and fates of a few dozen individuals in each conflict. They omit the stories and voices of those individuals most affected by the violence: the internally displaced people (IDPs) who spent weeks in the forest fleeing roving militias, the members of those militias hunting down their neighbors in interior, the individuals from rural villages whose relatives were killed, or who did the killing. The terror, suffering, and exhilaration of these periods are left out, replaced by grand narratives that discuss timelines, causal mechanisms, and the roles of political elites and their parties.

One of my main conclusions is that elite agendas and machinations were not as central to conflicts as many observers would have us think. The political fault lines in provincial towns, so often the subject of political analysis, were not always relevant to people trying to kill each other in the countryside, or to the rural people who came to wage war in urban settings. In her work on Ambon in central Maluku, Patricia Spyer (2002a, 24) has noted that "too little heed is given [in these political accounts] to the work of the imagination and the construction of knowledge in all of this and, specifically, to how these compel and propel particular actions and shape those who carry them out." Building on Spyer's observation, my goal is to shift the emphasis away from the politics of causation and explore how North Moluccans conceived, theorized, and constructed their knowledge of the conflict as they interpreted the events taking place around them. Spyer (2002a, 24) refers to these efforts at interpretation and knowledge creation as "hyper-hermeneutics," which she describes as a "compulsive need to interpret and mine just about everything for hidden meaning, to see any trivial occurrence as a sign or omen of what might come." The interpretive results of these hyper-hermeneutics shape the way people act and the decisions they make during conflicts. Thus rather than focusing on causation, I explore how these (re)interpretations of events, rumors, local histories, narratives, and performative acts of violence influenced how the conflict was lived, produced, contested, and remembered.

Regardless of the original contentious issues that start a conflict, people's reasons for taking part in it, or avoiding it, are based on fears, desires for revenge, possibilities of loot, or a wide variety of other reasons that change over time and space. A focus on high politics removes any meaning in the violence for those who perpetrated it, suffered through it, or in some cases both. For example, Klinken (2007a) argues that the post-Suharto violence in North Maluku and elsewhere in Indonesia was largely the result of struggles among a rising government-employed middle class over limited spoils. Although insightful in many ways and helpful for understanding issues of causation, Klinken does not explain why individuals throughout North Maluku who stood to gain little from these struggles, and were well aware of this, took up arms and attacked their neighbors or their own family members under the banner of religion. In these accounts, North Moluccans appear as the dupes of the elite, unable to interpret for themselves the events taking place around them and easily talked into committing morally reprehensible acts. We need to consider why people were willing to take actions in the name of ethnic or religious solidarity beyond simply linking it to issues of economic and political advantage. As Mamdani (2001, 7–8) has argued for Rwanda, even if instigations from above were pivotal in creating an outbreak of communal violence, that instigation could only succeed if the idea of the violence itself found resonance with the masses. We have to explore the historical and cultural construction of the points of difference that were called on in the violence and how those particular points of difference affected events. Explanations of the conflict should include the perspectives of those who did the killing, or witnessed the dying. These are the perspectives that shaped the violence as it spread and continue to influence the future of conflict regions, not the "objective" academic analysis based on media reports and interviews with regional and national elites.

Scholars who have moved beyond causation often focus on chronology, documenting "the who did what to whom, where, and when" aspects of the conflict. Most descriptions of violence in Indonesia, and elsewhere for that matter, tend to convey outbreaks of communal violence as a series of events and dates along a timeline. These timelines usually include only those events deemed important by the researchers and "leave out the witnesses, participants and events" that a particular author sees as marginal (Trouillot 1997). Since these accounts often build on one another, eventually a standard academic narrative of events, delineating the violence into stages or phases, develops. Oftentimes scholars put forth this stage-based narrative with little or no analysis of why particular events receive more prominence than others. These reified academic timelines seem to take over as that which needs to be explained, rather than narratives based on the events that participants themselves deemed important.[6]

Anthropological scholars of communal violence have long noted that a number of problems arise when analysts attempt to explain larger conflicts simply through historical blow-by-blow accounts that focus on the procession of events (Feldman 2003; Das 2006). In his analysis of narratives of violence in West Africa, Daniel Hoffman (2005, 338) argues that "it is only as a narrative convention that we attempt to delineate into discreet and successive temporal movements the act, its consequences, memorialization, and narration, rather than recognizing the constant interplay of each." People's understandings of the conflict were shaped by their experiences, as well as by information gathered after the violence had finished, such as rumor, media sources, or the conflict narratives of others. A narrow focus on chronology ignores that scholars almost always collect these accounts "after the fact," and thus narratives are concerned as much with the present and the future, as they are with the past.

Scholars also need to take into account that during the violence participants could only see the conflict from their particular position within it. They did not always know what was going on in other parts of the province, or even in the next village. The omniscient narratives presented in academic accounts or in NGO reports were unavailable to people caught up in the fighting and did little to shape their decisions. To paraphrase Bourdieu (1977, 106), the "privilege of totalization" won by the analyst through the compilation of a vast amount of information after the fact, was not available to anyone involved in the conflict.[7] Perceptions of who started the violence and why were based more on subjective experience, rumors, or hearsay than

on impartial fact-finding efforts. In North Maluku objective conflict narratives were often secondary to local understandings based on regional history
and experience, which were what fueled the spread of the violence, brought
about its cessation, and have continued to play a significant role in postconflict intergroup relations.

As I gathered information about the chronology of the conflict and com-
piled detailed maps and timelines, I quickly realized that the empirical
information I was collating often had little relation to the narratives I collected from participants. Unsurprisingly, Muslim and Christian versions of
the same events often differed substantially. When I presented these inconsistencies to Christians, they would scold me for being gullible, correct my
mistakes, and remind me that I should be more careful about accepting
Muslim accounts of the violence. When I would then present these versions
to Muslims, they would do the same. My informants were as agile in refuting my challenges to their versions of the conflict as the Azande were in
refuting Evans-Pritchard's (1937) questions about the efficacy of their witchcraft. Challenges to these accepted versions of events were easily swatted
aside with claims of conspiracies to hide the truth, or my failure to find that
one key informant who would provide incontrovertible proof.

The triangulation between various sources to uncover an objective account
of what happened, while valuable for putting together chronologies of the violence, is, I would argue, secondary to understanding people's conceptions and
experiences of what they "know" happened. They constructed their knowledge about what was happening around them from other, far less objective,
or even empirical, sources. These versions were not simply set aside when an
"objective observer" pointed out the errors or the logical inconsistencies in
their accounts. Stories of particular events, whether it be the killing of women
and children, or divine intervention, took on lives of their own and to a certain extent moved from rumor to established fact, regardless of empirical
verification or not (which in and of itself was largely irrelevant to many).[8]

Exploring Local Understandings of Collective Violence

My goal is not to present an exhaustive who-done-it of political elite involvement, nor to fact check the stories that I collected. I am not interested in
laying out a microhistory of the conflict from its outbreak in Kao-Malifut in

August 1999 to its end with the disappearance of the *Cahaya Bahari* in July 2000 (to pick arbitrary beginning and end points for the conflict).[9] The point is not which version of events is more accurate but rather how these versions affected people's subsequent understandings and actions, both during and after the conflict.[10] Although I still take into account political and economic issues related to the violence, I am more intent on exploring how particular versions of events came to be accepted, transmitted, and acted on, and how they came to supersede other possible explanations. I am less interested, for example, in the name of who wrote a false letter that led to rioting in the provincial capital than why people who read that letter reacted the way they did. I'm less concerned with who threw the first stone that led to large massacres than with local beliefs about who threw the first stone and why and how people reacted to and made sense of these events.

In contrast to the overriding concerns with causation and chronology prevalent in many political science works, other scholars of communal violence have turned to exploring the discursive construction of particular incidences of conflict.[11] These approaches look at how participants in a conflict perceive their situation and how they call on the past, as well as the present, to explain the violence they find taking place around them. In one of the first scholarly publications on the conflict in North Maluku, anthropologist Nils Bubandt (2000b) drew attention to the discursive construction of the violence in North Maluku as the focus shifted from a land dispute to religious differences. Building on Bubandt's insights, I explore why explanations of violence that focus on religious difference in North Maluku were and remain plausible to local communities, and the consequences of these religious interpretations. In part I do this through an exploration of the historical and cultural issues that gave this particular framing of the violence so much leverage that it came to supersede, and in some cases erase, competing narratives. I also examine the experiences of those caught up in the fighting and how their interpretations of these experiences shaped the ensuing conflict, the associated levels of violence, and postconflict dynamics in North Maluku.

Elizabeth Drexler's (2007, 2008) work on what she calls "the social life of conflict narratives" is helpful in this regard. In her analysis of the separatist conflict in Aceh in western Indonesia, she writes that "conflict situations are produced and perpetuated by various narrations of successive events that stand, not as object and description, but as spirals of interpretation and action. That some narratives come true is not evidence that those particular narratives are correct representations of the conflict, but rather signs of their discursive power to reproduce it" (Drexler 2008, 27). The ability of certain conflict narratives to change the way people see a particular set of events or a particular history is often tied to real or imagined historical points of contention that may or may not be related to issues of causation. No particular point of contention is necessarily guaranteed to become hegemonic in local understandings, rather it is through shared experience, discussion, and the hyper-hermeneutics of those caught in warscapes that people come to see violent conflict in a particular way.

In the case of religious violence, Hans Kippenberg (2011, 202), a historian of religion, has argued that in times of conflict the "religious language of the actors introduces new motivations for action and new courses of the conflict into the existing clashes of interests." In the North Maluku case I explore here, the conflict was no longer about development, dishonest migrants, stolen land, or jealous indigenous people, but about the continued existence of particular faith communities, ideas of holy war, and avenging insults to one's religion. As I will show, once North Moluccans came to frame the violence as religious, it shifted the course of the conflict and its very nature. As Kippenberg (2011, 200) notes "the framing of the [conflict] in religious language generates a corresponding way of acting, thereby creating a reality all of its own." In North Maluku, it provided participants with a different type of commitment to the conflict and its outcome.

Managing Memories

As other scholars of communal violence have noted, struggles to make sense of a particular instance of violent conflict or about its meaning does not end when the fighting stops (Brass 1996, 1997; Theidon 2000, 2003; Sorabji 2006). The struggle continues as various actors attempt to ensure that their understanding of what happened becomes the standardized version of events. These efforts to manage the memories of what happened often remove, or marginalize, the complexities of particular periods of violence. Ex post facto explanations may in some cases supplant earlier understandings and gloss over the nuances of recent history with monolithic narratives. In North Maluku, the narrative of religious conflict has marginalized the polysemic nature of the violence and placed the focus on Muslim-Christian conflict. In an earlier publication, I wrote that "such oversimplifications [of the conflict in North Maluku] do nothing to enhance our understanding of events" (Duncan 2005a, 80). However, in subsequent visits to North Maluku between 2004 and 2012, I have documented this very process of oversimplification taking place amongst those who participated in the violence. Although the homogenization of these narratives can obscure alternative experiences and understandings of the conflict, simply dismissing it, as I did in the past, fails to take into account the resonance of that particular framing and why its significance continued to appeal to North Moluccans. The metaphor of a lens is helpful here. Looking at the conflict in North Maluku through the lens of religion illumines some features of the violence while obscuring others. As they tried to make sense of their suffering and explain their victories or defeats, people on all sides have tended to narrow their focus to a narrative of religious conflict. This reductionism has taken place despite efforts by government officials and regional leaders to discount that same narrative.

Although detached observers can try to assess the origins and underlying political-economic issues at stake in the North Maluku violence, for Muslims and Christians it was an entirely different game altogether. They based their assessments of the conflict on their own experiences or those of their friends and neighbors. As a result, incompatible versions of what happened and contradictory notions of culpability pervaded the postconflict landscape of conflict narratives. People in North Maluku have a lot invested, both politically and emotionally, in having their version of events and their interpretation of the violence accepted by their own communities and by outsiders.[12] They have a vested interest in molding local memories of the violence to justify their own suffering and their past actions, and to help them reshape interfaith relationships in the aftermath of the conflict.

I find Steve Stern's (2004, 2006, 2010) work on memory in Chile after Pinochet helpful in exploring the management of memories that has taken place in postconflict North Maluku. In his analysis of how some memories of the past become widely shared, Stern coins the phrase "emblematic memory." He argues that memories become emblematic "because they purport to capture an essential truth about the collective truth of a society" (Stern 2004, 68). This sort of memory tells people not just what happened to them, but what happened to their neighbors, their families, or their religious brethren. People can see particular stories, or their own story, as emblems of a much larger narrative (Stern 2004, 68). These memories are also emblematic because many people believe them: "People find in them an anchor that organizes and enhances the meaning of personal experiences and knowledge. . . . People find their anchor credible in part because of validation by similar memory echoes in the public cultural domain" (Stern 2004, 68). Emblematic memory in part refers to the way memories assume a certain level of uniformity within a group. Stern (2004, 105) argues that "memory is the meaning we attach to experience, not simply recall of the events and emotions of that experience." This focus on the meaning of experience, rather than simply the recall of previous events, forces us to make a distinction between a positivist understanding of what happened during the North Maluku violence, the sort of narrative that one finds in a human rights report, and the way people experienced it as it was happening and understood it once it was over. The latter often describes a reality that, although less positivist, is no less real for those who believe it. Thus the idea that people believed a particular incident had taken place, and based their future actions or presumptions on its occurrence, was often just as important to understanding perceptions of the conflict as trying to figure out whether a particular incident had happened or not.

In the years following the conflict, people shared memories and tried to make sense of their experiences and sufferings—or the sufferings of others—at the same time as they tried to explain their victories or defeats. To borrow a phrase from Lemarchand (1996, 19), individuals and communities in North Maluku appeared to have "the need to adapt memory to explanation" as they sought to justify their actions during the conflict or to figure out why they had been singled out to be the victims of the violence. This idea of memory as explanation brings to mind, as Lemarchand (1996, 19) notes, Liisa Malkki's (1995, 54) concept of mythico-history, which she explains as "not only a description of the past, nor even merely an evaluation of the past, but a subversive recasting and reinterpretation of it in fundamentally moral terms." These mythico-histories are concerned, in part, "with the ordering and reordering of social and political categories, with the defining of self in distinction to other, with good and evil. . . . [They] seize historical events, processes, and relationships and reinterpret them within a deeply moral scheme of good and evil" (Malkki 1995, 55-56). This moral (re)evaluation of the violence in North Maluku has led to the elision and steamrolling of different narratives and focused the attention (what has become emblematic memories) on its religious dimensions.

My examination of how North Moluccans managed memories of the violence is not limited to what people said or wrote. I also explore how the religious narrative of the conflict affected people's decisions in the aftermath of the violence: in the reconstruction or lack thereof of villages, in decisions to return to their places of origin or not. On a much larger and more visible scale the importance placed on the religious narrative was evident in the ways some North Moluccan communities chose to memorialize those who died. Struggles over the meaning of the violence and its relation to religion were also evident in how some approached the idea of reconciliation. Certain segments of North Moluccan society argued that the revitalization of traditional customary law (*adat*, Ind.), one that forefronted cultural identities rather than religious ones, was the solution to preventing future violence in the region (Sjah 1999; Pemerintah Daerah Halmahera Utara and Dinas Pariwisata Halmahera Utara n.d.).

The Ethnography of Communal Conflict in Indonesia

Having explained the larger goals of this work, I should briefly note how this book fits with other work on the various communal conflicts that took place in Indonesia, particularly eastern Indonesia, at the end of the twentieth century. Let me stress again, however, that this is not a comparative work that seeks to explain all of the outbreaks of communal violence that occurred after the fall of Suharto. There are already three political science studies that attempt to provide overarching explanations, and I will leave further efforts toward that difficult challenge to others. In regard to North Maluku, these three studies have examined the events there to varying degrees as part of their efforts at broader models of conflict (Bertrand 2004, 114–34; Sidel 2006, 181–87; Klinken 2007a, 107–23). I have already addressed some of the faults that I see in these macroscopic approaches to understanding the conflict in North Maluku and will not rehash them here.[13] There are also numerous books, edited collections, and articles on communal violence published in Indonesian, some of which I will call on in the course of my discussion of North Maluku, particularly the work of the Indonesian sociologist Tamrin Tomagola (2000a, 2000b, 2000c, 2006) and Ruddy Tindage (2006).[14] Much of the writing in Indonesian, particularly on North Maluku, is rather partisan, but even these biased accounts provide insight into how various sides sought to control or influence the discourse about the conflict.[15]

On a more detailed level, Chris Wilson's *Ethno-religious Violence in Indonesia: From Soil to God* provides a microhistory of several major events that took place over the course of the violence in North Maluku. While there is much to be learned in Wilson's account, I have opted not to provide an in-depth critique of his book, pointing out where we agree or where I believe he has erred in his analysis (a subject that would be of little interest to those not working in North Maluku, and of even less interest to those of us who do). I made this decision because my project differs significantly from his in a number of ways. Wilson's book is an attempt to provide a detailed analysis of particular periods of the violence in North Maluku, seeking to explain a subset of the events that took place over the course of ten months from August 1999 through June 2000, the subject matter of chapters 3 and 4 in this book. His book focuses primarily on using a variety of political science approaches, such as resource mobilization theory and the idea of the security dilemma, to explain how the violence developed across what he (and others) refer to as the five "phases" of the conflict. As I have explained above in my discussion on the need to move beyond causation and chronology, I have a rather different aim in this book, which is to explore local understandings of the violence, in particular looking at why explanations of violence that focus on religious difference were and remain plausible to local communities and what the consequences were of these religious interpretations. Furthermore, my work is not focused solely on the ten months of conflict, but is equally, if not more so, concerned with postconflict dynamics in the decade or so since the fighting stopped.

As may be apparent by now, my approach to understanding conflict and postconflict dynamics has greater theoretical affinity to the work of my anthropologist colleagues who work in the region, such as Nils Bubandt, Patricia Spyer, and Lorraine Aragon. These studies have moved beyond issues of causation and chronology and explored the social, cultural, and political aspects of the various conflicts from perspectives grounded in long-term ethnographic fieldwork in the region that precedes these conflicts and continues in their aftermath. Patricia Spyer's (2002a, 2006b) work on the hyper-hermeneutics of those caught up in communal violence in Ambon and Maluku explores how Moluccans constructed their knowledge of what was (or soon would be) taking place around them. Elsewhere she has explored the use of Christian imagery in the postconflict situation and what that can tell us about how Christian communities situate themselves now that the violence is over (Spyer 2008). Spyer's analysis exemplifies the importance of religion and religious identity in eastern Indonesia that extends beyond looking at electoral politics and access to resources, precisely what I am exploring in this work.

Nils Bubandt has examined several aspects of the conflict, in particular the topics of framing and rumor. Although I do not agree with him about the importance of a millenarian narrative in the violence (Bubandt 2004), it will quickly become evident that I share many of his views about how the violence came to be seen as religious. Bubandt was one of the first academics to analyze the framing of the conflict in his work on shifting discourses of violence (Bubandt 2000a, 2000b). Along these lines he has also explored the topic of rumor in the early months of the fighting that both he and I (in chapter 3) argue strongly influenced this shift in framing (Bubandt 2008b, 2009). I build on Bubandt's observations on the discourses of violence by exploring how this framing affected people's future actions, and how this understanding of the conflict came to be, and remained, hegemonic both during the violence and in the aftermath.

Fieldwork

I gathered the data for this book over the course of several years of fieldwork in eastern Indonesia beginning with an exploratory visit in July 2000 and followed by eighteen months of fieldwork from June 2001 through November 2002. Initially, due to restrictions on travel, I lived in Manado, the capital of North Sulawesi, undertaking research among the more than thirty-five thousand internally displaced persons from North Maluku who had fled there in 1999 and 2000 (Duncan 2005b, 2008). These IDPs were virtually all Christian, although there were a few Muslim families from Ternate. They originated from numerous parts of North Maluku, but the bulk came from the islands of Ternate, Tidore, Morotai, Bacan, Mandioli, Obi, and the subdistrict of Oba in central Halmahera. They lived throughout the province of North Sulawesi, some in large camps in and around the cities of Manado and Bitung, and others in private homes. I focused on two particular camps, one in Manado consisting primarily of people from Ternate and

Central Halmahera, and another in Bitung, which was the largest camp with a mix of IDPs from throughout the province.

My other primary research sites were the subdistricts of Tobelo and Kao in northern Halmahera where I had connections from a previous year of fieldwork (1995–96). They were focal points of the violence in 1999–2000, which made them interesting research sites. Tobelo and Kao housed a large number of IDPs from all over the province, particularly from the islands of Morotai and Bacan, and the subdistricts of Oba, Weda, Galela, and Wasile. I also made numerous trips to nearby subdistricts, including Malifut, Galela, Jailolo, Wasile, Maba, and the island of Rau off the coast of Morotai to conduct interviews. I spent additional time in Ternate and Tidore. Throughout my fieldwork I made it a point to meet with local community members and with IDPs living in places where I lived and visited.

I followed up this initial period of fieldwork with visits in 2004 and early 2005. I then completed an additional four months of fieldwork in late 2005 with Modole communities and Javanese transmigrants in the western part of the Kao subdistrict. Although that research focused on a different project, I continued to gather information related to the violence. This period of research provided an opportunity for an in-depth exploration of how Modole communities, who took part in the violence from the beginning, understood the conflict. I made other visits in 2006, 2008, 2010, and twice in 2012 to follow up on outstanding questions. The breaks between periods of fieldwork provided me with opportunities to reflect on my data, reassess the various stories that people had told me, and return to challenge my assumptions with follow-up questions or explore new topics. Most important, my repeated field visits over the course of twelve years allowed me to take into account changing understandings of the violence, as well as to document how communities were recovering, rebuilding, and remembering.

The bulk of the research was carried out in Indonesian and North Moluccan Malay (the local form of Malay). In the subdistricts of Tobelo, Kao, and Maba, I used the Tobelo language when appropriate and necessary, particularly in interviews with the elderly and with Forest Tobelo communities. A previous year of field research in North Maluku in 1995–96 on the Forest Tobelo, the forest dwelling-foragers of Halmahera's interior provided valuable insight into the preconflict situation in North Maluku (Duncan 1998, 2001, 2002). These various periods of fieldwork spanning seventeen years have allowed me to look at ethnic and religious conflict in Halmahera diachronically with both pre- and postconflict periods of research in the region.

I have relied primarily on individual interviews, focus group discussions, general conversations, and participation in other activities for my data.[16] One initial challenge in my research in the immediate aftermath of the conflict was the reluctance of some Muslim communities to discuss certain aspects of the violence with me. They were willing to talk about the basic chronology, issues of reconciliation, their needs and complaints as IDPs, and broader issues of North Moluccan culture and history. The topic of the violence, beyond simple chronologies, however, was met with silence or with references about the need to "forget the past and focus on the future." This reluctance presented a stark contrast with the open and frank way that Christians discussed similar topics. After numerous attempts to gather this information myself, I hired two Muslim research assistants. I provided them with sets of questions, and in one case a survey, and sent them to various points in North Maluku on their own. Sabir Maidin, a lecturer from the National Islamic Theological School (STAIN, Sekolah Tinggi Agama Islam Negrei) in Manado, conducted interviews and surveys in Ternate. My second assistant, Muhammad Uhaib As'ad, a professor from Universitas Islam Kalimantan in Banjarmasin, conducted a wide range of interviews across the province with local communities and IDPs. It was clear from the latter's research that Muslims were no less inclined to discuss the violence, they were simply less eager to talk about it with an American, particularly in the immediate aftermath of 9/11.[17]

Orientation

The first part of this book presents a history of the conflict from the outbreak of violence in Ambon in 1999 to the end of major hostilities in North Maluku in June 2000. Chapter 2 contextualizes the conflict within the larger events in Indonesian and North Moluccan history that laid the groundwork for the beliefs and ideas surrounding the violence and the course that it took. It begins with a brief examination of the history of Islam and Christianity in the region and explores the legacies of the Dutch colonial missionary effort. I then look at the growth of reform Islam during the New Order and how these developments affected various populations in North Maluku.

Religion was not the only contentious issue in the region and the chapter ends with an exploration of the history of development in North Maluku in the latter half of the twentieth century and the changing nature of local politics as the New Order came to an end.

The next two chapters juxtapose the different ways Muslims and Christians described the course of the violence as it spread across North Maluku. Chapter 3 looks at how an ethnic conflict over land between indigenous people and government-sponsored migrants came to be viewed as one that pitted Christians against Muslims. I move beyond simply explaining this framing shift, and examine what exactly it meant for those taking part in the violence and how it influenced their actions. I then explore how the violence, with its new religious narrative, spread throughout the region, ending the chapter with an in-depth analysis of a reported massacre of children in a Halmaheran village, which I argue is pivotal to understanding the ensuing level of atrocities that followed. Chapter 4 continues my examination of chronologies of conflict by documenting the outbreak of violence in northern Halmahera. I then chart how the fighting spread throughout the rest of the province until the end of large-scale conflict in June 2000 after a massacre in northern Halmahera. In this chapter I pay particular attention to the religious nature of various acts of violence that were highlighted in people's narratives, such as forced conversions. Chapter 5 links my discussion of the conflict with its aftermath by exploring how the conflict came to a close throughout the region and how various communities dealt with the return of displaced populations. After noting the more general patterns that signaled the end of the fighting, I examine efforts to reestablish relations between Muslim and Christian communities in one of the most contentious areas of the province, northern Halmahera. I juxtapose official narratives of reconciliation with grassroots conceptions of peace and reconciliation, and how these terms are understood at the local level.

Chapter 6 investigates how North Moluccan communities managed the memories of the violence and how these memories were called on to explain the conflict, largely through the idiom of religious differences. I investigate postconflict reassessments of the violence through an examination of the notion of victimhood, exploring how the Muslim and Christian communities saw themselves as the primary victims irrespective of their roles in it. I focus on two particular themes, aggression and betrayal. These understandings of victimization were directly linked to perceptions of, and justifications for, the various types of violence committed during the conflict and their targets. I also look at how some communities and individuals have instrumentalized images of victimhood to achieve particular goals. Building on these notions of victimhood, chapter 7 explores how communities have dealt with those who were killed in the conflict. I focus on two different issues, martyrdom and the construction of memorials, and how Muslim and Christian communities understood each one.

A brief conclusion summarizes and elaborates on some of the main points discussed throughout the book, particularly those relating to the issues of religion, violence, and vernacular memory. One of my main goals is to illustrate that discussing how North Moluccans perceived the violence to be about religious differences does not require that we fall back on essentialism or notions of primordialism. I conclude by briefly revisiting my argument for the importance of taking into account local understandings and explanations of the conflict. I end with some final thoughts on how understanding vernacular memories of conflict might assist efforts at peace and reconciliation.

Chapter 2

Historical Preludes to the 1999–2000 Conflict

Most academic accounts of the violence in North Maluku provide historical background limited to the end of the New Order and the changing political landscape immediately after its downfall (Bertrand 2004; Klinken 2007a, 142).[1] North Moluccan history, however, does not begin with the fall of Indonesia's long-reigning dictator Suharto. Looking at the *longue durée* of regional history takes into account that North Moluccans are historically constituted subjects rooted in a history of social processes that precedes both the New Order period and the communal conflict that followed its end.[2] An understanding of more than four hundred years of colonial and post-colonial history that created the mixture of Muslims and Christians in modern North Maluku also allows us to examine how people called on these histories to shape or influence their understandings of the violence. I am not proposing a Lamarckian transmission of interreligious mistrust but rather am pointing out that prevalent historical narratives in the region often portray Christians and Muslims as antagonists, just as they were in the 1999–2000 conflict. One local observer compared the violence of 1999–2000 to

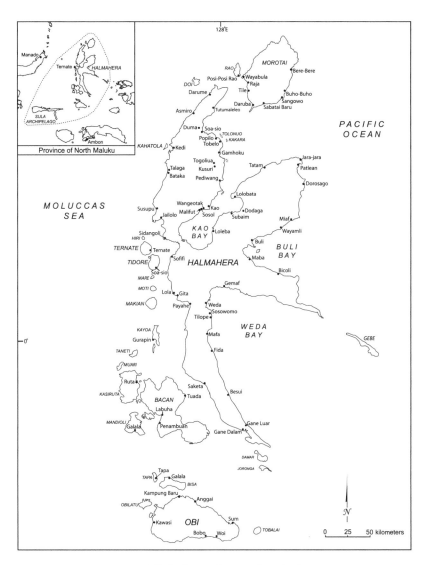

Map 2. Halmahera and surrounding islands

events that took place during the reign of Sultan Babullah of Ternate in the latter half of the sixteenth century (Alfatah 2003). When modern Protestant church leaders discuss the history of Christianity in the region, they often start with the 1520s (when the first Catholics arrived), rather than with the arrival of the first Protestant missionaries in 1866 (Haire 1981, 107). The long history of North Maluku would thus seem relevant to understanding the post–New Order conflict.

Although many descriptions of North Maluku start with rather clichéd references to the social harmony and peacefulness that pervaded the province prior to the outbreak of violence in 1999, the region has a long history of conflict and turmoil.[3] Forced migration as a result of armed conflict, while new to this generation of North Moluccans, has characterized regional history. Warring sultanates in the early modern period consistently resettled populations to make them more accessible and to control rebellious communities (Widjojo 2009). The Dutch did the same throughout the colonial period in the name of state control and as part of their efforts to dominate the spice trade. In the twentieth century, in addition to the horrors of the Second World War, North Maluku experienced a number of smaller conflicts, including a 1906 rebellion in Kao, a 1914 uprising in Jailolo, and disturbances during the Permesta rebellion in the 1950s.[4] Furthermore, as I will describe below, tension between Muslims and Christians, while rarely leading to violence, has played a significant role in shaping intergroup relations in North Maluku.

The Arrival of Islam and Christianity in North Maluku

Historically referred to as "the Spice Islands," North Maluku was once a global crossroads. Traders from Persia, India, China, and eventually Europe traveled to these tiny islands on the edge of the Pacific to buy cloves, which were available nowhere else. This trade brought great wealth and eventually four small kingdoms (Ternate, Tidore, Bacan, and Jailolo) developed and staked (often competing) claims over various parts of the region. Local tradition claims that Islam first arrived with a Javanese trader who convinced the ruler of Ternate to adopt the faith in the late fifteenth century (Amal 2002). Although the region's rulers converted to Islam, the religion did not spread far beyond the royal families or their traders. It held little sway with local populations and initially remained confined to the areas near the sultans' courts and in their trading centers on the coasts of Halmahera. The sultans attempted to assist the spread of Islam by appointing Muslims to serve in official capacities elsewhere in their domains (Amal 2002, 20–21). The Islamization of the sultans' trading posts on Halmahera and a reliance on Muslim officials served to create a point of distinction between the sultans' representatives and the island's interior communities who were not Muslim (Haire 1981, 100). For example, Platenkamp (2012, 6) notes that the distinction between Muslim and non-Muslim communities under the sultan of Ternate was already well established by the sixteenth century. Iberian and Dutch missionaries would later exploit this cleavage to their advantage (Haire 1981, 97–98).[5]

The Portuguese were the first Europeans to arrive in Maluku in 1512 and allied themselves with the sultan of Ternate. In 1521 the remnants of Magellan's expedition arrived in the region and the Spanish quickly aligned themselves with the rival sultan of Tidore. From the outset relations between the Iberians and the local sultans were filled with intrigue as the sultans used the Iberians as pawns in their local political struggles. The Iberians in turn used the sultans to further their own geopolitical agendas. The Europeans treated the populace poorly, often committing horrific atrocities on local communities and prominent members of the courts (Andaya 1993, 119). They also involved themselves in the internal affairs of the various sultanates. These intrusions into local politics and dynastic quarrels offended supporters of the sultans. As a result many in Maluku (and elsewhere in the archipelago), particularly those aligned with the sultans, turned to Islam as a vehicle for opposing the Europeans. To be pro-Islam, or to become a Muslim, was to support the sultans in their struggles with the Iberian powers. Ironically, the arrival of the Catholic Portuguese and Spanish fueled the spread of Islam in the northern Moluccas (Reid 1993, 143–50).

Although the majority of Europeans focused on the spice trade, a small number tried to introduce Catholicism. The sultans viewed these efforts with great suspicion and occasionally attacked villages that converted to the new faith (Villiers 1988, 594).[6] Despite this resistance, Francis Xavier traveled to the Moluccas and formally founded the Jesuit mission on Halmahera in 1546. Over the next twenty-five years of sporadic proselytization, the Jesuits enjoyed relative success and at one point claimed more than thirty-five thousand converts (Jacobs 1974, 135–36). This missionary activity came to a sudden halt in 1571 with the defeat of the Portuguese by Sultan Babullah of Ternate whose father, Sultan Khairun, had been assassinated by the Portuguese in 1570. After the Portuguese surrender, Babullah destroyed most of the Catholic settlements in the region to avenge his father's death.

By the end of 1573 virtually all Catholics in the northern Moluccas had been killed or had apostatized (Andaya 1993, 132).[7]

The Dutch East India Company (Vereenigde Oostindische Compagnie, or VOC) arrived in the northern Moluccas in the early years of the seventeenth century and eventually seized control of the spice trade from the Spanish in 1666. Unlike their Iberian predecessors, the VOC had no interest in evangelism and adopted a strict policy of religious neutralism (albeit tinged with anti-Catholicism). The Dutch even signed an agreement in 1610 with the sultans of Tidore and Ternate to deliver any Christian converts they found to the sultans for punishment (Hueting 1934, 6, cited in Haire 1981, 109). The VOC signed another treaty with the sultan of Tidore in 1657 declaring it would not promote Christianity in the region (Steenbrink 2004, 227). When the VOC went bankrupt at the end of the eighteenth century the East Indies became a Dutch colony. The Dutch government continued a policy of religious neutrality in the region for a number of years. They saw no need to challenge local Muslim leaders and possibly harm their trade relations or stir up trouble in, what was by that point, a region of little economic importance in the colony since the center for clove production had been moved to Ambon in the central Moluccas in the mid-seventeenth century.

The Dutch policy of religious neutrality remained in place for almost two hundred years until the mid-1800s. The change resulted from a growing concern with the spread of piracy in the eastern parts of the archipelago. Many of these pirates were from the Tobelo ethnic group in northern Halmahera, but they disrupted maritime traffic throughout the eastern half of Dutch possessions and raided villages as far away as central Sulawesi, Flores, and the southern Philippines (cf. Velthoen 1997; Warren 2002). The Dutch government allowed missionaries to enter the region with the hope of creating a more stable social atmosphere on the island that would prevent young men from taking to the sea to make a living (Haire 1981, 110). The sultan of Ternate approved this decision as these pirates often attacked his shipping. The Dutch government assigned the area to the Utrecht Missionary Society (Utrechtsche Zendings Vereeniging, or UZV), a missionary group affiliated with the Dutch Reformed Church. The first UZV missionaries received permission to work on Halmahera in 1866.

In consultation with Dutch authorities and the sultan of Ternate, the UZV established its first mission station in the northern part of Halmahera among the Galela ethnic group. Although the mission grew slowly among the Galela, it experienced significant expansion to the south among the Tobelo. Once Christianity had gained a toehold in the Tobelo region it quickly spread to other Tobelo-speaking areas around Kao Bay. The UZV slowly expanded their efforts throughout Halmahera and set up stations among the Tabaru, Sahu, Loloda, and Waioli in western Halmahera, and the Buli and Sawai in central and southern Halmahera. They had little if any success with groups that had already converted to Islam, such as the Maba, Bicoli, and Patani of the southeastern peninsula.

Missionary accounts of the period contain numerous references to Muslim anger at the spread of Christianity (cf. Fortgens 1904; Ellen 1906; Roest 1914, 33–36). In some places, the Islamic community responded to missionary success by increasing their own proselytization activities (*dakwah*, Ind.) aimed at communities that continued to follow indigenous ritual practices or at Christians who lived in mixed faith villages. In the 1920s the sultan of Ternate, Sultan Haji Usman Syah, who was known for being "very anti-Dutch" (which eventually landed him in exile in Bandung) appointed three imams to northern Halmahera and Morotai to stop missionary advances (Amal 2000, 24). In Galela, the imams focused on communities that had either refused Christianity, or those that had only partially accepted the new faith (Amal 2000, 28–30). These dakwah efforts met with some success and a number of entire villages, and parts of other communities, converted to Islam. Similar events took place on Morotai where the imam focused on villages that had not yet converted to Christianity. Dakwah efforts in Tobelo faced a different set of challenges as a large percentage of the region had already converted to Christianity due to UZV proselytization in the early 1900s and UZV headquarters was in Tobelo. Proselytization in Tobelo focused on mixed communities and eventually the population of several villages to the north of Tobelo converted, as did large segments of the various communities that make up the town of Tobelo. As part of these dakwah efforts, Muhammadiyah, an organization aimed at furthering the spread of reform Islam in Indonesia, established a branch in Tobelo in 1938 and opened a madrasa to compete against missionary-run schools (Amal 2000, 26). In that same year the three imams founded the Imam's Deliberative Council of the Tobelo District (Imam Permoesyawaratan Onderafdeling Tobelo, IPOT) as part of their effort to organize dakwah activities throughout northern Halmahera and Morotai (Amal 2000, 32).

The North Moluccan historian M. Adnan Amal describes Islamic proselytization in northern Halmahera and Morotai as attempts to directly compete with Dutch missionaries. One IPOT founder wrote that they created the organization to "counter the activities of the mission that was centered in Tobelo and Galela" (Amal 2000, 32). Thus we can see that in both the earlier Iberian phases of colonialism, as well as in the final decades of the Dutch colonial period, Christianity and Islam were in competition for converts. Muslim communities often equated this contest for converts with the struggle between themselves and their colonizers.

The Legacy of the Dutch Colonial Mission

Much has been written on the relationship between the colonial government of the Netherlands East Indies and Islam, and its differing treatment of Christians and Muslims (cf. Steenbrink 1993; Algadri 1994). Suffice it to say that in the aftermath of Indonesian independence, a certain amount of mistrust existed between segments of the Muslim and Christian communities throughout Indonesia. In the decades prior to Indonesia's independence, non-Christian nationalists often suspected that the affinities of Christians lay with the Dutch rather than their fellow Indonesians (Boland 1971, 224; Kipp 2000). Fatimah Husein (2005, 67) notes in her analysis of Christian–Muslim relations during the New Order: "The Muslim experiences during the colonial period left a deep wound in the Muslim memory regarding the Dutch as well as the Christians, and in turn provided the potential to ignite the flame of hatred within Muslim thinking." While possibly an overgeneralization, Husein's statement highlights that some Muslims did not trust their Christian counterparts, and in some cases "identified the Dutch and the Christians as two sides of the same coin" (Husein 2005, 67). In Maluku, where the Christian Ambonese had a long history of joining the Dutch colonial army, Muslims often associated Christianity with sympathy for the Dutch. In North Maluku, as demonstrated above, Christianity had long been seen as a handmaiden of imperialism.

The loyalty of Moluccan Christians to the Indonesian nationalist cause was questioned again in the 1950s when some Moluccans formed the Republic of South Maluku (RMS, Republik Maluku Selatan, Ind.) and declared independence from Indonesia. The RMS sought to establish an independent republic in the southern portion of the Moluccan archipelago, primarily focused on Ambon and surrounding islands.[8] Under the colonial government, the Ambonese, particularly Christian Ambonese, had constituted a large part of the Dutch colonial army. When the Dutch left, the Ambonese lost that special position. The privileged status of the Ambonese in colonial society had allowed many of them to secure bureaucratic positions throughout colonial Indonesia. Their presence across the archipelago led to resentment. Representatives from the RMS reportedly visited the sultan of Ternate in 1950 to recruit his support for the rebellion but he refused their invitation (Djaafar 2005, 150–52). The movement appears to have had few open supporters in northern Maluku, as people in the region did not want to replace their Dutch colonizers with Ambonese ones. Lacking support in the largely Muslim north, the RMS remained a primarily Christian movement centered in Ambon with only a few local Muslim supporters (Chauvel 1990, 361). Relations between the RMS and the Muslim community deteriorated during the brief period of RMS control of Ambon and in several instances RMS soldiers committed atrocities against Muslims (Chauvel 1990, 370–71). The RMS rebellion, however, was short-lived and the Indonesian military quickly retook Ambon.

The threat of an RMS rebellion resurfaced in 1999 when communal violence broke out in Ambon. Some Muslims accused the Christian militia of reviving the goals of RMS separatists for an independent South Maluku (cf. *Media Dakwah* 1999b; Aditjondro 2001, 115). The prominence of Christian Ambonese in the original movement, and a desire to link that separatist movement to Christian communities in the 1999 violence, led some Muslims in Maluku and elsewhere to refer to the RMS as the Christian Republic of Maluku (*Republik Maluku Serani*, Ind.) (cf. Kastor 2000). Radical Muslims, such as the leaders of the Java-based Muslim militia Laskar Jihad, seized on this supposed link between the remnants of the RMS now living in the Netherlands and the religious tensions on the ground in Maluku at the turn of the century. They used these fears of the RMS to argue that they were fighting for Indonesian national integrity rather than for purely religious motives. Despite the historical lack of support among North Moluccans for the separatist goals of the RMS, some Muslims I interviewed linked the 1999–2000 violence in North Maluku to this separatist agenda, or at least referenced it. The individuals who put forth this theory were usually more connected with national-level Muslim militia networks, such as Abu

Bakar Wahid Al-Banjari, the leader of the Pasukan Jihad in Ternate. Accusations of RMS involvement often correlated with the role of ethnic Ambonese
in the violence. Some Muslims saw Christian community leaders who were
ethnically Ambonese as having links with a larger RMS conspiracy.[9]

Two other rebellions during the Sukarno period also affected North
Maluku. The Darul Islam/Indonesian Islamic Army Rebellion, which
sought to establish an Islamic state found a small number of backers in
North Maluku. Darul Islam followers in Galela killed the village head of
Ngidiho, but they never gained much support among the populace and
were quickly eliminated by the Indonesian armed forces (Adeney-Risakotta
2005, 186). The Permesta rebellion of 1958–62, on the other hand, had a
significant impact on several regions of Halmahera, particularly the subdistricts of Kao and Ibu in northern Halmahera. Permesta (from Perjuangan
Semesta, Inclusive Struggle) was largely based in North Sulawesi and supported by ethnic Minahasans. Rather than a separatist rebellion, the supporters of Permesta were concerned with regional autonomy and the influence
of the Indonesian Communist Party (Henley 2007, 92). The rebellion had
supporters among Minahasan members of the armed forces stationed in
North Maluku particularly in Jailolo and on the island of Morotai, where a
large WWII airfield was of considerable interest to both sides in the conflict. Permesta rebels seized control of Jailolo for a short period in 1958, but
Indonesian counterattacks forced them to flee into the forested interior of
the Kao and Ibu subdistricts (Salim 1995, 97–101). In the interior they convinced some local people to join their cause, but others were more reluctant
to do so. Those who refused to join either fled deeper into the forest or were
resettled by the Indonesian army on the coast or in Tobelo until the hostilities ended (Leith 2001, 121–123).

Politicizing Religion in Indonesia and North Maluku

Since their independence in 1945 Indonesians have had a contentious debate
over the role that Islam and religion should play in the country. As the nation's
founders drafted the constitution, they disagreed on whether or not Indonesia should be an Islamic state. Some conservative Muslims argued that Indonesia should be based on Islam, and that Muslims should be obliged to follow
sharia law. Non-Muslim communities and many nominal and modernist

Muslims strongly opposed the idea of an Islamic state. In a contentious compromise, Indonesia's founders decided that rather than establishing a national religion, they would proclaim that Indonesia was a religious nation. The first principal of Indonesia's national philosophy, the Pancasila (The Five Pillars) thus became "Belief in the One and Only God" (*Ketuhanan Yang Maha Esa*, Ind.). As part of this principal the state (eventually) recognized five official religions (*agama*, Ind.), Islam, Protestantism, Catholicism, Hinduism, and Buddhism.[10]

A number of parties in Indonesia were not happy with this compromise, and in the 1950s and 1960s some elements of conservative Islam continued their struggle to establish an Islamic state. One result was the Darul Islam rebellions that broke out in various parts of the country, such as West Java, South Kalimantan, and South Sulawesi (Dijk 1981). In response to these ultimately failed rebellions the government imposed restrictions on conservative Muslim leaders throughout the archipelago. Despite these crackdowns, religious freedom was more prevalent under Indonesia's first President, Sukarno (1945–67), than it would be in later years. People who did not adhere to one of the official religions were left alone to a certain degree and allowed to practice their indigenous beliefs. Members of other religions were allowed to proselytize to whomever they chose with little interference from the government.

Adhering to one of the official religions became more important following a purported communist coup on 30 September 1965. In the wake of this failed coup, General Suharto presided over the annihilation of the Indonesian Communist Party, and an estimated 500,000 to 1 million people were killed. Since the Indonesian authorities made a conscious effort to equate communism with atheism as part of their anticommunist strategy, anyone who did not profess one of the officially recognized religions ran the risk of being seen as a communist. In the years immediately following the coup thousands of people across the archipelago joined Islam, Christianity, or one of the other recognized faiths. Numerous historical and anthropological accounts tell of large-scale "conversions" of people who feared being labeled as communists (Willis 1977; Hefner 1985, 246–47; Kipp 1993, 100–101). In North Maluku, some of the last villages that still followed indigenous ritual practices converted to either Christianity or Islam in the decade after 1965. In Jailolo, Fransz (1976, 70–71) reports that the Department of Religion gathered together all of the people in the subdistrict who still followed the indigenous religion (*agama suku*, Ind.). Under the watchful eyes of various government officials, these individuals were ordered to choose between Islam and Protestantism. Similar gatherings reportedly took place in Kao and in Buli (Fransz 1976, 71).

During the Suharto years religion played a significant role in local politics and patronage networks. State patronage and access to coveted positions in the civil service were, and still are at times, doled out along religious lines. In North Maluku, Muslims and Christians often talked of Christian versus Muslim control of the region and played close attention to the religion of government officials. Ethnicity was also important; however it often took a back seat to religion. Christian civil servants complained that their opportunities for career advancement were limited by their religion, while Muslim civil servants complained of the educational advantages that Christians had due to their perceived connections with the West.

During the early decades of his regime President Suharto saw political Islam as a threat to his rule and forced it out of the political sphere. With the removal of Islam from politics, many Muslims sought nonpolitical arenas in which to operate. Many of them looked to reform Islam with its focus on revitalizing the faith and purging it of local practices. As reform Islam grew in strength, some of its followers began to focus on the perceived threat posed by Christianity and worked to counteract or slow its expansion (cf. Hakiem 1991; Bruinessen 2003; Zubir and Siandes n.d.). In the 1990s, as Suharto turned to certain circles of these reform Muslims for political support, some Christians began to fear Islam's growing influence. In the last decade of the twentieth century these religious tensions erupted into violence on several occasions, resulting in the destruction of churches or mosques across the archipelago.[11]

These tensions had long been evident in North Maluku. Although Muslims and Christians each constitute approximately 50 percent of the population in central Maluku (Ambon and surrounding islands), the numbers are different for North Maluku, where 85 percent of the population is Muslim (Suryadinata et al. 2003, 110). Throughout the years, religion has often played a role in shaping intergroup relations. Villages are usually organized according to religion with Muslims and Christians living in separate neighborhoods. Furthermore, although marriage across ethnic lines is acceptable in North Maluku, marriage across religious boundaries is problematic. At times interfaith marriages have been seen as a strategy of religious expansion as one member of the couple, often the woman, will have to convert to the spouse's faith. A common story in North Moluccan Christian communities concerns a pamphlet that circulated in Ternate in the 1980s calling on young Muslim men to marry Christian women so they would have to convert.[12] Christians saw this pamphlet, or rumors of its existence, as evidence of larger plans to Islamize North Maluku.

Fears of a perceived Islamization of Indonesia and of North Maluku predated the fall of Suharto.[13] Christians noted a number of government policies and pieces of legislation that pointed to these plans. They cited the increasing amount of Muslim transmigrants being sent to the region as emblematic of the government's strategy to decrease the influence of Christianity in North Maluku.[14] Many North Moluccan Christians believed that the Indonesian government only allowed Javanese Muslims to take part in transmigration projects in the province as part of an effort to shift the population balance in favor of Muslims. In a similar fashion, a number of Christians also considered the Indonesian government's family planning program, which seeks to limit families to two children, as a threat. They argued that the government targeted this program at Christian communities in an effort to slow their population growth, while Muslims, they claimed, were largely left alone and even allowed to have multiple wives. They also saw evidence of these Islamization plans in the passage of two ministerial decrees from the Department of Religion in the 1970s: Number 70 on Guidelines for the Propogation of Religion and Number 77 on Foreign Aid for Religious Organizations in Indonesia.[15] Decree Number 70 made it illegal to proselytize to people who were already affiliated with a recognized religion or to distribute religious literature to them. Christians throughout Indonesia saw this legislation as a violation of their religious freedom and as an attempt to stop the spread of Christianity in the archipelago. As for Decree Number 77, which gave the Department of Religion control over foreign aid to Indonesian religious institutions, many Christians in Halmahera (and elsewhere in Indonesia) interpreted it as an attempt to usurp their financial support from the West.

Despite their majority status in North Maluku some Muslims in North Maluku had grown wary of the designs of the Christian community.[16] These fears have long been fed in North Maluku and throughout Indonesia by more radical elements of the Muslim community (Hefner 2000, 107–9; Bruinessen 2002). Local Muslims interpreted the Western aid that Christian churches received, the presence of European teachers at the local theological seminary, as well as the continuing presence, albeit a small one, of Western missionaries in the region as evidence of this threat. One Muslim community leader from Tobelo explained the dangers these missionaries posed to Muslims:

> According to me, what happened in Tobelo was a religious war [*perang agama*, Ind.]. Before the war happened, Christian missionaries from the West had been coming to Tobelo for a while. They established the KGBI Foundation [Kerapatan Gereja Baptis Indonesia, Ind., the Convention of Baptist Churches in Indonesia]. After they established their foundation, it was easy for them to enter [the region]. Missionaries came to Tobelo, and wherever there were Muslim pockets they built churches. . . . That is what I mean when I say it was a purely religious war [*perang agama murni*, Ind.]. They had these plans from the beginning—to convert the Muslims to Christianity. . . . If there had not been a physical war, there would have been a psychological war [*perang murut saraf*, Ind.] and in five or ten years all the Muslims would have been Christians . . . . So this was a religious war. They built schools for Christians and our teachers were Christian. They taught our children how to pray like Christians. (Ternate, September 2002)

The American-based nondenominational Protestant New Tribes Mission, which began working with Forest Tobelo communities in Central Halmahera in the 1980s, experienced this mistrust firsthand. During the early years of the mission's work the provincial government sent a small security detachment to their mission station to investigate rumors that they were training the Forest Tobelo (long feared for their marital prowess) as an anti-Muslim militia that would cleanse the region of Muslims. It turned out that a local man, vying for control of land, had spread the rumor. The government reaction, however, provides some insight into local Muslim anxiety about Christian expansion.[17]

The growth in the number of Christian denominations in North Maluku also became an issue of concern for some in the Muslim community. Not being fluent in the politics of church fission or the differences in Christian doctrine, they did not see the proliferation of new denominations as evidence of the fracturing of the Christian community. They saw the construction of these new churches as efforts toward the eventual Christianization of the region. Muslims often expressed suspicion about why small communities of Christians needed more than one house of worship per village, or large churches for small congregations. Some argued that these churches would have to be filled with people somehow, and that meant Christians would have to expand their proselytization efforts to the Muslim community.

Along with these continuing fears about the designs of the religious other, the nature of Islam and Christianity in North Maluku changed as well. As reform Islam gained ground throughout Indonesia, it also spread across North Maluku. A study undertaken in the 1980s noted that reform Islam had gained a strong following among Muslim youth in Ternate (Kiem 1995). The same can be said for Tidore where reform Islam gained adherents in the 1980s and 1990s, particularly among Tidorese schooled in Makassar and among those who became civil servants (Probojo 2010).[18] These changes in the Islamic community affected Muslim-Christian relations. In their efforts to institute a more "pure" Islam, some proponents of reform Islam are criticized for being less tolerant of cultural diversity. In addition to purging Islam of adat practices, reformists consider secularization and Western influence as serious threats.[19] They often see Christianity as the prime example of this influence. Christians noted that as local Muslim communities adopted a more orthodox Islam there was a significant impact on intercommunity relations. Prior to the spread of reform Islam in North Maluku, many Muslims took part in Christmas and New Year's celebrations and Christians attended Lebaran festivities marking the end of the Islamic fasting month of Ramadan. However, in 1981 the Indonesian Association of Ulama released a *fatwa* declaring it forbidden (*haram*, Ind.) for Muslims to take part in Christian holidays and much of this interaction ceased. A frequently cited example was the unwillingness of Muslims to eat in the homes of their Christian neighbors, or in some cases even to accept tea and cookies, an important mark of hospitality in the region. This refusal to accept hospitality, or even to exchange visits with their Christian neighbors led to a deterioration in relationships between the two groups.[20] In particular, the perceived growing intolerance of reform Islam led some Christians to see it as a threat to their well-being.

It was not only Islam that was changing. The Protestant Evangelical Church of Halmahera (GMIH, Gereja Masehi Injili Halmahera, Ind.), the successor of the Dutch mission church, has long held a near monopoly over Protestant Christianity in North Maluku. It remains the dominant church in the province, with the exception of Ternate, Tidore, Obi, Bacan, and the Sula Archipelago, which are under the Protestant Church of Maluku (GPM,

Gereja Protestan Maluku, Ind.). However, in the last decades of the twentieth century other denominations began making inroads. These new churches, such as Seventh Day Adventists, Baptists, and Pentecostals, forced the GMIH to pay more attention to the needs and interests of its parishioners. The GMIH grouped Islam with these new Christian churches as a threat and possible drain on its flock, particularly in the case (albeit rare) of interreligious marriages. I am not arguing that the establishment of new churches radicalized the GMIH, simply that the new churches pushed the GMIH into a more proactive role as it lost its monopoly over the Christian community.

These new Protestant denominations were far less tolerant of indigenous practices that continued to coexist alongside Christianity. Much like its colonial precursor, the GMIH has a rather ambivalent relationship with pre-Christian practices and often focuses more on cooptation than eradication (cf. Bubandt 2005). The newer denominations also tend to be less tolerant of highlighting the similarities between Islam and Christianity. Dieter Bartels (2003, 2010) observed these developments in both the Muslim and Christian communities in Ambon as new migrants to the region brought with them new forms of Islam and Christianity in the 1970s. He warned that "extremists among [these religious purists] demand the 'purification' of religion from beliefs which are not in line with pan-Islamic or pan-Protestant beliefs. Thus they have launched attacks on beliefs that God is one and the same for Christians and Moslems, and they have demanded the discontinuance of ancestor veneration and most of *adat*—all of which would lead to a further weakening of interfaith ties" (Bartels 1977, 324–25).[21] I recorded a number of church sermons in North Maluku in the 1990s, none of them at GMIH churches, in which preachers differentiated between the Christian and the Muslim god, pointing out the superiority of the former. In some cases, preachers specifically argued against the Indonesian government ideology of Pancasila ("The Five Principles"). They considered Pancasila misguided since it implied that Islam and Christianity were in some ways equal, which they argued was not the case.

Despite these tensions, there were positive aspects of interfaith ties. In some parts of North Maluku, particularly in Tobelo and Galela, many families have Christian and Muslim branches. Some of these multifaith families stem from interfaith marriages, while others are the result of decisions made earlier in the twentieth century. As Christianity and Islam spread through northern Halmahera, some families split their allegiances, due to individual choices, or from parent's decisions to cover their bets by having half of their children become Christian, and the other half Muslim. Muslims and Christians often cited these close family ties when expressing their disbelief that communal violence engulfed northern Halmahera. Religious communities in North Maluku also have a long history of assisting each other. When Muslims built new mosques, Christians often helped or provided some funding, and the same went for Muslim aid for church construction. In earlier years it was not unusual for Christians and Muslims to take part in each other's religious holidays. Some Muslims would attend Christmas festivities, and Christians would take part in festive activities associated with Ramadan. For example, in Ternate in the 1990s Christians took a turn playing the mosque drums to announce the beginning of fasting and Muslim youth groups would occasionally take part in Christmas singing contests. However, what it meant to be a Muslim or Christian Tobelo or a Muslim or Christian Galela slowly changed over the last half of the twentieth century. Categories that were once more fluid and open were reified as religious identities were politicized and interactions such as those mentioned above became less prevalent or more problematic.

Religious tensions in preconflict North Maluku were not limited to Muslim-Christian disagreements. Conflict between Christian denominations was just as pronounced. The GMIH considers North Maluku (with the exception of the islands of Tidore, Obi, and Bacan) to be its territory when it comes to Christian congregations and has often worked to prevent the opening of new churches.[22] When the New Tribes Mission began proselytizing to Forest Tobelo communities in central Halmahera in the 1980s, local GMIH leaders saw their efforts as a threat to continued GMIH dominance. They made several bureaucratic attempts to have the missionaries removed from the region without success. The establishment of a new church in a community with an existing GMIH church was, and still is, bound to create friction and can lead to violence. To cite but one example among many, in the early 1990s in the village of Pumalanga in the subdistrict of Maba, tensions developed when a young man returned from his travels and established a Charismatic congregation in his community. His neighbors referred to it derisively as the "hand-clapping church" or the "crying church" based on what they did in their services. Similarly within the Muslim community, as elsewhere in the archipelago (cf. Woodward 1989), modernists and traditionalists often disagree over the proper way to practice Islam and whether or not adat practices or local flourishes to Islam are acceptable (Kiem 1995; Probojo 2010).

It should be apparent by this point that North Moluccans have long considered religion something of a zero-sum game. The Dutch missionaries in the 1860s had started a fierce competition between Christian missionaries and Muslim leaders to attract followers until the last sedentary communities converted to one or the other by the mid-1970s. Something that benefited one group was seen to diminish the prospects of the other. Christians were, and remain, often fearful that they would be victimized by the numerically superior Muslim community, while Muslims feared the spread of Christianity that would reduce their numbers. This perception is not limited to Christian-Muslim interaction but also appears in relations between Christian denominations that zealously guard their congregations lest anyone be tempted to switch allegiances. It is also evident amongst some of the few remaining non-Christian forest-dwelling communities who have taboos that restrict their interactions with practicing Christians.

Religion represents more than simply differing doctrines. Tensions between Christians and Muslims were not always about institutions and theology. Conflicts also arose over small everyday practices such as food, space, noise, and youth peer groups. The segregation of villages into Christian and Muslim sections frequently leads young men to interact primarily with others from their own religion. As a result, conflicts between young male peer groups often followed religious lines, and in some cases were interpreted as religious-based aggression. During my 1995–96 fieldwork in Central Halmahera, Christian villagers in the village of Bebseli in the Maba subdistrict described frequent brawls between their youth and Muslim youth from the neighboring Buli village of Wayamli. They talked about these fights as examples of Muslim aggression and intolerance. Behavior during religious holidays, particularly when Ramadan coincides with the Christmas and New Year period (called Tahun Baru in North Maluku), is also a bone of contention between the adherents of different faiths. The tension arises from the different nature of the two celebrations. Whereas Ramadan is a time of fasting and piety, Tahun Baru is essentially the reverse; festivities run from Christmas through early January and the period is marked by large amounts of eating, drinking, and dancing beginning early in the afternoon and extending well into the evening. Finally, the presence of pigs and dogs in a village, or the sale of pork or dog meat at local markets, or its prohibition, had also been a frequent source of conflict.

We can see that, to a certain degree, religious differences demarcated virtually every sphere of social life in North Maluku. Political, cultural, ethnic, educational, and social differences were often organized around religion. I would go as far as to say that a religious identity is a necessary aspect of being a North Moluccan from both a social and legal perspective.[23] This does not mean that tensions between religions are primordial ones that North Moluccans cannot escape; it simply calls attention to the numerous ways that religious differences shape and organize life in the region. At the most basic level, ethnicity and religion are often one and the same—to be Tabaru, Modole, Pagu, Sahu, or Tobelo Boeng is to be Christian, to be Tidorese, Makianese, Patani, or Bicoli is to be Muslim. Some ethnic groups are divided, such as the Galela, Tobelo, and Sawai, but for most, religion and ethnicity are intertwined. From a young age, daily life reinforces people's religious identity, and just as important, highlights religious differences. With the exception of a few larger towns, such as Ternate and Tobelo, and a few villages, such as Dokulamo in Galela, people live in religiously segregated communities. Peer youth groups are largely defined by these religiously segregated communities. In larger towns those Christians who can afford it go to Christian or Catholic schools, while some Muslim children attend a *pesantren,* or a madrasa. Beginning early in life, an individual's social networks—his kin, his neighbors, his classmates, his friends—are often from the same religious background. Moving beyond education, North Moluccans usually marry someone from the same faith community, as interreligious marriages are discouraged. They then often call on religious or ethnic-based patronage networks if they want to enter the civil service, the main nonfarm/nonfishing form of employment in North Maluku. These patronage networks were particularly strong in Ambon, which prior to 1999, was the capital of a larger Maluku province that included northern Maluku. Thus anyone hoping to rise above the local level in the civil service, or education, needed to be tied into these larger religious patronage networks in Ambon.[24] Furthermore, as I have discussed throughout this chapter, these differences are reinforced by various government policies that serve to strengthen religious identities, whether it is the government's insistence that everyone affiliate with a recognized religion to enjoy the full benefits of citizenship, or the mandatory religious classes in public schools that call attention to religious differences. Although the social mosaic of North Maluku is divided by a multiplicity of identities (based on class, politics, ethnicity, race, religion, language, regionalism, fealty to a particular sultan, gender, and education, to name but a few), religion represented one of the more prominent divisions that permeated social life in the region and affected the lives of virtually everyone in the province at the end of the twentieth century. I would argue it is the one aspect of identity for which every North Moluccan has to put forth a claim. Individuals can ignore their ethnicity if they choose, claiming some sort of pan-Halmaheran identity as some did in the 2000 census (Suryadinata et al. 2003, 155). Individuals can also forgo their linguistic identity as younger generations choose not to learn local languages and instead rely on North Moluccan Malay or other local variants of Malay. Political parties can be avoided or dismissed, as can allegiance to sultans. Religion, however, is a required identity from both a legal and social perspective. Unless a person is one of the few non-Christian Chinese or one of the ever-shrinking number of Forest Tobelo who continue to follow indigenous ritual practices, you are either Christian or Muslim. Even if you are simply an "identity card Muslim" or an "identity card Christian," or what they refer to in Indonesia as *Islam KTP* or *Kristen KTP*, you still have to choose a religious community with which to affiliate.[25] As we will see, once the violence focused on religious differences, these affiliations and identities became nonnegotiable.

Development and Local Communities during the New Order

Religion was not the only point of contention in North Maluku. The rapid development of Halmahera beginning in the 1980s but with roots in earlier decades had also laid the groundwork for anger and resentment. Despite the prominence given to mining in analyses of the conflict, the primary extractive industry in the region has been timber. The Department of Forestry divided the island into large forest concessions for various (largely Jakarta-based) timber companies in the 1980s. As was common in Indonesia under the New Order, local communities who had previous claims to forested land received little, if any, compensation. The other major government-sponsored development has been transmigration. Prior to the outbreak of conflict in 1999, there were eighteen transmigration sites on Halmahera with more than twenty-eight thousand transmigrants (KWP-MDTPPH 1995, Lampiran 2). The government had plans to increase the number of transmigrants to more than sixty-eight thousand. A major complaint with the program (apart from religious fears among the Christian population discussed above) was that indigenous communities, which had been around for decades, remained without basic infrastructure (paved roads, electricity, schools beyond the elementary level), while the new Javanese migrants had almost all of these amenities prepared for them before they arrived. The government also expanded plantation agriculture on Halmahera at the end of the century. These efforts included industrial timber plantations (*hutan tanaman industri*, Ind.) aimed at producing wood pulp in several parts of Halmahera. In Galela, the government supported agribusiness, and in 1991 a conglomerate called Global Agronusa Indonesia established a banana plantation aimed at the export market (Risakotta 1995). This plantation covered thirty-five hundred hectares of land that many local farmers were coerced to sell. These projects usually disenfranchised local people of their land rights while enriching regional and Javanese elites. Many of these development plans have required the removal of communities from their land and their resettlement elsewhere. In addition to bearing the brunt of these land expropriations, local communities have also been affected by the deterioration of common resources, such as rivers and coastal fisheries due to ensuing environmental degradation. The anger surrounding these dislocations would resurface as violence spread across the island in 1999–2000.

More recently mining has come to play a significant role in the North Moluccan economy, but that had been far more localized prior to the outbreak of violence in 1999. A gold mine located in the subdistrict of Kao run by an Australian and Indonesian consortium called Nusa Halmahera Mineral (referred to locally as NHM) holds a contract of work covering thirty thousand hectares. Mining operations began in 1999 and some observers argued that competition over mine profits, kickbacks, and employment opportunities at the mine may have played a role in increasing tensions between Kao and Makianese communities that led to the initial outbreak of violence in 1999 (Abdullah 2003, 132; Wilson 2008, 57; D'Hondt 2010, 6).

Over the last decades of the twentieth century communities in North Maluku began to see that New Order style development was not necessarily working for their benefit but was aimed more at enriching regional and Jakarta-based elites. The nature of these enterprises, and the impact that they have had on local communities, demonstrated rather unequivocally that the central and provincial governments were not interested in the development of local communities as much as they were in making a profit. Risakotta's (1995) research on the establishment of the Global Agronusa Indonesia banana plantation exemplifies this approach. The development of the plantation led to the halt of a successful agricultural extension project that had benefitted local farmers. In these businesses the workers, especially the ones with high paying jobs, were often brought in from outside the region. The few jobs created by these development initiatives often became a source of tension.

A detailed look at government projects in the subdistrict of Kao from 1970 through 2000 demonstrates how little local communities benefited from development. Beginning in 1975 the government moved approximately nineteen thousand Makianese settlers to southern Kao after the Indonesian Institute of Vulcanology predicted that the volcano on their home island of Makian was going to experience a major eruption. Eventually sixteen Makianese villages, complete with their original names, sprang up around the village of Malifut. As is often the case in Indonesian resettlement schemes, this land actually belonged to indigenous groups in the area. In this instance, the indigenous Pagu people claimed most of the land and were not pleased with its annexation by newcomers. The Pagu are one of the several indigenous groups in the Kao subdistrict, the other three major groups being the Modole, the Tobelo Boeng, and the Toliliko (sometimes referred to as the Kao which includes the Kao Islam).[26] Some Forest Tobelo communities also live in Kao, both in the interior and resettled on the coast.

The resettlement of the Makianese was just the beginning of the reallocation of Kao lands. Jennifer Leith (2001) documents how in the 1980s the government essentially demarcated the entire land area of Kao for other economic purposes. The government gave the harvest rights to the large sago swamp in the subdistrict's interior to a government-run timber plantation (Leith 2001, 187–89). The Department of Forestry gave concessions to various timber companies that covered the entire subdistrict. This total was later decreased, not in recognition of local claims, but because it contradicted other government plans for the region. After logging, the government designated more than fifteen thousand hectares as part of the transmigration program, often against the wishes of local communities (Leith 2001, 201). A number of indigenous villages in the region lost land to the project, and others were entirely absorbed into transmigration settlements.

Some of those that were not absorbed were resettled (in some cases involuntarily) on the coast (Leith 2001, 148). Thus development in Kao did little for local communities except to move them out of the way.

In a number of cases religion and ethnic differences became superimposed on the economic tensions created by these New Order development projects. People looked at larger government programs and found a religious facet in how they were implemented and how they would affect the religious makeup of the region. Christian communities believed the transmigration program to be part of larger government plan to Islamize North Maluku. Some Christians and Muslims interpreted the relocation of the Makianese to the Malifut region as an effort to stop the southward spread of Christianity. Tensions at the banana plantation in Galela also reflected the religious divide, as Muslims resented a perceived dominance of Christians in the plantation workforce (Adeney-Risakotta 2005, 72). In Kao-Malifut, employment at the gold mine became an issue of contention between the Makianese and their Kao neighbors.

Decentralization and Its Impact on North Maluku

The context of development and its role in regional politics in North Maluku shifted rather abruptly after the fall of Suharto in 1998. In 1999 the Indonesian government passed new laws on regional autonomy and decentralization that transferred a large amount of fiscal and political responsibility to regional governments, including control over revenues from natural resource extraction.[27] Decentralization held much promise for North Maluku, particularly since the region that now makes up the province consisted of only two rather large districts prior to 1999. The district of North Maluku, with its capital in Ternate, contained the northern and southern peninsulas of Halmahera, most of the surrounding islands (Ternate, Makian, Morotai, Bacan, Obi, and others) and the Sula Archipelago to the southwest. The district of Central Halmahera with its capital in Soa-Sio, Tidore, covered the island of Tidore, and the central part of Halmahera, including the subdistricts of Oba, Weda, Maba, Wasile, and Patani. The announcement that North Maluku would become an independent province in 1999 heightened the expectations surrounding decentralization. Having their own province had long been a goal of the North Moluccan elite. Initial attempts to establish themselves as a separate province from Ambon had begun almost as soon Indonesia gained its independence from the Dutch. These plans were stifled by the temporary inclusion of North Maluku in the Dutch government's failed attempt to establish a Republic of Eastern Indonesia (Negara Indonesia Timur, Ind.), in which the Residency of Noord Molukken (which largely corresponds to North Maluku) would be a separate province. The rebellions that took place in eastern Indonesia during the Sukarno period also hampered these efforts, as the national government often saw demands for a new province as part of larger separatist agendas. During the Permesta revolt authorities jailed several local campaigners for a separate province of North Maluku claiming they were subversives working in league with rebels (Djahir 1966, 16).

The new province announced in 1999 consisted of the island of Halmahera and surrounding islands, such as Ternate, Tidore, Obi, and the Sula Archipelago to the southwest. The establishment of a new province brought with it competition over the location of a new provincial capital, the creation of new district and subdistrict boundaries, and the selection of regional officials. The tensions that arose around these issues often mirrored preexisting fault lines in North Moluccan society. I would argue that rather than creating new points of contention, decentralization exacerbated these fault lines, such as tensions between Christians and Muslims or political competition between competing factions in the province. For example, the people of Ternate and Tidore, historic rivals, argued over which should be the new provincial capital (*Manado Post* 1999b; *Ternate Pos* 1999b). Regional political differences were also evident in the question of who would become the first governor of North Maluku. Two of the main contenders were the sultan of Ternate, Mudaffar Sjah, an ardent supporter of Golkar, the political party of the New Order military dictatorship, and the regent (*bupati*, Ind.) of Central Halmahera based in Tidore, Bahar Andili, a career civil servant aligned with the United Development Party (PPP, Partai Persatuan Pembangunan, Ind.), a Muslim-centered opposition party (*Gatra* 1999; *Manado Post* 1999a).

Although some accounts of the violence in North Maluku have focused on decentralization (Klinken 2007a, 97–123), they do not take into account local understandings of regional autonomy in 1999, which remained largely confused. The larger project of decentralization only came to fruition in 1999, the same year that violence broke out in North Maluku. As late as

2002, high ranking officials in various parts of the province remained rather uninformed about the true nature of decentralization and what it meant for them and their communities. At the local level, understandings were even less coherent. It would seem premature to argue that large numbers of people in North Maluku, even the political elite, were instantly aware of the ramifications of decentralization.

Uncertainty and the Possibility of Violence

Despite the presence of religious tensions in North Maluku, the New Order policies on religion and on development appeared to work, and Suharto was able to hold together a diverse nation for more than thirty years, albeit with an iron fist. However, during the final years of his rule signs of religious, political, and ethnic tensions began to appear across the archipelago. Some of these conflicts resulted in the burning of places of worship. Many of these burnings took place in Java, but they also occurred in South Kalimantan, Kupang, and elsewhere (Tahalele and Santoso 1997). Individuals looking for signs of larger religious conspiracies also found verification in the rising tide of communal violence in the eastern half of the archipelago in the last years of the twentieth century. Christians found evidence of plans to Islamize Indonesia in the violence in Ambon, Poso, and the various church burnings, while Muslims saw their vulnerability exposed in Ambon and Poso and in Indonesia's withdrawal from East Timor in 1999. The politicization of religion during Suharto's New Order regime, and his repression and manipulation of Islam, allowed people in North Maluku to interpret these events in 1999 and 2000 in a particular way that made religious violence seem plausible.

In addition to fears of the religious other, the violence that surrounded the final years of Suharto's reign called attention to possibilities of violence. The large-scale killings of Madurese in West Kalimantan in 1997 demonstrated that the armed forces had lost their ability to maintain control and, subsequently, their ability to inspire fear in local communities. In his work on the killing of sorcerers in Banyuwangi, East Java, anthropologist Nicholas Herriman (2006, 370) notes that his informants cited the presence of "opportunities" (*kesempatan*, Ind.) to explain why they took part in the killing of suspected sorcerers. They pointed out that the decline in the power of the police and the army after 1998 had opened up opportunities for violence, and some believed that they could act with impunity. I would argue these various incidences of collective conflict throughout the archipelago (i.e., in Poso, Ambon, West Kalimantan, East Timor, and the anti-Chinese riots in Java and elsewhere) made violence a viable option for North Moluccans. During the height of the New Order, people in North Maluku largely had to follow the dictates of the government and accept its policies. Their options were few in the face of state threats of violence. In contrast, the fall of Suharto and the failure of the armed forces to stop communal conflict elsewhere in Indonesia opened the door for the possibility of bloodshed. Once this door was opened, it was hard to shut. As North Moluccans dealt with their own misgivings or hopes during the early years of democratic reform (*reformasi*, Ind.), the collective violence that appeared to be spreading across the country arrived on their doorstep with the outbreak of fighting in Ambon in 1999.

Chapter 3

FROM ETHNIC CONFLICT TO HOLY WAR

On 19 January 1999, a fight between a Christian bus driver and a Muslim passenger in Ambon, the capital of Maluku Province, escalated into widespread violence throughout the city. Although initially a conflict between local Christian Ambonese and Muslim migrants (mainly Butonese, Bugis, and Makassarese), it eventually took on religious overtones pitting Muslim "white" forces against Christian "red" forces.[1] This first outbreak of violence, which lasted until March 1999, eventually spread throughout Ambon Island and much of central Maluku and displaced thousands of people. The fighting erupted again in July and spread to other parts of the province, including the neighboring islands of Seram and Buru. As violence spread across central Maluku, most of the region that would soon become the province of North Maluku remained calm. A few days after the initial outburst of violence in Ambon, a small confrontation occurred in the town of Sanana on the island of Mangole in the Sula Archipelago (*Ternate Pos* 1999a). This incident resulted in the deaths of several people and a small amount of property destruction, but it did not spread outside of Sanana, and the Sula

Archipelago avoided violence throughout the rest of the conflict. Although North Maluku remained peaceful, tensions were rising as news and rumors about the violence in Ambon spread. As the fighting continued, North Moluccans who lived in Ambon, along with other forced migrants from the island, began to flee north to escape the violence. They arrived in North Maluku with tales of atrocities that they shared with others. These stories heightened the sense of apprehension pervading the region as people worried about the possibility of the conflict spreading north.

Tensions increased in North Maluku in May 1999 when a document titled "The Protestant Church of Maluku Invasion Map for Ternate" (Peta Penyerangan Gereja Protestan Maluku (GPM) di Ternate, Ind.) began circulating in Ternate, the largest city in the region. The map purported to show Christian invasion plans for seizing Ternate. Local security forces, however, soon discovered that the map, taken out of a church report, actually illustrated the distribution of GPM members in the city, rather than points of attack (Nanere 2000, 54). Several weeks later on 24 June a small fight broke out on Halmahera between the villages of Talaga and Bataka in the Ibu subdistrict between Muslims and Christians influenced by internally displaced persons (IDPs) from Ambon (*Media Dakwah* 1999a; Nanere 2000, 54–56). Neither this clash, the incident in Sanana, or the circulation of the "invasion map" created the large-scale impetus for violence that subsequent events would, but they were indicative of increasing tensions in the region. At this point, however, many people in North Maluku continued to see the dispute in Ambon as an Ambonese problem.

The Beginnings of Ethnic Violence in North Maluku

Large-scale violence in North Maluku began in the Kao-Malifut region in northern Halmahera when conflict broke out between Makianese transmigrants and the indigenous population. The conflict revolved around the passage of Government Regulation No. 42/1999 that created a new Malifut subdistrict (*kecamatan*, Ind.) for the Makianese in the southern half of the Kao subdistrict. The Indonesian government had moved the Makianese to Kao beginning in 1975 to protect them from a predicted catastrophic volcanic eruption on their home island of Makian. The indigenous Pagu claimed most of the supposedly empty land that the government had given to the migrants.

Over the next twenty-five years, relations between the Makianese and their new neighbors were rarely more than cordial. Paul Taylor, an anthropologist who did research on Halmahera in the 1970s and 1980s, noted that by 1977 "it was clear that tensions were building" between the Makianese and the indigenous population (Taylor 2001). At various points in the 1980s, violence broke out between indigenous villages and Makianese settlements. In general, the indigenous people remained upset over the loss of their land and offended by what they perceived to be the privileged treatment given to the Makianese by the local government. They also complained that the Makianese had a tendency to steal land by expanding their garden borders every year. The Makianese reputedly used their better understanding of land law to accumulate land from less knowledgeable farmers in Kao and Tobelo. People in Kao also accused them of being culturally insensitive and religiously intolerant.[2]

In response to these accusations, the Makianese argued that the indigenous people were lazy and resented the Makianese for their economic and political successes. The political accomplishments of the Makianese were as significant as their economic achievements. Several Makianese civil servants had attained key positions in regional government prior to 1999, while others held positions as subdistrict heads (*camat*, Ind.) of several important subdistricts, including Tobelo and South Morotai. The Kao were not the only ones who resented Makianese political successes. The resentment was (and remains) widespread throughout North Maluku spanning both ethnicity and religion. For example, in 2001 an unsigned pamphlet titled "Lets Greet 2002 by Opposing the Makianization Movement" ("Mari Kita Sambut Tahun 2002 dengan Melawan Gerakan Makianisasi," Ind.) circulated in Ternate and Tidore lamenting the undue influence of the Makianese.

The Makianese had been lobbying for their own subdistrict for almost twenty-four years before the government passed Law 42/1999.[3] These lobbying efforts, led by the Makianese elite in Ternate with the support of Makianese students at the provincial university, paid off in 1999 with the passage of Law 42/1999. The Makian Malifut subdistrict implemented by the new legislation would contain all sixteen Makianese villages settled since 1975, six villages from the subdistrict of Jailolo to the south, and five Pagu villages from Kao (the villages of Sosol, Tababo, Balisosang, Gayok, and Wangeotak).[4] The Pagu and the other indigenous groups in Kao were not pleased with this decision. They had no desire to be ruled by the

Makianese or to be separated from their indigenous brethren with whom they shares traditional ties.

The indigenous people of Kao have a strong sense of unity based on their adat belief that the four "tribes" (*hoana*, Tobelo / *suku*, Ind.) of Kao (the Modole, the Pagu, the Toliliko [which includes the Kao Islam], and the Tobelo Boeng) cannot be divided. They base this sense of unity on an historical conflict with Dutch forces in the region in the early twentieth century. As explained by the sangaji of Kao in 2006, the people of Kao had revolted against the Dutch in 1906 when colonial authorities arrested the sangaji of Modole for failure to collect taxes.[5] Angered by the arrest of their leader, the Modole recruited the Kao Islam, Pagu, and Tobelo Boeng to join them in an attack on a Dutch barracks located in the village of Kao. They killed a number of soldiers, before forcing the Dutch to flee. During the skirmish, the Dutch killed seven indigenous people, three Muslims and four Christians.[6] The Kao claim that their unity had enabled them to chase off the Dutch. After the battle, they buried the seven individuals in a single grave to serve as a reminder of this unity. The communal grave can still be seen in the village of Kao.

Many in Kao regarded the inclusion of the four Pagu villages into a new Makianese-controlled subdistrict as an affront to this historical unity. They did not consider the creation of a new Makian Malifut subdistrict as redistricting (*pemekaran*, Ind.), a process that would soon be common throughout Indonesia, but rather as a seizure (*perampasan wilayah*, Ind.) of their traditional lands. With these views in mind, Kao leaders voiced their strong opposition to the redistricting (cf. *Ternate Pos* 1999c). The government, however, ignored these protests just as they had disregarded past Kao protests about land expropriation for transmigration or other extractive purposes discussed in the previous chapter (DHV Consulting 1982, 40, as cited in Leith 2001, 201). The various groups in Kao never presented a serious problem to earlier government projects (apart from the few very small rebellions under Dutch rule), and government officials in Ternate saw no reason to expect anything different in 1999. It appears that the Makianese, as well as the political elite in Ternate, assumed that the indigenous ethnic groups in Kao would accept the inevitable once the new subdistrict boundaries were established.

This time, however, the Kao were determined to prevent the redistricting. Unfortunately, the Makianese were equally determined to see that it took place, and Makianese solidarity was just as strong as it was among the

Kao. The Makianese had the advantage of better organization and better connections due in part to the Association of Makian-Kayoa Brotherhood, an organization established in the 1970s to organize Makianese migrants wherever they lived in the province.[7] Adeney-Risakotta (2005, 218) argues that the networks established by this association enabled the Makianese to gain significant influence in the North Moluccan civil service during the New Order, which they used to ensure that the initiative moved forward. Tensions surrounding the redistricting increased throughout July and August 1999 and were inflamed by Makianese actions in Ternate. For example, a group of Makianese and Kayoan students from Khairun University issued a threat to the people of Kao over the Ternate branch of Radio Republik Indonesia: "Whoever tries to prevent the implementation of regulation 42/99 will face the Makayoa [Makianese and Kayoan] students" (Suara Peduli Halmahera 2000b). These students also held demonstrations in Ternate in support of the new subdistrict. Some in Kao argued that these protests spurred the Makianese in Malifut to be more confrontational in the belief that they had widespread support from others in the region.

Threats of violence forced the local government to cancel the 18 August inauguration ceremony for the new subdistrict. Despite the cancellation, fighting broke out that day between Makianese villages and the Pagu villages of Sosol and Wangeotak. Exactly how the conflict started remains uncertain as both sides blame the other for instigating it. The Kao claim that the Makianese attacked the two recalcitrant villages and burnt them to the ground. Some Makianese assert that the people of Sosol invaded the Makianese village of Tahane on 18 August to prevent the redistricting and these actions forced them to retaliate. Other Makianese, however, say they invaded the two Pagu villages because people from those communities kept antagonizing them while they worshiped in their mosques or worked in their gardens. Eventually this antagonism proved too much. One man from Malifut explained:

> As far as I know, these actions were attempts to anger the Makianese. Then one night they came to Tahane and started screaming: "Muslim motherf*#ers, if you are men come out and fight." I heard it myself. If they had just said, "Makianese come out and we will fight you," we would not have paid any attention. We just would have thought they were sinners. However, they

came with weapons and they were ready to fight. That night we had to hold out. We started throwing rocks at each other between the two villages. In the morning, because we could no longer control all of our people and since we had resisted all night, we decided to invade them before they invaded us. But before we attacked them in the morning, they had already attacked us at night, by throwing bombs and other things. . . . Eventually we decided that we were better off invading them first. At 6:00 a.m., we invaded them from Tahane. (Tahane, September 2002)

The violence continued for three days until the police and army intervened. The fighting resulted in one death and the complete destruction of Sosol and Wangeotak, which forced several hundred IDPs from these villages to flee to the subdistrict capital of Kao. In an effort to prevent further violence, the district head of North Maluku and the sultan of Ternate traveled to Kao on 21 August. The government hoped the sultan of Ternate, a traditional figure still revered in Kao, could use his influence to help resolve the conflict. During negotiations, the people of Kao expressed their desire that the Makianese vacate Malifut in three days. The sultan promised to take their concerns to the government, implicating himself as a Kao supporter in the eyes of Makianese, a fact that would become particularly salient later in the year.

The security forces set up a barricade between the two groups to maintain the peace while negotiations to resolve the dispute took place. Unfortunately, during this break in the violence the central government passed legislation that made North Maluku a new province.[8] Regional leaders quickly switched their focus to the establishment of the new province and the related spoils (the demarcation of district borders, the selection of a governor, the location of a provincial capital, and so forth).[9] They appear to have forgotten about the resolution of the Kao-Malifut dispute. Left to themselves, the people of Kao and the Makianese remained at odds and tensions simmered. During this time, the Makianese say they felt threatened by the reputed arrival of armed Christian supporters of the Kao from throughout North Maluku. The people of Kao denied this accusation. Kao leaders, well aware of the dangers of religious instigation due to the violence in Ambon, assigned Muslim Kao to guard churches and Christian Kao to guard Kao mosques. No one, however, thought to take such precautions to prevent conflict between the Makianese and the Kao.

Years of tension and built-up resentment had taken their toll on the indigenous people of Kao. The destruction of Sosol and Wangeotak was the final affront. They felt they had to remove the Makianese from the region, and they had to burn Malifut to the ground as the Makianese had done to Sosol and Wangeotak. Many in Kao argued that if they did not respond to this transgression, and the government created the new district, the Makianese would simply ask for more in the future. A group of local elite decided to pursue all available options to achieve the removal of the Makianese or, at the very least, the revocation of decree 42/1999. According to local accounts, they settled on three options: diplomacy, the courts, or conflict. In the name of diplomacy, they created "Team Nine," a group of nine local leaders that went to Ternate to argue against the new subdistrict and the continued presence of the Makianese to no avail. This failure did not come as a surprise, as North Moluccans believe that the Makianese have a lot of sway in the government and the civil service. Pursuing the legal option by contesting the new law in court was prohibitively expensive in a country well known for its corrupt judicial system. For some in Kao, the failure of the first two options left violence as their only recourse. In turning to violence, they considered three possibilities: magical assaults, guerrilla attacks, or a full-scale invasion of Malifut. They claim they implemented magical attacks and guerrilla warfare hoping to avoid an all-out assault on Malifut. They gathered everyone from Kao with strong magical power (*ilmu gaib*, Ind.) and used these powers against the Makianese. They maintain that they had great success, and these magical attacks supposedly killed a few Makianese every night. Others claimed that they also started harassing the Makianese in their gardens and in the forest, although I never interviewed anyone who talked about taking part in these activities. This reputed violence continued for several weeks. Before they could judge their success and decide whether to launch a full-scale attack on Malifut, the Makianese attacked them.

The Kao claim that on the Sunday morning of 24 October the Makianese invaded Kao. According to this version, a small group of Makianese went to the checkpoint established by the army between the two sides and asked for permission to harvest their copra on the other side of the boundary. The authorities let them through. They then joined other Makianese who had traveled through the interior for a planned invasion. A number of Kao Muslims, who had been assigned to watch the border during Sunday services, quickly confronted them. The Muslim Kao held off the Makianese until reinforcements arrived after the end of church services. The Kao then launched a counterattack that destroyed numerous homes in Malifut. On 25 October the Kao, now with reinforcements from the Modole and other villages in the interior continued their attacks until the entire population of Malifut fled to Ternate or took refuge at local military installations. During and after the attack, the Kao set fire to all sixteen villages, leaving only the mosques untouched. The Kao were vehement that they did not destroy a single mosque, despite the Makianese destruction of churches in Sosol and Wangeotak in August.[10] The Kao placed an emphasis on the nonreligious nature of events. They noted that their side consisted of both Muslims and Christians. They often mentioned the competing shouts of "*Allahu Akbar*" between the Muslim Kao and the Makianese during the fighting. Furthermore, the Muslim Kao remained allied with their Christian neighbors throughout the violence in North Maluku, even after religion became the focus of the conflict.

In contrast, the Makianese argued that once the people of Kao had assembled an arsenal and mobilized upward of seven thousand people from the neighboring subdistricts of Tobelo, Ibu, and elsewhere, they attacked without provocation. The attack caught the people of Malifut by surprise. They were overwhelmed and forced to flee to Ternate. Many Makianese focused on the reputed arrival of large numbers of Christian supporters from outside of Kao to take part in the attack and argued that these reinforcements were mobilized by the GMIH Synod in Tobelo. Several Makianese admitted that they were on the verge of going on the offensive themselves, but the Kao moved first. One village head noted: "We had no food because we were scared to garden. We decided that rather than die of starvation, it was better to fight them. But before we could do anything, they attacked us." Despite Makianese claims about the mobilization of Christians from elsewhere in North Maluku, the Kao remained adamant that the violence in August and October 1999 was about the redistricting initiative. To substantiate their argument about the nonreligious nature of the violence, people in Kao noted that as interior communities traveled to the coast during those early days of the conflict, they passed through Muslim Javanese transmigration settlements. During these trips, indigenous communities did not threaten or harass the Javanese, a fact that the Javanese confirmed during interviews in 2005.

Regardless of the religious differences between the Kao and the Makianese, Muslims and Christians elsewhere in North Maluku consistently pointed out that the violence in Kao-Malifut was a local problem between ethnic groups. In interviews with non-Makianese Muslims, I found similar responses. When one of my research assistants referred to the Makianese simply as "Muslims" in discussions of the Kao-Malifut violence he was often stopped and corrected by non-Makianese Muslims and told that it was not Muslims, but Makianese:

> RESEARCH ASSISTANT: So the first invasion and burning was done by the Muslim Makianese. They burned churches?
>
> BAPAK: Yes, it started that way.
>
> RESEARCH ASSISTANT: So the Muslims attacked first?
>
> BAPAK: The Makianese ethnic group, not Muslims [attacked first]. We are not talking about Islam.
>
> (Ternate, September 2002)

Other Muslims referred to subsequent violence in Ternate, Tidore, and Central Halmahera as the work of the Makianese, not of Muslims. For example, they would speak of the "Makianese attacks" on central Halmahera that followed the violence in Ternate and Tidore.

So how did the focus of the violence shift from redistricting to religion? The Kao Islam and Christians in North Maluku argue that the Makianese shifted the focus to religion to gain support from the broader Muslim community in the province, many of whom disliked the Makianese. The Makianese argument is similar. Although the original dispute was over redistricting, they argue that the Christian Kao turned it into a matter of religion to gain support for their planned invasion of Malifut. The use of red headbands by the Kao lent credence to this argument. Although the color red has long been associated with warfare and bravery in Halmahera, it was also the color of the headbands used by Christian militias in Ambon. Makianese could point to this similarity and argue that the violence was religiously motivated. Another point of contention was the aid that IDPs from Sosol and Wangeotak received from churches in Tobelo and Galela. Some of the Makianese, as well as Muslims elsewhere in the region, conflated this help with military assistance from the larger Christian community. This confusion as well as rumors that Christian militia from Tobelo and Galela were moving into Kao to assist their religious brethren inserted a religious dimension into some people's interpretation of events.

Several commentators have focused on the role of an Australian-owned gold mine opened in the Kao subdistrict in 1997 (Alhadar 2000; Klinken 2001, 6; Thalib 2001, 59; Abdullah 2003; Wilson 2008, 56–59). Tomagola (2000a) and Abdullah (2003) both claim that tensions over jobs at the mine were a factor in the outbreak of violence. The indigenous people felt that the Makianese received preference in the allocation of jobs for local people.[11] Tomagola also argues that the indigenous people were upset that the redistricting would place the mine in a new Makian Malifut subdistrict. He fails to note that regional autonomy legislation would have sent mine revenues to the district government, not the subdistrict government. Along these lines, another report claims that the former vice regent (*wakil bupati*, Ind.) of North Maluku had suggested that Malifut be named the capital of a new district of North Halmahera, so it would be in control of mining revenues (Suara Peduli Halmahera 2000b). The report argues that these rumors contributed to the violence. However, if the provincial government made Malifut the district capital, it would receive the mine revenues regardless of subdistrict boundaries, making the location of the goldmine a nonissue. These objections do not take into consideration local level misunderstandings of the legislation.

Another argument made by commentators, including the Indonesian sociologist Tamrin Amal Tomagola (2000a; *Sabili* 2000b), focuses on the Makianese resettlement as part of a government effort to block Christian expansion into southern Halmahera. Tomagola based his argument on the presence of the GMIH Synod in Tobelo to the north. He fails to note that for several decades prior to 1975, the GMIH had dozens of congregations throughout southern and central Halmahera. The placement of a large Muslim community in southern Kao would have had little effect on the actual expansion of Christianity. Many Christians in northern Halmahera, however, believed that the resettlement of the Makianese was part of larger government plans for the Islamization of North Maluku. Christians were not the only ones who inserted religion into their understanding of the resettlement. Some Muslims believed the government placed the Makianese in southern Kao in an effort to stop the Christianization of Halmahera. Makianese believed that since their resettlement Christians had seen them as a "thorn in their flesh." One Makianese official argued that Christians in Tobelo would have tried to cleanse Halmahera of Muslims long ago if it had not been for the large Muslim presence in Malifut.

The Changing Master Narrative: From Ethnic to Religious Conflict

After the destruction of Malifut, approximately fifteen thousand Makianese IDPs arrived in the city of Ternate. The IDPs were less than welcome in Ternate and the sultan wanted them to go back to Halmahera or to continue on to the nearby island of Makian. The majority of the IDPs eventually moved into the southern part of the city, home to a large number of migrants from Tidore and Makian. Once settled they began sharing tales of the atrocities they had suffered with the local population. The anger and fear generated by these stories, alongside the ongoing violence in Ambon, increased tensions in the city. To exacerbate the situation, the Makianese IDPs had poor relations with the sultan of Ternate and his supporters. They considered him an ally of the ethnic groups from Kao due to his perceived favoritism in the Kao-Malifut dispute. Rumors also circulated that the sultan had encouraged the Kao to invade Malifut. Many Christians and Muslims in Ternate said that the Makianese IDPs began a reign of terror shortly after their arrival seeking revenge for the events that had transpired on Halmahera. These actions included attacks on students from Kao at the local university, threatening phone calls to Christians in Ternate, assaults on people in the streets believed to be from Kao, the disruption of church services, and the stoning of Christian homes at night. Makianese community leaders, both from the IDPs that had recently arrived, as well as Makianese who had long been resident in Ternate, worked with IDPs and other Muslims in an effort to coordinate their efforts against Christians in Ternate. Christian civil servants I interviewed in a Manado IDP camp described office meetings where their Muslim boss told the Christians to leave the room before meetings began. They argued that these meetings focused on the planned riots or on the drafting of a suspicious letter that would appear on the scene in October.[12]

Some segments of the Muslim community in Ternate were unhappy with these developments. They considered the Kao-Malifut issue to be a political problem rather than a religious one and one that had little to do with the people of Ternate—Muslim or Christian. However, the presence of so many IDPs increased the level of tension in a city already on edge, as one Muslim resident of Ternate explained:

> It was very tense. At that time, people were already thinking that this was the beginning of the [coming] destruction [*kehancuran*, Ind.]. The first signs [of the impending violence] appeared at that point, because [the Makianese IDPs] arrived in a very sad state. They had nothing. Some only had the clothes on their backs. They were placed in people's homes. In my opinion, that was the government's mistake. The government should have anticipated [the impact that the IDPs would have on people] and should have put them in a place where they could not associate with other people in the city, so no social flare-up would arise. The information they brought with them was often not filtered by people [in Ternate] and was received in its raw state. Some thought that we had already been attacked by the Christians and all kinds of stuff. That is what caused religious sentiments to arise. (Ternate, September 2002)

To make matters worse, in late October a contentious letter began circulating in Ternate and Tidore that ultimately shifted the attention away from ethnicity to religion. The letter was popularly known as "Bloody Sosol" (Sosol Berdarah, Ind.) in reference to the Makianese destruction of the Pagu villages of Sosol and Wangeotak in August 1999 (see appendix A). Bubandt (2009) reports that people woke in Ternate to find copies of the letter strewn throughout the streets. Others told of men standing on street corners handing the letter out to passersby. It contained plans for the removal of the Muslim Makianese from Halmahera and the establishment of Christian control over the island, particularly over northern Halmahera. The letter was supposedly sent by the "Head of the Maluku Synod" from the GPM, one Semi Titaley, to the "Head of the Halmahera Synod in Tobelo." The letter, dated 29 July 1999, provided a religious-based explanation for the events that had taken place in Kao-Malifut earlier in October.[13]

Although rather facile and at times nonsensical to the outside observer, the letter brilliantly played on various fears and rumors present in North Maluku at the time, as well as utilizing older ethnic and religious stereotypes.[14] It began with an exhortation to the Evangelical Protestant Church of Halmahera to use the situation created by new regional autonomy legislation and the current disputes over the placement of a new provincial capital to take revenge for the Makianese destruction of Sosol and Wangeotak and to occupy the area around the future capital city. The letter pointed out that "from the perspective of geography North Maluku and Central Halmahera are wedged between Central Maluku (Ambon), North Sulawesi (Manado), and Irian Jaya that are already majority Christian areas," making it ripe for becoming a majority Christian province as well. To aid this endeavor the author claimed that church efforts had ensured that the province of North Sulawesi "is ready to give [the islands of] Sangir and Talaud to North Maluku" due to their cultural and historical connections. The small islands that make up the Sangir and Talaud archipelagos are located to the north and northwest of Sulawesi and stretch to the border with the Philippines. Both of these island groups are the place of origin of large numbers of migrants in North Maluku—both on Halmahera and in Ternate (Raharto 2000). Furthermore, both of these island groups are almost 90% Protestant (Ulaen 2003, 101). The addition of the Sangir-Talaud islands would provide the Christians of North Maluku with a "force that will be larger than what the other ethnic groups in North Maluku and Central Halmahera could handle."

The contents of the letter played on Muslim concerns by appealing to their fears of a Christian takeover. The author of the letter claimed that Christian militia members (Laskar Kristus, Ind.) from North Halmahera had already met with representatives from the Protestant Church of Maluku in Ambon to devise a "strategy for the return invasion of Bloody Sosol." Part of the plan included gathering strength from every Christian area in North Maluku. The reputed Ambon meeting tied the violence in Kao to the larger conflict in Ambon, making a religious explanation for the violence that much more sensible. It served to strike fear into the Muslim community, by noting that the end goal was to create a "Christian giant" in North Maluku. The letter purported to show that the violence was not just about the Makianese, as the Christian community would have them believe but would affect all Muslims in the province. Furthermore, building on images of savagery and atrocity circulating in Ternate and Tidore from the incidents in Kao-Malifut in early October, the letter also notes that the much-feared Forest Tobelo would also be encouraged to take part in the violence. These forest-dwelling foragers are spread throughout Halmahera and have a fierce reputation that strikes fear into the hearts of many coastal communities (Duncan 2001). The Makianese are supposedly quite scared of these forest-dwellers (Lucardie 1985, 72). The possibility of their participation added an additional degree of fear to the letter. It also helped explain the purported savagery of what had taken place in Kao-Malifut and would take place elsewhere if Christians gained the upper hand.

The letter was at its most inflammatory in the final section when it discussed the goal of the operation and how it would be undertaken. It stated that Christian militia must evict the Makianese, who were referred to as "tall, smart, hard-working, brave and very fanatic Muslims," from the island of Halmahera, in a sadistic way "that will cause trauma and depression." The letter urged Christians to "check identification cards along the Trans-Tobelo highway and speak with sympathy to [people from non-Makianese] ethnic groups to change their understanding, so that the ethnic division in the conflict will be more obvious later." The last portion of the letter details the goals of the war strategy and is worth quoting at length:

> By adhering to the pattern of war set out in the points in part B (War Strategy) then
> - The Makianese ethnic group will not find support from other Muslims in North Maluku/Central Halmahera.
> - The Muslim community that we have long known as a unified power will be torn asunder by the strength of its own ethnic groups.
> - The Makianese ethnic group, the Islamic giant of North Maluku and Central Halmahera, will be defeated by our multi-ethnic coalition, tied together by our Christian faith. This process will create a new giant that will rise with the face of the indigenous ethnic groups of Halmahera with the blood of Jesus the Savior, who is coming at the third millennium to complete the golden triangle of Maluku, North Sulawesi, and Irian Jaya, which has always been conducive to the work of the Church.
> - The defeat of the Islamic giant of the land of Halmahera (Malifut) will be a barometer for other ethnic groups to open a front in a new war, that will have these effects:
>   1. The Ternatan, Tidorese, Bacan, and Sanana ethnic groups will be amazed and the fear of the giant of Christ will run rampant.
>   2. Other Muslim ethnic groups will be reluctant and scared to enter North Halmahera.

The contents of the letter played brilliantly on current events, as well as on a number of religious and cultural fault lines in North Moluccan history. One Muslim from Ternate commented on his initial reaction:

I immediately knew that the person who wrote this letter was intelligent. He had to have had anthropological insights, sociological insights, and insights on mass psychology, only then could he have made a letter like this. If he didn't have this knowledge he could not have done it. Furthermore, whoever wrote this knew all about the cultural and ethnic differences of North Maluku. The letter had an extraordinary effect on people who did not really understand [what was taking place]. So the author of this letter was not just anyone. (Ternate, September 2002)

This persuasiveness of the letter overshadowed the numerous errors it contained, some of them rather obvious. For example, the letter notes that the churches had begun planning a strategy for the "return invasion of Bloody Sosol" at the end of July 1999, yet the destruction of Sosol took place in mid-August. Other obvious errors, particularly to Indonesians who are used to the importance of official letters in the nation's byzantine bureaucracy, include the lack of letterhead and the lack of an official stamp, two crucial aspects of any written correspondence. Other errors were less obvious, particularly to a Muslim audience, and dealt with church issues, or particular ways in which Christians would have written the letter. Both Protestant churches implicated in the letter quickly denied its authenticity and issued statements that decried it as a blatant attempt at provocation.[15]

Despite the denials, many Muslim readers looked past the mistakes and considered the letter to be evidence of the church's role in the Kao-Malifut violence. As one Muslim man from Tidore told me during an interview in Manado in 2001, "People believed the letter was real because it proved what they had seen historically. The letter itself may have been a forgery, but its contents showed the true nature of Christian plans to take over the province." He explained that people believed the letter largely because it essentially told them what they thought they already knew from personal experience and from history. Dutch missionary efforts in the region during the colonial period and the continuing interaction between the GMIH and Western churches had many convinced that there was a long-term conspiracy to Christianize the region. The letter also drew a link between the events in Kao-Malifut and the violence in Ambon. These connections led many Muslims in Tidore and Ternate to accept its authenticity. Photocopies of the letter, or rumors of its existence, circulated throughout both islands and continued to foment anger and fear in the Muslim community.[16] Since the letter said Christians would deny the religious nature of the violence, Muslims who read the letter and believed its contents were prepared to discredit the nonreligious explanations put forth by Christians.

The letter and associated rumors increased anxieties in Ternate and Tidore, both of which were already tense from the violence in Ambon and the presence of IDPs from Malifut.[17] Rumors of impending violence spread throughout late October and small acts of violence and intimidation began to take place in Soa-Sio, Tidore, and Ternate. Tales of pelted homes, interrupted church services, and mysterious and threatening phone calls put the community, particularly Christians, on edge. Despite constant reassurances from local authorities concerning their safety, people began to prepare for the worst. Some began to leave for Manado or Tobelo. As one Christian IDP woman from Ternate recounted:

> As early as 25 October, there were already signs that the violence was coming. That day someone threw a rice sack soaked in gasoline on the steps of the church in Kalumata [a neighborhood in Ternate], but luckily people were around and put it out. [One day] someone came to my house, knocked on the door, and asked who lived there. My son said it was the people from Tidore checking their address list so they knew which houses to burn. I prepared for the attacks by setting aside lots of dish soap [used to put out kitchen fires in Indonesia], and wet rice sacks to help put out any fires. However, my son convinced me that I had to leave. (Manado, October 2001)

Those who did not leave began to stockpile food in their homes so they could stay indoors if there was trouble.

To ease the tensions in Tidore, on 3 November local officials in Soa-Sio arranged a meeting to let Christian ministers explain the inflammatory letter and reassure the Muslim community that they presented no threat. Most Christian leaders were too afraid to attend. The few who went to the meeting quickly left in fear for their own safety, they said, due to the anger permeating the rather large Muslim crowd. Local officials had invited the head of the GPM in Tidore, Reverend Risakotta, but he initially refused to attend due to a fear for his safety. Eventually the chief of police went to Risakotta's home and brought him to the meeting. Before he could finish explaining the letter, someone cut the electricity and the angry crowd attacked and killed him. A riot ensued as the crowd left the meeting and, augmented by others, preceded to burn Christian homes and churches. Local security forces were unable, or unwilling, to stop the rioters.[18]

Throughout Soa-Sio, Christians ran to police stations or other military installations to seek refuge. Others recalled hiding in the grass or in the homes of friendly neighbors and watching as the mobs destroyed their houses. Pak Okens (a pseudonym) from Tidore recalled how he heard of the impending riot when someone who had fled the meeting where the Reverend Risakotta had been killed knocked on his back door at around 10:30 p.m. They were told to flee quickly before the rioters arrived and killed them all. Pak Okens and his family ran out the back right before a Muslim mob surrounded the house. They took cover in a neighbor's home and watched as the mob pelted their house with stones, shouted "Allahu Akbar," and yelled for them to come out. Pak Okens said he was prepared to sacrifice himself to save his wife and children if the mob found them in the neighbor's house. At 1 a.m. it started raining which helped to disperse parts of the crowd. Pak Okens used the opportunity to send someone on his motorbike to the district police headquarters (Kapolsek, Ind.) and seek help. This effort failed, because another mob was already planning to burn down the district police headquarters, which was filled with other Christians seeking shelter. He then watched as rioters returned and burnt his home to the ground. Eventually members of the armed forces arrived at 6 a.m., after negotiating city roads barricaded with rocks and palm trees. Pak Okens and his family ran into the car as the police held back the mob. Eventually the Indonesian Navy evacuated the remnants of the small Christian community from Tidore to Bitung in North Sulawesi. When the smoke cleared, nine people were dead and almost every Christian home and three churches had been destroyed (Nanere 2000, 66).

As Tidore burned, the situation in Ternate, with a much larger Christian population, remained tense. The local government did its best to reassure the Christian community that they had nothing to fear. It sent cars though the city with loudspeakers telling everyone to remain calm. Despite these assurances, violence broke out in the early hours of 6 November. Christians in Ternate say they awoke to the sight of hundreds of armed Muslims in the streets wearing white headbands (similar to those worn by the Muslim side in Ambon) ready to attack their homes. Despite the rumors, threats, and violence in Tidore, many Christians said the sight of Muslim rioters still took them by surprise. What astonished them even more was that the mobs outside of their homes were made up largely of Muslims from other parts of town who they did not know. This evidence of the organizational aspect for the rioting confirmed for many Christians that the riots were not spontaneous. As the rioters burned and looted Christian homes and churches, Christians sought protection in police stations and army bases throughout the city. Others took refuge in the northern parts of Ternate City controlled by supporters of the sultan.

The inability or unwillingness of the security apparatus to take control of the situation rendered them powerless. According to eyewitnesses, during the rioting the police were focused on protecting their own families and guarding the places where Christians had sought protection. In response, the sultan of Ternate deployed approximately four thousand of his customary palace guard (*pasukan adat*, Ind.), also called yellow troops (*pasukan kuning*, Ind.) due to the color of their traditional uniforms. The pasukan kuning consisted primarily of ethnic Ternatan Muslims from the northern part of the city or from the countryside where supporters of the sultan lived. When the violence began, the pasukan kuning did their best to protect Christians from the rioters. IDPs from Ternate repeatedly noted that if the pasukan kuning had not taken to the streets, the rioters would have massacred them, or as one Christian from Ternate said: "The power of God was working through the sultan." These efforts earned them and the sultan a pro-Christian reputation; an issue that would arise again in December. The Indonesian Navy eventually evacuated more than ten thousand people to North Sulawesi and Halmahera.

Despite the help offered by friendly Muslim neighbors, or the role that the sultan of Ternate's customary guard played in protecting them as they fled, Christians in Ternate say they were left with little doubt as to why they were being persecuted. Christian accounts of the riots focused on the religious nature of the violence, the calls of "Allahu Akbar" from rioters and mosque loud speakers, the insults hurled at them based on their religion, the destruction of churches, and the anti-Christian graffiti scrawled all over the city. One woman recounted how rioters tossed the corpse of her brother onto the stairs of a church and, in reference to the story of Jesus Christ, yelled, "Tell your God to bring you back to life. If your God is so good, tell him to bring you back to life." Although in the aftermath of the riots, some in the provincial government or in Jakarta blamed the violence on provocateurs from elsewhere, the events of early November left little doubt in the minds of North Moluccans that this conflict had become one about religion and the rhetoric of religious differences quickly subsumed issues of elite machination or larger political objectives.

The riots in Tidore and Ternate mark the point where the master narrative of the conflict definitively shifted from being about ethnicity and redistricting to being about religion for all sides involved. Although some Makianese had attributed religious motives to their enemies from the start, others, both Christians and Muslims, had denied these accusations. Prior to the riots, the non-Makianese in the region maintained that the conflict was about a border dispute based on ethnic differences. They argued that Makianese claims to be the victims of religious-based violence were a transparent attempt to gain support from the larger Muslim community. After the events of early November, however, all sides considered themselves involved in a religious dispute that pitted Christians against Muslims. Tambiah's (1996, 192–93) notions of focalization and transvaluation are helpful in understanding what happened to the master narrative of the conflict. Focalization occurs as understandings of local conflicts are removed from their particular contexts in time and space. Once the suspicious letter appeared in Ternate, Muslim communities began to set aside the particulars of the Kao-Malifut violence (issues of border disputes and migration histories) and focus on the Muslim-Christian aspect of the conflict. Christians did the same after the riots in Ternate and Tidore. The second process, transvaluation, occurs as individual conflicts and disputes are incorporated into a larger, extralocal context. Local conflicts expand to include a much larger number of extralocal adversaries involved in larger conflicts that are only remotely connected to the original dispute. In North Maluku, participants began to see the conflict between local communities as part of a broader struggle between Muslims and Christians throughout Indonesia, including the ongoing religious violence in Ambon. Some even began to see it as part of a global struggle between the two faiths. Tambiah (1996, 192) notes that focalization and transvaluation quickly turn outbreaks of violence into "self-fulfilling manifestations, incarnations, and reincarnations of allegedly irresolvable communal splits." After Ternate and Tidore, the new master narrative of the violence as a religious conflict quickly became self-fulfilling throughout North Maluku.

In looking at this transition I also find Elizabeth Drexler's (2007, 2008) work on what she calls "the social life of conflict narratives" helpful. Drexler (2008, 27) writes that "conflict situations are produced and perpetuated by various narrations of successive events that stand, not as object and description, but as spirals of interpretation and action." In the case of North Maluku, local Muslims reinterpreted the ethnic conflict between the indigenous people of Kao and the Makianese as one based on religious differences and then acted on perceived slights to the larger Muslim community. In turn, Christians interpreted the events in Ternate and Tidore as evidence of the religious basis of the conflict and acted accordingly. Once the ideas and rumors swirling around the suspicious letter began to take hold in Ternate and Tidore, the spiral of interpretation and action made this explanation of the violence self-evident. Muslims began to find evidence of Christian plots, and Christians found evidence of Muslim ones. Drexler (2008, 27) also notes that just because "some narratives come true is not evidence that those particular narratives are correct representations of the conflict, but rather signs of their discursive power to reproduce it." In the North Maluku case, people examined events that were taking place around them in light of local histories of interfaith relations. When presented with the narrative of religious violence in 1999, it made sense to many, proving what they already knew. In fact, some argued that the idea of a religious conflict made more sense than the idea of one based on a land dispute between the Kao and the Makianese. The indigenous communities in Kao had been pushed around for decades, and it seemed unlikely that only now would they strike out at one of the more politically powerful ethnic groups in the region. Surely religion had something to do with it.

The Violence Spreads to Central and Southern Halmahera

After Tidore and Ternate the violence, now coded as religious, shifted to Halmahera when Muslims from Makian and Tidore, now referred to as white troops (*pasukan putih*, Ind.) due to their white headbands, attacked Christian villages on that island. They argued that they had to protect Muslim communities from possible Christian aggression. However, the small Christian communities in the coastal areas of central and southern Halmahera presented easy targets for the white troops to redirect their anger and continue to take revenge for the slights done to the Makianese in Kao, which were now seen through the lens of religion rather than ethnicity. With the arrival of these white troops, violence soon broke out between Christian and

Muslim communities in the southern and central parts of Halmahera (including the subdistricts of Oba, Weda, and Gane Barat). The small Christian communities in these regions were quickly overwhelmed and, after little resistance, fled or hid in the interior. Those that fled, often had to travel for several days or weeks through the island's interior to reach safety, some coming out on the coast of Kao Bay in the subdistrict of Wasile, others reaching safety after coming out on the coast of Weda Bay. These IDPs eventually ended up in North Sulawesi, on the island of Bacan, or in the Tobelo subdistrict.

Among those arriving in Tobelo were IDPs from the village of Payahe in the southern part of the Oba subdistrict. As the displaced from Payahe trickled into Tobelo in late November and early December, they brought with them horrific stories that they shared with their anxious hosts. In addition to the standard tales of betrayal, murder, and flight through the forested interior, they told a particular story about the murder of young children that became a staple (and remained so at least through 2012) in Christian accounts of the conflict in North Maluku. One IDP woman from Payahe I met in Tobelo described it as follows:

> When they attacked us [in Payahe], we were not ready. We had no weapons. A few days before they invaded some people had threatened to attack us, but the village head and the police told us we did not need to worry. Some of us were scared, but they said they would protect us. They lied. . . . When they [the Muslims] attacked us, they had lots of weapons, guns, and bombs. All we had were machetes, bows, and arrows. We could not fight them off so we had to run into the forest. . . . Not everyone got away. They caught some young children and killed them for no reason. They tied the wrists of the small children and put them in rice sacks. They took them out into the ocean and tossed them in the sea. When they ran out of fuel, they beat the children to death with wooden beams. The same way people kill a dog. (Tobelo, 2001)

I recorded this same story from a wide variety of IDPs from the Payahe region, as well as numerous other Christians from North Maluku.[19] Another man, a prominent minister from the GMIH church, in a discussion about issues of victimhood noted: "Even we are not as sadistic as them. Small children tied up and put in sacks with rocks and drowned in the ocean . . . taken out to sea in motor boats where they were tied up and drowned." This story about the murder of children, whether based in reality or on rumor and exaggeration, outraged Christians in Tobelo and elsewhere. Christians throughout Halmahera frequently cited the example of Payahe when discussing the subsequent violence in Tobelo. The riots in Ternate and Tidore had been a tragedy, but it was more about the destruction of property and a violation of trust than a loss of life. That changed in Payahe. For example, when asked about the intensity of the fighting in Tobelo one Christian IDP in Manado noted: "We saw what they [the Muslims] did in Ternate and Tidore. Then we heard about Payahe where they killed those children. . . . We realized that if we did not kill them, they would kill us. That is why so many Muslims were killed in Tobelo, people were angry about Payahe. They wanted revenge." Christians used Payahe to justify some of the atrocities committed in Tobelo. On numerous occasions when questioned about the killing of women and children, I was told that these actions were simply a response to what Muslims did in Payahe, and therefore acceptable. Muslims from Tobelo corroborated the effect that these stories had on the atmosphere. Many noted how tensions increased after the Payahe IDPs began arriving. According to some Muslims sources, it was at this point that many Christians started arming themselves.

Whether or not the atrocities in Payahe actually took place, the story remained an accepted fact among the Christian population at large in the decade after the violence. Nearly three years after the violence, one could still see a few places where people had spray-painted "Payahe" on the walls of burnt out mosques and destroyed Muslim homes in the Tobelo region. The particular details of the Payahe violence gave the story its power. If the story had been about some children killed in the course of fighting it would have been tragic, but it would have been one tragedy among many and would not have attained the defining role that it did. Ironically, the violence committed against Muslims in Tobelo, in part a reaction to the violence in Payahe, provided Muslims with the same sort of pivotal incident that rallied others to their cause and justified future actions.

Changing Justifications and Changing Modes of Violence

To merely note that the framing of the violence changed does not provide much insight into subsequent events and does not move us far beyond instrumental explanations of the violence, unless we look at how religion and religious beliefs affected the way violence was actualized. To simply equate the religious aspect of these conflicts with larger political goals fails to account for how religious beliefs influenced people's understanding of the conflict, the justifications it provided them, and the acts they were willing to commit in its name. If the religious understanding of this violence was based simply on political categories, how do we explain the willingness of people to sacrifice their lives to protect their place of worship? How do we explain the prevalence of ideas about martyrdom in the aftermath of the conflict? We can only explain these actions and these understandings if we pay attention to the meaning invested in them by participants. In his work on religious violence, Hans Kippenberg (2011, 200) argues that actors "who advocate religious interpretations of a conflict alter the course of that conflict." He notes that the framing of a conflict "in religious language generates a corresponding way of acting, thereby creating a reality all of its own" (Kippenberg 2011, 200). In the case of North Maluku, people found their meaning in religious interpretations of the conflict and these shaped their subsequent actions. As soon as the rioters in Ternate and Tidore began attacking Christian homes chanting "Allahu Akbar" or shouting out insults to Jesus Christ and Christianity, they created a new conflict. As Muslim militias attacked small Christian communities in Central Halmahera, they were, to borrow Kippenberg's phrase, creating "a reality all of its own." Although North Moluccans were quick to point to the role of politicians and provocateurs in the outbreak of violence in Ternate and Tidore, someone had to write and distribute the letter, these shadowy political machinations were quickly overshadowed by religious differences, which many came to see as the primary root of the conflict. Notions of peaceful coexistence quickly fell by the wayside, even as Muslim friends and neighbors helped them escape in some cases.

The shift in framing altered the meanings inherent in the violence, as well as the nature and goals of the conflict for many of those involved. People began to call on a religious discourse to understand the conflict—one that privileged their views and their community—as well as bringing into play religious practices based on certain moral and ethical ideas taken from that religious discourse. Christians began to compare current events to biblical stories, or to mine their knowledge of Christianity for justifications or ways of understanding the violence and their role in it. Christians struggled to explain some of the atrocities their community had committed. A common explanation that arose was as follows: "The Muslims slapped us in the face and we turned our cheek and took a step back. They slapped us again, so we turned our other cheek and took another step back and then we found the Old Testament. Forward. Revenge. An eye for an eye, a tooth for a tooth." Others compared their persecution with the nature of persecution in the Bible. Ministers pointed out that North Moluccans were not the first Christians to experience violence at the hands of others. After the violence that took place in Tobelo around Christmas in 1999 (discussed in the next chapter), which was often referred to as a "Bloody Christmas" (*Natal Berdarah*, Ind.), ministers noted that the first Bloody Christmas had taken place with the birth of Jesus Christ when King Herod ordered the death of all children born on that day. When rumors of another Bloody Christmas circulated amongst Christian IDPs in North Sulawesi in 2001, ministers returned to these themes and placed people's suffering within a biblical context.

This shift sacralized the violence. People were now killing in the name of religion and there was less need to feel remorse for their actions and less need to hesitate. In interviews and discussions, members of the Kao community noted the change in intensity as religious differences replaced ethnic grievances. When they were initially fighting the Makianese as part of an ethnic conflict, their goal was to remove them from the region. Thus when they invaded Malifut they only killed those who insisted on resisting. Others were allowed to flee, and encouraged to do so. That changed when the conflict became a religious one. At that point, they did their best to ensure that no one escaped. When people did flee, they were often hunted down. When they took refuge in mosques or elsewhere they were killed. I am not arguing that religion makes people more violent, the atrocities committed between Madurese and Dayaks during the ethnic conflict in Central and West Kalimantan around the same time exemplifies that ethnic differences can lead to atrocities as well. Instead, I am arguing that in this particular case, people looked to religion to help explain what was going on around them and to decide what the proper reactions were. The nature of events, when placed alongside regional history, albeit one now looked at selectively for evidence of the current conflict, led people to turn to their faith and community.

The increase in the intensity of the violence was accompanied by a shift to targets of a religious nature. During the violence in Kao-Malifut, the Kao had made it a point not to burn the mosques when they destroyed Makianese villages. After the violence in Ternate and Tidore, where rioters destroyed Christian places of worship, attackers from either side now took as their main objective to destroy churches or mosques. Religious leaders were also singled out. It became a goal to kill ministers, religious teachers, imams, or hajis. Rumors abounded as to the rewards offered for the heads of ministers and priests, or the efforts to which Christians would go to kill respected Muslim teachers or hajis and desecrate their corpses. Another popular target was individuals who had converted from one religion to another. According to Christian accounts, Muslim militias specifically targeted recent converts and Christians described their own efforts to find and kill their recently converted relatives. These different views of appropriate behavior on the battlefield did not necessarily apply for all participants, but it did for many, including those who were deciding the course of the conflict and taking the lead in committing acts of violence. These changing ideas and practices did not take place immediately but took hold as the conflict spread out from Ternate and Tidore.

Prior to the shift, participants often relied on magical powers (ilmu gaib, Ind.) to enhance their fighting ability. These powers were acquired from deceased ancestors, traditional healers, or others renowned for their esoteric knowledge. Once religion became the basis of the conflict, people still wore protective charms; however now the protection from magical power was augmented by that coming from the Muslim or Christian God. Ministers prayed over and baptized amulets to give them God's power. Christian fighters wore bibles or vials of water blessed by a minister around their necks or posters of Jesus Christ across their chests for protection from harm. When faced with trouble in battle, Christian fighters told stories about prayers or quotations of Bible verses that allowed them to prevail. One Christian fighter from northern Halmahera explained: "God takes care of those who believe in him, we are proof of that. . . . I slashed a fellow two times [with my machete], but did not wound him. Then, I took my machete and said the Lord's Prayer, and cut him in half [with one swing]." Others resorted to using Muslim taboos against their Muslim enemies. People dipped their arrows in pig blood before they shot Muslims, or painted the blades of their machetes with it. They argued that the pig blood would defeat any Islamic charms or spells used by their enemies. Fighters on the Muslim side had similar practices to protect themselves from harm. Some wore headbands with verses from the Koran or carried pieces of paper with Koranic verses in their pockets for protection. Others said certain prayers, or recited certain passages from the Koran a specified number of times, or a series of passages in a prescribed order, to protect them from harm. They took part in purification rituals prior to entering battle to make them bulletproof. These often consisted of having water poured over them by a religious specialist to make them immune to harm from steel weapons such as bullets, arrows, or machetes.

As religious perceptions of the violence came to the fore, people on both sides also began to see the conflict as a form of holy war. Christians believed they were fighting in the name of their God, for his glory, and with his support. Their main goal was to maintain a Christian presence on Halmahera. Some Muslims believed they were fighting a holy war as well and that they were waging a jihad to protect Islam in North Maluku from the Christians. One young Muslim man from Java explained rather succinctly: "This is a religious war. And because of this we have to face them with the spirit of jihad." Both Christians and Muslims began to consider those who died in the fighting as religious martyrs.[20] Both sides interpreted these claims to martyrdom by the other as evidence that their enemies were seeking to annihilate them, and that their plans were grounded in irrational and unchangeable religious justifications. The only recourse was to destroy them first if possible and any actions taken to this end were morally justified.

The religious nature of the violence continued to feed on itself, taking cues from other conflicts in Indonesia and even from transnational sources.[21] Christians saw themselves as a religious minority in the world's largest Muslim country fighting against government plans for the Islamization of Indonesia. The final goal of this strategy was the removal of all Christians from North Maluku so that "the sound of church bells would never be heard again." They linked their struggle to other episodes of religious violence in Indonesia, such as Ambon and Central Sulawesi. Christians talked of government plans for the implementation of Islamic law, forced conversions, and compulsory veils. Muslims felt a similar threat and argued that they were fighting against larger regional agendas for the Christianization of eastern Indonesia, a theme highlighted in the suspicious letter that had circulated in Ternate and Tidore. Muslims remembered and shared half-forgotten stories of earlier warnings about plans to Christianize North Maluku. One Muhammadiyah official in Galela recounted how in 1983 someone had visited him from the Muhammadiyah branch in Ambon and warned him that Christians were happy with their progress in North Sulawesi and Maluku and were now going to focus on gaining control of North Maluku. He had forgotten about the warning until the 2000 violence. Muslims pointed to the fighting in Ambon and Poso as other examples of Christian aggression, and they also noted the secession of East Timor, which some argued was evidence of larger Western plots to dismantle a Muslim Indonesia.

Both sides began to see themselves as part of a global struggle between Islam and Christianity. Christians in north Halmahera often associated themselves with Israel. They would argue that like the Israelis, they were a small religious minority under threat from a much larger Muslim population who sought to destroy them. Their ability to take control of and defend large parts of northern Halmahera from much a larger and better-armed Muslim force enhanced this resemblance in their eyes. Throughout Christian-held areas one could see paintings of the Israeli flag and graffiti reading, "Welcome to the new Jerusalem" and "Long live the second Israel." In Muslim controlled areas, in addition to anti-Christian and anti-Jewish graffiti, there was also anti-American and pro-Iraqi graffiti as Muslims linked their sufferings to the struggles of other Muslims throughout the world.

Some Muslims in North Maluku latched on to conspiracy theories linking the violence in Maluku to a larger "Zionist-Christian" plot to destroy Indonesia. They portrayed the Christians as fighting with the support of Western nations and in some cases receiving military aide directly from Israel. One of the more widespread Muslim versions of events quotes a Christian minister in Tobelo shouting, "Don't be afraid, because we will be helped by the Netherlands, England, and Australia. Make Tobelo the second Israel" as he led his parishioners in a massacre of Muslims (Ahmad and Oesman 2000, 76). On the island of Morotai, Muslim communities taunted fleeing Christians by shouting, "Where are your American friends now?" Christians made similar claims about foreign aid for the Muslim side from the Middle East, Pakistan, or Afghanistan. I collected numerous stories from Christians about sightings of Pakistani or Afghan mujahideen taking part in the fighting or distributing weapons. Christians cited the presence of dates or empty date boxes as evidence of support from the international Muslim community. Whether such aid existed or not is an entirely different question, but many on both sides were convinced it did, and they were not easily dissuaded.

In conclusion, the shift in the master narrative of the conflict from being an ethnic one to being one based on religion was more than just a simple shift in classification. It had an impact on the way the conflict was fought, the way it was resolved, and the way it will be remembered. Understanding how this shift in coding took place, and the affect that it had, provides a better understanding of the conflict. It shows that instrumentalist accounts that see religion as simple mobilization tools for politicians fail to capture the meaning of the violence to people involved and why they undertook the actions that they did. Simply noting that religion is a place marker for other differences—whether political or economic—is not sufficient. It removes any other social meaning from acts of violence. In North Maluku, religion provided a matrix through which people made sense of what happened around them as the violence spread across the province.

Chapter 4

MASSACRES, MILITIAS, AND FORCED CONVERSIONS

As violence spread across central and southern Halmahera at the end of 1999, tensions increased in the more populous subdistricts of Tobelo and Galela in northern Halmahera. These communities had started to worry about the spread of the conflict soon after the fighting began in Ambon and IDPs from central Maluku began arriving in the region. As the capital of the former province of Maluku, Ambon was the regional center for higher education and civil service opportunities. As fighting spread through the city and across the island, people with family in Halmahera fled north for safety and brought with them tales of Muslim-Christian clashes. Initially people in northern Halmahera looked at the events in Ambon as an Ambonese problem that did not concern them. However, the riots in Ternate and Tidore and the subsequent fighting in central and southern Halmahera made conflict in northern Halmahera seem increasingly inevitable to some. As the year came to a close the region was awash in rumors about impending violence. Christians feared Muslim plans for a "Bloody Christmas"

(Natal Berdarah, Ind.) and similar stories of a "Bloody Ramadan" (*Ramadan Berdarah*, Ind.) had Muslims expecting the worst.

The steady trickle of Christian IDPs from other parts of North Maluku into Tobelo with their tales of death and destruction exacerbated these tensions. Muslims in Tobelo cited this influx of forced migrants and their influence on local communities as one of the main causes of the eventual outbreak of violence. They argued that these displaced people were suffering from the trauma of their experiences, and many of them were well armed.[1] The anger these IDPs had toward Muslims in general and their desire for vengeance threatened to overwhelm traditional ties between Christian and Muslim Tobelo. The IDPs saw no difference between Muslims in Tobelo and those who had chased them from their homes in Oba or Ternate. They were not to be trusted and were a legitimate target for revenge. Although some Muslims regarded this developing tension as the unfortunate by-product of newly arrived and traumatized people, others saw a more nefarious initiative in this influx of forced migrants. One Muslim IDP from Tobelo in Ternate noted "There was the problem of IDPs [*pengungsi*, Ind.] from West Gane, East Gane, and other villages. They were all brought to Tobelo. That is what makes me think it was all organized. Why weren't the IDPs taken somewhere safer, somewhere more neutral? Like Manado? Why were they all brought to Tobelo?"

Muslims accused the GMIH of actively bringing the IDPs to Tobelo to augment their forces for a planned attack on the Muslim community. As one Muslim man from Gorua explained, "There were definitely suspicions on both sides, but the Christians had already brought lots of people from other areas into Tobelo. They called them IDPs. . . . But if we look at the day the conflict started, it was only an excuse to add to their strength . . . to add to their strength and destroy us." Local authorities made the same mistake that officials had made in Ternate. Rather than house the IDPs in one location, they placed them throughout the subdistrict to minimize the burden on local communities, or as one man explained: "Every village got a truckload of IDPs."[2]

As stories of violence circulated throughout Tobelo, Christians grew angrier and more distrustful of their Muslim neighbors. A Christian leader remembered the impact of IDP narratives on rising tensions:

> I remember in [my village] the first IDPs [from Central Halmahera] to arrive were from the village of Gumi in Oba. They arrived with the subdistrict

head, 170 people, and this was in addition to those who had preceded them from Ternate. If I am not mistaken there were 4,000 IDPs in Tobelo. It added to the difficulty of preventing [conflict] because while we worked from one direction to prevent the violence, from another direction, forced migrants told their stories about the atrocities [*keganasan-keganasan*, Ind.] that they had experienced and [these stories] heightened the emotions of those that heard them. (Manado, July 2001)

A staple component of these narratives was the promise from Muslims and government officials (largely Muslim as well) that they would protect their Christian neighbors. Almost inevitably, IDPs later witnessed these same people taking part in the violence or simply standing by and watching as the violence took place. The moral of these stories appeared to be that it was unwise for Christians to trust their Muslim neighbors or officials.

Aware that Christian communities were upset by stories from the displaced, a number of factions in Tobelo and Galela stepped up efforts to prevent the outbreak of violence. One group of individuals created the interfaith Forum for Solidarity in North Halmahera (Forum Solidaritas Halmahera Utara, Ind.) to combat rumor and innuendo. Others thought customary tradition, that is, adat, might be the proper tool to prevent conflict. In March 1999 Christian and Muslim members of the community formed the Hibualamo Adat Council (Dewan Adat Hibualamo, Ind.) to mediate rising tensions in the region. This organization tried to use adat, in particular the adat notion of *hibualamo* (big house, Tobelo), as a tool for conflict prevention. Hibualamo refers to a type of meeting house that used to exist in Tobelo communities and served as a place of mediation between different villages, different religions, or members of the community. The hibualamo, ideally, had served to integrate the various factions of Tobelo society. As religious institutions, the colonial government, and then the Indonesian government took over these mediating functions during the twentieth century, the hibualamo were relegated to serve as ceremonial locations for festive gatherings, such as weddings. Eventually, the structures began to fall into disrepair until the last one was destroyed in the 1950s or 1960s. With the disappearance of the physical structure of the hibualamo, only the idea remained with its focus on unity, but by the 1990s, even that had faded.

Leaders in Tobelo hoped a return to this idealistic philosophy of inclusion would unite Muslims and Christians in Tobelo in the face of religious provocation. They believed adat was the key to preventing the violence because, as one Muslim leader explained: "Tobelo adat does not distinguish between Christian and Muslims, it only pays attention to who was wrong and has to pay a sanction." The council consisted of village adat leaders (*kepala adat*, Ind.), politically powerful individuals, and various other influential (and ethnically Tobelo) members of Tobelo society. As one of their first activities, they held a communal feast to highlight their unity. They also began to hold meetings across the subdistrict to help maintain the peace. Other sectors of society got involved as well, including a group of young men who formed the Young Generation of Hibualamo (GEMAHILO, Generasi Muda Hibualamo, Ind.) to prevent violence among youth, something they thought older elites were unable to do. Fights between (often-intoxicated) youth from various neighborhoods have long been common in Tobelo town and elsewhere in Halmahera. As neighborhoods tend to break down along religious lines, some feared that these brawls could escalate into full-scale communal conflict.

Community leaders in Galela, north of Tobelo, undertook similar efforts in response to these rumors. After the violence in Kao-Malifut, a number of community leaders in Galela had formed the Galela Association for Harmony (Ikatan Kerukunan Masyarakat Galela, Ind.) in an attempt to prevent the outbreak of violence. As one Muslim member of the association explained:

> We had a program aimed at socializing the people about anticipating the impact of the violence that had taken place in Ambon and Malifut. We wanted them to know that what happened in Ambon and Malifut.... whatever had taken place there, [it had] happened there, not here. We did not need to be provoked or influenced by those events. We did it in churches, at meetings of the Family Welfare Movement [Pembinaan Kesejahteraan Keluarga, Ind.], in mosques. It was even more than that, since we did it in two groups as Muslims and as Christians. We also did it in the village administration building. I did one at the PT Global [banana plantation], then in Mamuya, together with subdistrict-level government officials [Muspika, Ind.] from the Christian side. We said we did not want what happened in Ambon to happen in Galela. What happened in Ambon, that was Ambon. Here we would stay friends. But, the Muslim side thought that most likely it [staying friends] would not happen. (Soa-sio, Galela, September 2002)

Despite these efforts throughout the subdistrict, interfaith tensions continued to simmer. Distrust between Muslims and Christians in Galela grew as rumor, innuendo, and actual violence spread across other parts of the region. The Bloody Sosol letter that had sparked the riots in Ternate and Tidore also circulated in the Galela subdistrict and put people on edge. After the August violence in Kao-Malifut, Muslims in Galela misinterpreted Christian aid for displaced families from Sosol and Wangeotak as the provision of arms for Christians in Kao to attack Muslims in Malifut (Adeney-Risakotta 2005, 244). Interactions and misinterpretations such as these heightened the tensions between the two groups and continued to thwart efforts to foster a wider sense of security between interfaith communities.

Back in Tobelo, increasing levels of mistrust led a segment of the Christian community to demand that all people of Tidorese, Makianese, and Kayoan descent leave the Tobelo subdistrict until the government restored order throughout the province. They based this demand on their belief that members of those particular ethnic groups, rather than Muslims in general, were the main instigators of violence. In response, some Muslims demanded that all Ambonese Christians leave town.[3] Neither demand was met. In an effort to calm the situation, a number of provincial leaders, including the sultan of Ternate and the governor, visited Tobelo town on 7 December to meet with local leaders and attend a peace rally. The organizers hoped the rally would prevent the outbreak of violence as well as convey their concerns to the regional government. Prior to the arrival of the delegation, some community leaders had taken a large white banner throughout the Tobelo subdistrict and asked people to sign it with messages of harmony. They brought this banner with its hundreds of signatures to the gathering as a sign that both Christians and Muslims were committed to peace.

Despite the multifaith emphasis planned for the meeting, the rally had overtones of Christian power. As the visitors from Ternate walked to the stage, protesters, mostly Christian IDPs, blocked their path with signs demanding an end to the violence. One sign read: "Muslims are our brothers, but the Makianese, Kayoan, and Tidorese are trouble-makers, [they must] leave Tobelo."[4] A representative from the Tobelo adat council gave a speech in which he threatened "migrants to the city," by which he meant Muslims from Makian and Tidore, if violence broke out. He also demanded that the government rescind Law 42/1999 that established the subdistrict of Malifut. A large group of students from the GMIH theological seminary located in Tobelo also attended the meeting. After marching to the rally in pseudo-military formation, a number of them gave fiery speeches demanding action.

Several other members of the community gave more moderate speeches. They pledged to maintain the peace and to stop attempts at disrupting interreligious relations. The rally, however, failed to ease tensions and both sides continued their preparations for conflict. One Muslim leader in attendance interpreted it as an extreme example of "Christian arrogance."

As 1999 came to an end, violence persisted in central and southern Halmahera and rumors continued to circulate in Tobelo and Galela. People expected to be attacked at any moment. As others have noted in central Maluku (cf. Spyer 2002a, 204–6; Hagen 2006, 196) efforts to prevent violence, or to prepare for it, essentially hastened its arrival as each side listened to rumors, armed themselves, and searched for evidence of the first strike. Every piece of evidence that could be interpreted as proof that the other side was preparing for an attack was cited as a warning, regardless of its banality. When people saw Muslims or Christians gathering at houses of worship outside regular meeting times, they interpreted it as planning sessions for an invasion. Attempts to guard places of significance to one side or the other were seen as acts of aggression rather than cautionary moves. Christians considered almost any sign of white clothing as proof that Muslims were preparing jihad uniforms for their militia. Cars moving along the highway at night were evidence of clandestine meetings, even when these trips were undertaken by conflict prevention organizations. Conflict seemed inevitable and often an overriding sense of inevitability is enough to make something happen.

Violence in Tobelo

On the night of 26 December the fighting began in Tobelo. It remains uncertain exactly how the violence started, no formal investigation was ever undertaken, and the results of any such investigation would most likely have been dismissed by whichever side was found to have thrown the first stone. Christians claim that Muslims began stoning Christian homes in the Gosoma neighborhood of Tobelo town, and they were forced to retaliate. Muslims claim the exact opposite. Regardless of how it started, the situation quickly spiraled out of control as these disturbances convinced both sides that they were under attack.[5] The sight of Muslims and Christians seeking refuge in mosques and churches was interpreted as evidence of mobilization, as both sides had accused the other of stockpiling weapons in their respective houses of worship. The appearance of people wearing red (Christian) or white (Muslim) headbands also convinced many that the long expected attack was underway.

Once it began, Muslims, who constituted a large percentage of the urban population in Tobelo town, quickly gained the upper hand. Most of the town's Christian population fled to the south where they rallied their forces. In the following days Christian militia from the southern part of the Tobelo subdistrict and from the Kao subdistrict launched a counterattack. They managed to take control of the town by 28 December in some of the most brutal fighting of the conflict. As one Muslim man described it:

> At that time between the burning and massacring of Muslims and Christians, I saw how human life had lost its value. It was so easy for a man to kill a man, as if people no longer valued humanity. There was only inhuman behavior and no dignity. Everyone was overcome with ferocity. Those who were Muslims had to kill Christians, and Christians had to kill Muslims, even if they were brothers. Brotherhood no longer existed. There were only Muslims and Christians. All the tools of war had to be used to kill and destroy. Tobelo was like Judgment Day. (Ternate, September 2002)

As Christians gained the upper hand, a number of Muslims took refuge in the main mosque, called Mesjid Raya, in the center of town where they were surrounded. A Christian man present at the fighting said that many of the Christian fighters did not want to accept their surrender:

> There were thousands of them [in the mosque]; old people, women, and children. The red troops had already routed them. They were surrounded in the mosque. Two people at the mosque still resisted. They were both killed. . . . We discussed what to do with the people in the mosque. Some wanted to kill all of them and someone threw a bomb in the mosque that killed many people. That was when the army showed up. . . . They quickly loaded all of the people from the mosque onto their trucks and protected them. If the army had not shown up at Mesjid Raya, we would have killed them all. We would have killed all of them. They did not resist any longer once they entered Mesjid Raya, but we wanted to kill all of them. (Tobelo, May 2002)

The army evacuated the Muslims from the mosque and other places throughout Tobelo town and took them to the army base north of town. From there, the government eventually evacuated the survivors to Ternate.

Fighting also took place to the south of Tobelo town. Christians from neighboring villages attacked the small Muslim community in Gamhoku and killed dozens of Muslims taking refuge in the church and destroyed their homes. The village of Gamhoku is a one of the larger villages to the south of Tobelo town and one of the only mixed-faith villages. As violence spread across the region both religious communities in Gamhoku felt pressure from their religious brethren elsewhere to prepare for an attack on their neighbors. However, the Christian and Muslim families of Gamhoku (many of whom were related) decided to follow the example set by the Kao and remain united. Both sides agreed to protect each other in the event of an attack from outsiders. These plans fell apart when several Muslims from Gamhoku skirmished with some Christians from a nearby village. This fight resulted in two Christians getting injured. The Muslims from Gamhoku returned to town and were instructed by their Christian neighbors to take refuge in the church for fear of reprisals.

Eventually a large contingent of fighters from the neighboring villages of Upa and Pitu arrived to avenge the injuries. Christians in Gamhoku were unable to maintain control over the situation and the people from Upa and Pitu proceeded to attack the church. As the outsiders were attacking, some Christians from Gamhoku frantically tried to save their Muslim family and friends and managed to carry a few off to safety, while others fled into the forest. Estimates on those killed range from thirty to seventy-seven people. In subsequent years, Muslims from Gamhoku claimed that the killings had been planned in advance because Christians wanted to prevent Gamhoku Muslims from setting up road blocks. Christians supported this argument and noted that Muslims in Gamhoku had built road blocks to inspect passing vehicles for weapons on several occasions prior to the violence.

As the fighting raged in Tobelo town and the southern part of the subdistrict, violence broke out between Christians and Muslims in several villages north of town as well, including the villages of Gorua, a mixed Christian and Muslim village, and the Muslim village of Popilo. After Christians defeated the Muslims in Tobelo town, they reinforced Christians living to the north and joined the attacks on Gorua and Popilo on 31 December. The Christians were able to rout the Muslims from Gorua, and many of those Muslims who survived fled north to the neighboring village of Popilo. Popilo, however, was under attack by Christian militias from the north as well as from the south. Muslims who did not flee sought refuge in the village mosque. One survivor explained that the wounded, women, and children fled to the mosque because they thought they would be safe there. Christian militia members argued that those who fled to the mosque were not seeking refuge, but rather regrouping and continued to shoot at them or threaten them from inside the mosque. Christian militia attacked the mosque and killed almost everyone inside, including women and children. Survivors from Popilo told me that more than 150 Muslims were killed inside the mosque that day. Those who managed to escape fled to the local army base, to the subdistrict of Galela, or to the island of Morotai.

Another part of the Christian strategy was to control the Trans-Halmahera Highway, the only road that runs between Kao and Tobelo. One obstacle to that plan was the largely ethnic Tobelo Muslim community of Togoliua located along the highway in the southern part of the subdistrict.[6] The presence of this large Muslim community had prevented reinforcements from the Kao subdistrict from using the highway to aid Christian militia in the early days of the violence in Tobelo. Christians claim that the Muslims in Togoliua blocked the road with felled coconut palms; as a

Figure 4.1. Christian militia, referred to locally as "red troops" (*pasukan merah*, Ind.),
pose for a photo before heading off to battle, Tobelo subdistrict,
North Maluku. January 2000. Photo by Ci Mey.

result militia from Kao had to travel by boat to bypass Togoliua. Leaders of the Christian militia wanted to ensure that troops from Kao could return home safely once the fighting ended. People in the Christian village of Kusuri also claim that people in Togoliua had sent taunts to neighboring Christian communities to provoke violence. Muslims in Togoliua maintain that they were the victims of a preemptive attack that lacked any clear motive other than religious cleansing. The subsequent fighting led to the complete destruction of the village. During the invasion, members of the overwhelmed Muslim community, including a large number of women and children, retreated to a mosque in the village that was subsequently burnt along with most of those taking refuge within. Muslims who were able to escape fled into the forested interior where many were killed by pursuers. Those who were not killed were captured and turned over to the security forces.

These massacres in Popilo and Togoliua provided Muslims with a rallying point and a level of anger that would aid in the recruitment of others to their cause and provide significant motivation in their quest for revenge. A common refrain in interviews with Muslims involved in violence after the massacres in Tobelo was a desire to avenge these killings. A young Muslim woman who took part in later attacks in 2000 in which dozens of Christians were killed explained it this way:

> For me, a jihad to defend religion is the responsibility of all Muslims. Let alone when Christians massacre Muslims whenever it suits them. We have to fight and retaliate. We destroyed [the village of Duma] and it's large church as revenge against Christians. Actually the Pasukan Jihad's last goal was to destroy Tobelo which is the base for the Christianization of North Maluku. Christians should not try to hurt Muslims. Muslims will rise up and defend themselves. (Popilo, September 2002)

Graphic accounts of the killings in northern Halmahera were published in a local newspaper and fanned the flames of Muslim anger (*Ternate Pos* 2000c, 2000d). Images of the burnt out mosques and footage of Indonesian soldiers and bulldozers pushing corpses into mass graves were published in a variety of national Muslim magazines (cf. Kompak-Dewan Dakwah 2000) and became a staple of the inflammatory VCDs that were popular in Indonesia and on the Internet in the early 2000s (Spyer 2002c).

Violence in Galela

As news of the fighting in Tobelo reached Galela on 26 December, communities frantically made more attempts to prevent the spread of the violence to their villages. These efforts, as the others before them, failed and fighting broke out between Christians and Muslims in the village of Dokulamo on 27 December. The Christians in Dokulamo, aided by reinforcements from the nearby villages of Duma and Soa Tabaru, were able to defeat the Muslims and take the village. Prior to attacking Dokulamo, troops from the village of Duma had already routed Muslims in the neighboring villages of Ngidiho and Gotolamo. In the wake of these clashes Christians eventually controlled most of the interior of the Galela subdistrict. The majority of the Muslim population retreated to the subdistrict capital of Soa-Sio where they were joined by thousands of Muslim IDPs from Tobelo.[7] Although estimates vary, the violence in Tobelo and Galela most likely led to the deaths more than one thousand people.[8]

The success of Christian militia in Tobelo and Galela convinced some Christians that they should launch an attack on the subdistrict capital of Soa-Sio in Galela to eliminate the last Muslims in the region. The Muslims in Soa-Sio were surrounded. Christian militia from the interior of Galela controlled the area to the north and west of the town, while militia from Tobelo had total control over the Tobelo subdistrict to the south. They planned to sweep into Soa-Sio from all directions and destroy the last remnants of the Muslim community. The Christian militia would then move across the strait to the island of Morotai to secure Christian communities there. However, at this point Christian leaders in Tobelo called for a brief respite to install traditional war leaders (*o kapita*, Tobelo), to rest, and to ponder their situation.[9] Some leaders argued that enough blood had been shed, while others were eager to press their advantage while they still had the initiative.

During the lull in fighting, the army took steps to "protect" the local population. Soldiers set up a blockade along the highway between Tobelo and Galela to hinder any large scale invasion from the south. They also forcibly removed almost all of the Javanese transmigrants from the subdistricts of Kao and Tobelo. Soldiers told the Javanese that they were being evacuated to protect them from Makianese militia who were supposedly planning to attack them for not joining their cause. They evacuated all of the Javanese from Tobelo and Kao, irrespective of their religion. The army did not, however, evacuate other transmigrant communities in Halmahera (in places such as Weda, Wasile, and Maba) and some did get caught up in the conflict. Christian Javanese transmigrants in the Dodaga region of Wasile were killed or chased from their homes by Muslim militia.[10] Other Javanese transmigrant communities were located either in Muslim-controlled regions, such as Gane Timur, or Gane Barat, or in areas that largely escaped the conflict entirely, such as Maba.

A Political Interlude: Violence in Ternate

In addition to the fighting between Christians and Muslims that took place throughout Halmahera at the end of the year, clashes broke out again in Ternate City. On 27 December residents of Ternate witnessed an outbreak of violence that contradicted the interreligious character of the larger conflict in North Maluku. The renewed fighting in Ternate pitted the Muslim supporters of the sultan of Ternate against his Muslim Makianese and Tidorese opponents. Tensions between these two factions had been running high since the riots in November when the sultan of Ternate had re-created and deployed his customary palace guard also known as yellow troops (*pasukan kuning*, Ind.). The sultan's forces had become the de facto guarantors of order in Ternate after the Indonesian security apparatus had collapsed during the November riots. After the departure of the Christian community, the pasukan kuning continued to play a major role in maintaining order. Some people accused the sultan of using his troops to further his own political agenda under the guise of providing security.[11] Supporters of the sultan argued that the pasukan kuning and a related group called the Sultan Babullah Youth Organization (Generasi Muda Sultan Babullah, Ind.) simply arrested and interrogated provocateurs who were trying to upset the peace. Their opponents viewed it differently. They alleged that the pasukan kuning kidnapped and tortured members of the Makianese and Tidorese community who openly opposed them (Forum Komunikasi Masyarakat Propinsi Maluku Utara Makassar 2000; Tomagola 2000c; Hoda 2000, 31–32). These abuses at the hands of the pasukan kuning angered the Makianese and Tidorese and added to the lingering resentment toward the sultan for his alleged favoritism of the Kao in the Kao-Malifut dispute and his supposed pro-Christian stance.

This growing antagonism eventually led to open violence in late December when some residents from the migrant neighborhood of Kampung Pisang in Ternate, a well-known stronghold of opposition to the sultan, attacked a group of the sultan's troops in response to an assault on one of their community members. In retaliation for this attack, the next day the pasukan kuning burnt down large parts of Kampung Pisang. News of the destruction of Kampung Pisang and additional attacks on migrant communities in Ternate reached Tidore and reinforcements rushed to help their Makianese and Tidorese brethren fight the sultan's forces.

The troops from Tidore wore the now familiar white headbands worn by Muslim forces in the religious conflict that had been raging across North Maluku for the last two months. Thus Muslim white troops (*pasukan putih*, Ind.), opponents of the sultan of Ternate, were engaged in hand-to-hand combat in the streets of Ternate with the mostly Muslim pasukan kuning of the sultan. The much larger pasukan putih were able to overwhelm the sultan of Ternate's troops. The battle ended with the defeat of the pasukan kuning on the steps of the sultan's palace and the surrender of the sultan himself to the sultan of Tidore who was called in on 29 December to calm things down and prevent the burning of the sultan of Ternate's palace. The sultan of Ternate eventually left the island when people began calling for his arrest as an instigator of the December violence (*Jawa Pos* 2000). Some Muslims in Ternate and Tidore claimed the sultan of Ternate sparked the conflict with his opponents to prevent reinforcements from leaving Ternate and Tidore to aid Muslims in northern Halmahera. If people from Ternate and Tidore were busy fighting the sultan's troops in Ternate City, they argued, they would not be able to help their Muslim brethren in Tobelo or Galela. Thus as pleas for aid were coming in from Muslims in Tobelo hundreds of people were involved in intrareligious fighting in the streets of Ternate City.[12]

As news of Muslim defeats in Tobelo and Galela arrived in Ternate, local Muslims, joined by thousands of newly arrived IDPs from northern Halmahera began to plan how to avenge the massacres in Tobelo and to return the displaced to their homes. The man chosen to lead this effort was Abu Bakar Wahid Al-Banjari, a civil servant from the village of Tomolou on Tidore. The militia that these people eventually formed was referred to as Pasukan Jihad (Jihad Troops), and because they wore the white headbands that Muslim militia had donned in the fighting throughout eastern Indonesia, they were often referred to as white troops (pasukan putih, Ind.)

The Violence Spreads throughout North Maluku

In the first weeks of 2000 the conflict continued to spread throughout northern and central Halmahera. In the last days of 1999 and the first few days of 2000, Christian militia destroyed every Muslim community in the subdistricts of Ibu and Sahu. The violence in Sahu and Ibu was minimal as most of the Muslim communities had fled to Ternate before the outbreak of hostilities due to their small numbers. Fighting also took place throughout the subdistrict of Jailolo to the south of Kao where Christian communities battled local Muslims along with Muslims from Ternate and Tidore before being defeated. In the Loloda subdistrict on the northern tip of Halmahera fighting broke out in January and February. Christian militias were able to take control of most of the mainland and forced several hundred Muslims to take refuge in Ternate. In contrast, the Muslim community on Doi Island off the coast of Loloda maintained that island as a Muslim stronghold throughout the conflict. The unrest also spread to central Halmahera when clashes broke out in various villages in the subdistrict of Wasile forcing a large number of Christian IDPs from southern Wasile to flee across Kao Bay to Kao and Tobelo, and a much smaller number of Muslim IDPs from northern Wasile to flee to Morotai

Clashes broke out on the island of Bacan to the south of Ternate as well in late January. How the fighting began in Bacan, again, varies depending on who you ask. Muslim sources claim it began when someone threw a fire-bomb into the Al-Khairaat Pesantren in the subdistrict capital of Labuha on 25 January. Christians claim it began when Muslims started burning down Christian homes in Labuha that same day. The violence eventually spread throughout Bacan destroying several villages and causing thousands of Muslim and Christian IDPs to flee to the district capital of Labuha, the province of North Sulawesi, or to Halmahera. The government eventually established an IDP camp in the village of Panambuang on Bacan to house approximately thirty-five hundred Christian IDPs from Bacan and neighboring Gane Barat. Violence also broke out on the nearby island of Mandi-oli forcing Christian IDPs to flee to North Sulawesi and elsewhere.

In February the violence spread across the island of Morotai off the northeast coast of Halmahera. Southern Morotai had been tense since thousands of Muslim IDPs from Tobelo and Galela had arrived in the last days of 1999. Widespread rumors led many to believe that both sides were planning an attack. At end of February clashes broke out in and around the subdistrict capital of Daruba. The Christian community fled to the nearby air force base where they were held for several months. The unrest spread up the east and west coasts of Morotai and several Christian villages and Christian neighborhoods in the South Morotai subdistrict, as well as several villages in the North Morotai subdistrict, were destroyed.[13] Hundreds of Christian IDPs joined those from Daruba at the air force base. Others fled to the nearby island of Rao where several thousand IDPs from all over Morotai took refuge in the village of Posi-Posi Rao. Muslims threatened to invade Rao several times, but never did. A local Chinese merchant hired a company of marines to guard the island and their presence prevented any large-scale attack.[14]

Other parts of the province were not so fortunate. In mid-February violence broke out on the island of Obi to the south of Halmahera. The situation on Obi had grown tense as soon as the violence had broken out in Ambon in 1999 since many of the children who had been schooling in the capital returned to their various villages. The riots in Ternate and Tidore and the violence in Tobelo and elsewhere had made people even more anxious. Rumors and evidence of the impending violence seemed to be everywhere on the island. For example, in one village on Obi, Christian villagers said that shortly after the violence began in Ambon three men with identity cards that identified them as being from Java arrived with briefcases of money, but were unable to explain where they were from, or what their purpose was to the satisfaction of the villagers. According to the story, the locals killed them out of suspicion. The Obi IDPs who related this story argued that that they must have been provocateurs. Some people were scared enough that they left for Manado prior to any fighting. Eventually clashes took place in six villages on Obi and the nearby islands of Tapa and Bisa between 17 February and 3 March leading to the complete destruction of several villages.[15] This period of fighting ended with an attack on the largely Christian village of Bobo on the south coast that was repelled. These various attacks forced several thousand primarily Christian IDPs from Obi to flee to Tobelo, North Sulawesi, Tanimbar, and Papua.[16] During this same period, several villages were destroyed in fighting in Gane Timur in southern Halmahera.

North Maluku on the National Stage

News of the unrest in North Maluku had an impact throughout a nation already distressed by the ongoing violence in Ambon. The destruction of the Muslim community in Tobelo in December 1999 and the savagery of the violence shocked Muslims across the country. On 4 January the newspaper *Republika* (2000d) ran its widely cited article about the massacres in Tobelo with the provocative title "Three villages invaded, women raped, 800 Muslims massacred overnight."[17] The article referred to the violence as a "humanitarian tragedy that smelled of genocide" (*tragedi kemanusiaan berbau genocide,* Ind.) and described how women were raped in the streets and 80 percent of the men in Gorua, Popilo, and Luari were killed.[18] The violence in Tobelo and the seeming inability or unwillingness of the government to address the killings in Ambon increased Muslim anger. Some were convinced of President Wahid's inability to handle the situation when he drastically downplayed the number of fatalities in Halmahera, claiming at one point that only five people had been killed (*Media Dakwah* 2000; *Republika* 2000d; Thalib 2001, 36). His statement contrasted with mainstream media accounts (*Kompas* 2000c) and those in more radical Islamic publications (*Suara Hidayatullah* 2000; *Kompak-Dewan Dakwah* 2000; *Sabili* 2000a) that detailed the horrific nature of the violence and the large number of victims. Muslim leaders demanded the government take action.

Within days these appeals culminated in a large demonstration organized by Muslim politicians around the National Monument in Jakarta that called for a jihad to save Moluccan Muslims.[19] The rally, called a Million Muslim Religious Gathering (*Tabligh Akbar Sejuta Umat,* Ind.), was said to have attracted as many supporters as its name would indicate. A number of prominent members of the Indonesian political scene spoke at the rally. Among these was Amien Rais, leader of the Indonesia's largest Muslim organization Muhammadiyah, and the speaker of the People's Consultative Assembly. Rais took to the stage and said he supported the call to save the Muslims in Maluku. His appearance at the rally, and a subsequent photo of him on the cover of a major news weekly, was proof to many Christians in North Maluku that forces in the national government had clearly sided with the Muslims (*Forum Keadilan* 2000a).[20] Christians in North Maluku were not surprised when, on at least one occasion, they found a flag from

Rais's political party, the National Mandate Party (Partai Amanat Nasional, Ind.), on the corpse of a slain Muslim fighter.

In response to this call for jihad, the Laskar Jihad, one of the more prominent Muslim militia organizations involved in post-Suharto communal violence, was formed on 30 January 2000 (Hasan 2002, 159). The Laskar Jihad was created as the paramilitary wing of the Communication Forum for the Followers of the Sunnah and the Community of the Prophet (FKASWJ, Forum Kommunikasi Ahlus Sunnah wal Jama'ah, Ind.) headed by Ja'far Umar Thalib, a Muslim preacher who had spent time in Afghanistan.[21] Although founded in 1998, the FKASWJ did not announce the existence of its paramilitary wing until after the violence in Tobelo. The Laskar Jihad began publicly recruiting volunteers to send to eastern Indonesia and established training camps in several parts of Java. At a rally on 6 April, titled "Jihad: A Final Effort to End the Christian Moluccan Uprising" (*Jihad: Upaya Terakhir Mematahkan Gerakan Pemberontakan Kristen Maluku,* Ind.), Thalib announced that three thousand Laskar Jihad members were ready to depart and a further seven thousand were in training (*Forum Keadilan* 2000c). After the rally, Thalib marched to the presidential palace with his supporters and demanded to meet with President Wahid to discuss the crisis in Maluku. Wahid agreed to see him and five of his associates (including the leader of the Pasukan Jihad in North Maluku, Haji Abu Bakar Wahid Al-Banjari), but they were "rudely thrown out" (*diusirnya dengan kasar,* Ind.) after they delivered their demands (*Kompas* 2000b; Thalib 2001).

After this meeting, the national government made some perfunctory moves to shut down Laskar Jihad training camps in Bogor and elsewhere. Despite these efforts and presidential instructions to prevent their departure, approximately one thousand Laskar Jihad members left for Maluku in April and May from Surabaya and Jakarta (Hasan 2002, 186). A few Laskar Jihad troops reportedly arrived in North Maluku where they were incorporated into local militias.[22] Extralocal militias such as the Laskar Jihad played a much smaller role in the conflict there than they did in Ambon.[23] Their effective media wing, however, essentially co-opted the actions of the local Pasukan Jihad into their larger narrative of Laskar Jihad involvement in eastern Indonesia.[24] The connections between Abu Bakar Al-Banjari, the head of the Pasukan Jihad based on Tidore, and Thalib helped people who read national papers equate the two militias.

Although Wilson (2008, 155–59) goes to great lengths to argue that the Laskar Jihad was not present in North Maluku, for Christian communities engaged in violence with local Muslim militia the difference was negligible. They saw little difference between the local Muslim militia (Pasukan Jihad, Ind.) and extralocal Muslim militia or Muslim organizations such as the Laskar Jihad. Christians often used the terms *laskar jihad* (jihad paramilitaries), *pasukan jihad* (jihad troops), and *pasukan putih* (white troops) interchangeably in their narratives of violence. Since Christians often saw the events in North Maluku as part of a wider pan-Indonesian effort to Islamize the entire country, the origins or ideological particularities of the attacking militia were seldom important. Furthermore, many Christian communities were convinced of the participation of non-Moluccans in the violence, whether as part of organized militia sent from elsewhere, or simply as individuals who had taken it on themselves to join the violence. They based this belief on a wide variety of evidence, such as identity cards found on the bodies of slain Muslim fighters, graffiti in destroyed Christian communities marking it as the work of people from Java or Sumatra, admissions from Muslim associates, or simply rumor. One friend of mine had a folder filled with photos and photocopies of identity cards, business cards, and other identity papers that were taken off of corpses after battles that identified individuals as originating from outside North Maluku. In one group discussion I had about the final attacks on the village of Duma, everyone noted the presence of outside fighters, particularly a large contingent of Madurese who kept shouting "We are from Madura and are thirsty for your blood." Thus in the minds of many Christians, for all intents and purposes, the Laskar Jihad was involved in the violence in North Maluku.

As I noted previously, Christians also believed that Muslims from outside of Indonesia participated in the violence. I collected numerous stories about the involvement of Afghans, Arabs, and Pakistanis. IDPs from Dodaga in Wasile claimed that a number of Afghans had appeared in town to train local Muslims about protection magic for the upcoming violence. A Christian village head from Morotai said the subdistrict head had told him about Pakistanis traveling around the island in the months before the violence distributing weapons and Korans. My research assistant from Ternate told stories of strangers with long beards and Arab clothing showing up in that city up to two years before the violence. They worked as vegetable traders and traveled all over the province. After the violence began, he realized they were preparing for the conflict by learning the roads and paths and by buying boats for use in future attacks. Although it is important to note after the fact that outsiders and the Laskar Jihad played a minimal role, it remains important to understand what people believed at the time of the violence, and which many still believed in the aftermath. Explaining the lack of a major Laskar Jihad presence does little to explain how Christians coped with the issue during the violence and understood events around them.

After the violence had ended Christians continued to talk about outsiders in the region. Benny Doro, a prominent fighter on the Christian side, claimed that local Muslims from Galela had visited him in 2002 to request his aid to chase out extralocal troops that would not leave now that the violence was over. Christians often cited the presence of lone young men, usually Javanese, in villages in Galela as further evidence for the continuing presence of these outsiders. In mid-2002 I traveled to a Muslim village north of Tobelo to conduct some surveys with a Christian Galela research assistant. We reported to the village head and asked him and others in his house fill out a survey (due to the postconflict circumstances we chose to rely on snowball sampling for the survey). He then directed us to a nearby barracks that housed a number of recently returned families. We introduced ourselves, explained the survey, and asked if any of the men or women present would be willing to participate. A few people asked to see the survey and began reading and discussing it. As we sat on the bamboo platform discussing the questions, a young Javanese man (evident from his accent) approached and demanded to know what we were doing. He insisted on seeing my business card, which I gave to him. After perusing it he climbed up onto the platform where the others were seated and began to walk around kicking the surveys and asking what they were. After I explained the purpose, he responded that had I been present in the village at the time of the US invasion of Afghanistan he would have certainly killed me and I was rather lucky I had been elsewhere. I asked him where he was from, but before he could answer others in the group quickly explained he was a transmigrant. I asked which settlement he lived in, but by this point he was hustled off by some bystanders and the people I had hoped to survey slowly dispersed. At this point my research assistant quietly suggested we should leave. During the short trip home he was adamant that the fellow in question was a member of Laskar Jihad and he recounted at length how large numbers of these militia members had stayed behind after the violence had ended throughout North Maluku. Despite my uncertainty on the matter, he had no doubt and once back in Tobelo town the story quickly made the rounds among his neighbors and friends. Although a simple anecdote, it should be clear to the reader by this point that anecdotal evidence held great sway in North Maluku.

On the Muslim side, my research assistants collected accounts from Muslims about fighters from outside North Maluku coming to take part in the fighting. Abu Bakar Wahid said his troops included some Javanese. His son recounted some "mysterious Acehnese" soldiers that accompanied them during the fighting in Galela in mid-2000. This reference to Acehnese fighters correlates with (but does not necessarily validate) Christian accounts of mysterious Acehnese units sighted during the conflict. Despite the presence of small numbers of extralocal militia members, the vast bulk of Muslim forces were made up of local community members.

Forced Conversions

During the first half of 2000, another type of story started circulating regarding the religious nature of the North Moluccan violence. Narratives of savagery and atrocities on either side had become common by that point, but as the violence continued to spread across the province people began to hear stories about the forced conversion of individuals, or in some cases of entire communities.[25] Some of these reports included stories of people being killed because they refused to change their religious affiliation. Christian accounts of forced conversion included circumcision and the taking of Muslim names, while Muslims focused on people being force-fed pork or dog meat and compelled to attend church. Others told of people converting, supposedly of their own initiative to save their lives in the face of impending violence. These narratives fit well with larger fears of Islamization and Christianization that were prevalent at the time. Furthermore, they drew more attention to the religious aspects of the violence. North Moluccans pointed out that it was difficult to argue that the conflict was not about religion if one group was forcing another to convert. If it was about land, politics, or something else, there would be no need for these forced conversions.[26]

The stories that caught people's attention were about entire communities forced to convert under the threat of death. These narratives described how a militia invaded a particular village and survivors were offered the choice of conversion or death. One of the better-known examples was the Christian village of Lata-Lata on the small island of the same name off the coast of Bacan in southern Halmahera.[27] Muslim militia from the island and elsewhere invaded the village of Lata-Lata on 5 February 2000. Although the Christian community tried to fight off the attackers, they were vastly outnumbered and fled into the interior. Eventually more than fifteen hundred Christians came out of the forest and surrendered to the Muslim militia. Once they had surrendered the minister and some of his assistants were taken away and executed. A young man from Lata-Lata who I interviewed in North Sulawesi said that some Muslims later told him that militia members received fifty million Indonesian Rupiah for the minister's head. The militia leaders then gave the people of Lata-Lata the choice of converting to Islam or dying. The majority of them chose to convert; those who refused were killed. The converts were drenched in salt water to cleanse them, instructed in how to say the *shahada* (the Muslim profession of faith), and eventually all were circumcised. They were then given Muslim names. Little by little, however, some of the new converts escaped to Ternate, North Sulawesi, or Halmahera. One of the young men I interviewed had escaped under the pretense of going on a shopping trip to Ternate, where he then boarded a boat to Bitung in North Sulawesi. From elsewhere in North Maluku, Christians reported incidences of their family members or neighbors being killed after refusing to convert. I collected information about other examples of forced conversions from Gane Barat, Oba, Morotai, Galela, and the small island of Doi off the coast of Lololda.

One of the more frequently cited examples of forced conversion to Christianity concerned conversions in the village of Togasa in the northern part of Galela. In fact the people who converted to Christianity were not from Togasa but from the neighboring village of Tutumaleleo. Tutumaleleo consisted of Muslim Galela as well as a large group of Muslim Sangirese migrants. The latter returned from the Philippines to Indonesia in the 1980s and settled in Halmahera along with a number of Christian Sangirese. Many of the Sangirese in Tutumaleleo only converted to Islam after the government resettled them in Halmahera and they decided to forgo their indigenous ritual practices. As the violence spread across northern Halmahera in 2000 the Galela in Tutumaleleo asked their Sangirese neighbors to join them in an attack on the Christians in Togasa. The Sangirese refused, citing their family connections with Christian Sangirese. At this time Christian militias from villages in southern Galela had religiously cleansed most of southern Galela, except for the capital, and were threatening to move north. As a result, Muslim villages in the area lived in constant fear of attack. One evening after the Sangirese went to sleep, their Galela neighbors slipped out of town. When the Sangirese discovered that they had been abandoned they fled into their gardens and the nearby forest to hide. They were too scared to seek refuge in Soa-Sio with the Muslim IDPs who had abandoned them, and they feared Christian militia. The Sangirese believed that their Galela neighbors hoped that they would be overwhelmed and killed by Christian militia as punishment for refusing to attack Togasa. After a week of hiding, one man went to the village of Togasa to surrender to Christian militia and eventually all of the Sangirese, as well as some others who had taken refuge in the forest, were brought to Togasa. After a few days, the Sangirese asked a minister to baptize them. They said it was an act of free choice. The minister initially refused their request but after repeated appeals, and after he checked with his superiors at the GMIH Synod, he agreed to baptize them, but only if each family signed a letter saying their conversion was voluntary. In total 150 people converted to Christianity. Some then joined Christian militia and took part in the fighting around Togasa when Muslim militia from Morotai and Soa-Sio attacked in March and April 2000.[28] My research assistants also recorded accounts of Muslims from the villages of Gamhoku and Togoliua who were forced to convert to Christianity. In some cases Muslim individuals or Muslim families who lived in Christian villages converted at the outset of the violence, or shortly thereafter, as a matter of survival. In one small village south of Tobelo there were only two Muslim households. When the violence broke out in Tobelo these two families, thirty-eight individuals in total, fled to their gardens and hid for five days. Eventually a local Chinese businessman coaxed them out of the interior. At that point, the head of the family decided that converting to Christianity was their best chance for survival and they did so.

What Happened to Agency?

At this point, some readers might argue that I appear to be saying that participants in the North Moluccan conflict were driven by ancient religious hatreds inherent in North Moluccan society and that I have removed any sense of agency from their actions.[29] This is not the case. My goal thus far has been to explore how the discourse of the conflict shifted from one focused on ethnic conflict to one that focused on religious differences, thus I have been exploring the broader warscape of North Maluku to examine how people across the province interpreted and reacted to events (both the real and the fantastic). Individuals and communities displayed a multiplicity of reactions to the conflict around them or the one they thought was just over the horizon. With this goal in mind, I have focused on those parts of North Maluku that succumbed to violence. The way that people responded to the discourse of religious violence and the violence itself varied across the province and even within villages. As anti-Christian riots swept Ternate and Tidore, some Muslims took part in their planning, other individuals quickly joined them once they began, while still others were forced to take part with threats of violence. Other Muslims protected their Christian neighbors or sat on the sidelines not taking part at all. While some in Tobelo town grabbed their machetes, spears, or bows and arrows and ran toward the violence, others fled to army bases or police stations for protection. Some North Moluccans embraced the idea of religious violence and sought out opportunities to take part in attacks against the religious others. They not only fought to protect, or retake, their village, but traveled to other villages, even other subdistricts, to take part in the fighting. Not every community, however, reacted to rumors or direct threats with preemptive or defensive violence. The most obvious choice some people made as tensions swept the region was to leave their homes in advance of any open conflict, whether that meant leaving the province or moving to another part of North Maluku where they felt more secure. Others fled in the face of overwhelming odds as majority communities attacked or expelled them. Some of these people spent the rest of the conflict living in IDP camps. Other forced migrants joined militias in their place of refuge and continued to take part in the fighting. A third set moved back and forth between conflict zones and IDP camps.

Fighting or fleeing were not the only options available to people. Some people stayed in North Maluku and worked on conflict prevention or resolution, as exemplified by the efforts at conflict prevention in Tobelo, Galela, and elsewhere mentioned above. Rather than succumb to calls for violence, these individuals worked to prevent bloodshed or stop it once it started, often at great risk to themselves.[30] They traveled into hostile territory to meet with like-minded individuals across the religious divide when doing so exposed them to violence from their religious enemies, as well as their own religious brethren who refused any moves toward peace or reconciliation. Others simply refused to take part in the fighting based on ambivalence or what they claimed was a moral opposition to the violence. One young man from a village in Tobelo subdistrict refused to join his village militia because he did not agree with the morality of the fighting. He claimed that this decision led to death threats from his neighbors, forcing him to leave the village. A carpenter who lived in a nearby village also refused to fight because he believed it did not fit with his understanding of Christianity. As his neighbors prepared to go off to battle they insisted, rather ominously he recalled, that he accompany them. They dismissed his complaints about the immorality of the violence, and he only avoided taking part by convincing them that someone needed to protect the village while the rest of the men were gone. In Ternate a large number of people were caught up in the violence in one way or another, while others did their best to continue with their lives despite the conflict that engulfed the province. A number of people found this rather trying and left on their own accord, moving to places such as Manado, Surabaya, or Makassar until the conflict was over.

In some cases entire communities were able to opt out of the violence. As mentioned earlier, the Sawai ethnic group avoided bloodshed because Muslim Sawai refused to join in attacks on their Christian Sawai neighbors. In this particular case the discourse of ethnic solidarity superseded that of religious differences. The Christian community on the island of Kakara off the coast of Tobelo made the decision to protect their Muslim neighbors until they could be evacuated to safety, while their neighbors on the mainland did otherwise. Finally, with the exception of the villages of Jara-Jara and Patlean, the entire subdistrict of Maba in eastern Halmahera, for reasons that remain unclear, was free of violence for the entirety of the conflict despite high tensions and local provocation.[31] In some cases these refusals to participate led to reprisals, as it did for the Sangirese Muslims of Tutumaleleo who were left to be massacred by their neighbors. In other instances, such as among the Sawai, it prevented conflict. Decisions to take part and decisions to accept or reject the hegemonic narrative of the conflict as one based on religious differences, varied across the province. Individuals and communities called on a variety of sources, such as historical narratives, rumor, religious ideology, and adat, in making (or accepting) decisions in response to, or in preparation for, the conflict. They were not driven by a religious version of primordialism but rather by processing ongoing events in light of their own historical understandings of intergroup relations in the region (which was variously based on cultural, ethnic, religious, geographical, or political differences), as well as their own personal needs—which in turn could be based on economics, kinship, or other factors.

The Fall of Duma and the End of Large-scale Violence

In mid-2000, although sporadic attacks continued throughout North Maluku, the bulk of the violence had shifted to the northern part of Halmahera as the Pasukan Jihad focused on avenging the massacres in Tobelo and returning Muslims to their homes, while Christians in the region worked to prevent them from doing so. During April and May Muslim forces in Galela were augmented by militia from elsewhere in North Maluku, particularly IDPs from Tobelo. They concentrated their efforts on defeating the last pockets of Christians in the subdistrict after which they hoped to converge on Tobelo. Eventually Muslim militia destroyed most of the remaining Christian communities in Galela. In the wake of these attacks, Christian IDPs fled to Tobelo or retreated to the village of Duma where they decided to make their last stand. The people in Duma were left to fend for themselves as army blockades prevented large-scale reinforcements from Tobelo. They had numerous opportunities to leave and in several instances were reportedly offered safe passage. They did not take these opportunities, however, and over the course of several community meetings decided to stay and fight. After one major attack in May in which Muslim militia destroyed part of the village and killed fifty-eight Christian militia members, some survivors suggested that the women and children should be sent to safety. According to a number of people I interviewed who were present at the meeting, village leaders (*tokoh masyarakat*, Ind.) denied them permission saying "We should not flee, it is better we all die to together" (*Jangan kita mengungsi, biar saja kita mati sama-sama*, Ind.).

Leaders argued that they had to defend Duma until "the last drop of blood" (*titik darah penghabisan*, Ind.). Unfortunately for them, the Muslim militia in the region remained equally determined that they be removed from Galela. They sought to gain a secure hold over the entire subdistrict, as well as to exact revenge for earlier violence in Tobelo and Galela. The people of Duma had played a significant role in the violence since it began on 27 December. Militia from Duma had been involved in attacks on Muslim communities throughout Galela in late 1999 and early 2000, and many Muslims considered them the main instigators of the violence. Furthermore, Muslims accused them of committing a number of atrocities. The destruction or defense of the last remaining Christian village in Galela became a rallying point for both sides.

The fate of Duma was more than just a matter of strategy. Muslims and Christians were well aware of Duma's significance in the religious history of Halmahera. Since Dutch Protestant missionaries had acquired their first North Moluccan converts in Duma in 1896, it had been considered the birthplace of Protestantism in the region. The missionary who had overseen these initial conversions was buried in the village cemetery. As a result Christians viewed it as a place they had to defend, while Muslims singled it out for destruction.[32] Abu Bakar Wahid al-Banjari, leader of the Pasukan Jihad, told one of my Muslim research assistants that they had targeted Duma, in part, because it was a "missionary center" (*pusat missionaris*, Ind.).

In late May and early June Muslim militia launched a number of unsuccessful assaults on Duma. They eventually ended the standoff with a successful attack on 19 June. The small army detachment stationed in the village was unwilling, or unable, to stop the attack despite desperate pleas from the people of Duma. Muslim and Christian witnesses claimed that a few soldiers actually took part in the violence. When it was done, 150 people, including many women and children, had been killed as the Christians were defeated. Much like the massacres in Togoliua and Popilo in Tobelo, the killing did not stop when the fighting ended. One Muslim participant explained what happened next:

> They could not run because they were surrounded. We made a decision that there were Christians that had to be killed, and those that we did not need to kill. We did it according to the rules of religion. Old people, children, and

women would not be killed. We put them in carts and sent them off. . . . The others were placed in the big church. They were placed in the church and arranged. They were given a chance to pray. There was an order from the leader of the militia [*panglima perang*, Ind.] that whoever had magical powers [*orang jin*, Ind.], someone who was a mystic—who could kill these people, they should go ahead and kill them in the church. (Ternate, September 2002)

In some cases however, Muslims from surrounding villages jumped into the fray to rescue their relatives when possible. Muslim militia spent the next week undertaking mopping-up operations in the region looking for survivors still in hiding, who when found were most often killed.

Any discussion of the North Maluku violence must mention the disappearance of the *Cahaya Bahari* passenger ship on 29 June 2000, since it was the last large-scale loss of life related to the conflict. As hundreds of IDPs from Galela, many of them seriously wounded, arrived in Tobelo the confidence of some began to falter. The anxiety turned to full-scale panic with the circulation of a map that purported to show the details for an upcoming Muslim invasion of Tobelo. The map was supposedly found in the bag of a slain Muslim fighter and its authenticity was not questioned. The discovery of the map and the fall of Duma convinced many people in Tobelo town that it was time to leave. At the point the only way to get to Manado was on the *Cahaya Bahari*, a rather dilapidated passenger ship. According to a former crew member, the ship, originally designed for 250 passengers, left Tobelo harbor on 28 June with more than 550 people on board. Most of the passengers were IDPs from various parts of Halmahera, including a large number of survivors from Duma. The ship was last heard from on 29 June, reporting that it was taking on water and its pumps had failed. Search and rescue operations were launched, but after more than three weeks of searching only ten survivors were found (*Kompas* 2000a).

The lack of debris from the ship led many Christians in Tobelo to believe that the sinking of the *Cahaya Bahari* was no accident and rumors abounded as to its fate. Some argued the Indonesian Navy sank the boat to hide the survivors of the massacre at Duma. Others claimed Pasukan Jihad troops captured the ship at sea and killed all on board. One man claimed to have met an eyewitness who saw the captured ship brought to the island of

Doi off the coast of Loloda where Muslim militia unloaded the passengers and executed them on the beach. Supposedly at low tide some of their bones were still visible. Some relatives of those who perished believed that Abu Sayaf or the Moro Islamic Liberation Front from the Philippines had captured the ship. I met one man whose wife had perished with the *Cahaya Bahari*. He had traveled all over Mindanao to meet with representatives of Abu Sayaf and the Moro Islamic Liberation Front to search for information regarding the ship's fate, with no success. I also knew several women who as late as 2005 refused to consider themselves widows because they were sure that eventually they would be reunited with their husbands who had worked onboard.

A State of Emergency

The killings in Duma and the continuing violence throughout North Maluku and Maluku led Indonesia's President Abdurrahman Wahid to declare a state of civil emergency in both provinces on 27 June 2000. A state of civil emergency allowed the government and security forces to close the region to nonresidents, establish naval blockades, impose curfews, and conduct household searches for weapons (International Crisis Group 2000b, 10n32). The government thought these actions would enable the armed forces to establish control over the two provinces. The level of violence in North Maluku decreased sharply after the implementation of the state of civil emergency (the same was not true, however, in Maluku). According to Muslim sources, their plans for a major attack on Tobelo lost support once news reached Galela that President Wahid had declared a civil emergency. Furthermore, large numbers on both sides had become tired of the fighting. The declaration of a state of civil emergency and the arrival of even more armed forces made a continuation of the violence through large-scale attacks untenable and unappealing to many.

The main reason the violence stopped, however, was because the destruction of Duma, the last Christian village in Galela, essentially divided the two sides into their separate corners. As each side had been pushed into its own enclaves, they became more and more unassailable and neither was strong enough to defeat the other. Christians held most of the northern peninsula outside of Galela and Jailolo, including Tobelo, Kao, Ibu, Loloda, and Sahu. It appeared that local Muslim militia could do little to take it away. Muslim attempts to invade Kao from the south had failed several times and further attempts had been abandoned. Christians had also come to the realization that they were not going to be able to expand their area of control either, particularly with the army guarding the border between Christian and Muslim militias at the border of Tobelo and Galela. They settled in to defend what they already had. Muslims were left in control of Ternate, Tidore, most of Jailolo and Galela, southern Morotai, and large swathes of central and southern Halmahera (the districts of Oba, Weda, Patani, Gane Timur, and Gane Barat) and most of Bacan and surrounding islands. Other parts of the region remained a patchwork with Christian and Muslim communities divided, but interspersed.

In the end several thousand people were killed and more than 220,000 were displaced during the violence. Those displaced by the fighting went to a number of places based on religious identification. North Moluccan Muslims fled primarily to Ternate, the Galela subdistrict, southern Morotai, and Bacan. The Christian diaspora was more widespread and covered at least four provinces (North Maluku, Maluku, North Sulawesi, and Irian Jaya). Within North Maluku, Christian IDPs were concentrated in the subdistricts of Tobelo and Kao, and on the island of Rao off the west coast of Morotai. Outside of North Maluku approximately thirty-five thousand mainly Christians IDPs fled to the province of North Sulawesi (Duncan 2005b). Other Christian IDPs fled to Maluku and Papua, in particular Sorong and Manokwari.

It is only in hindsight that anyone knew that the fall of Duma would be the last incident of large-scale violence in the region, and the situation on the ground remained uncertain. Despite the implementation of a state of emergency, North Moluccans remained cautious. They had seen the armed forces and the government fail too many times in their efforts to stop the conflict. People still thought that violence could erupt at any point, despite the presence of army and marine units. Furthermore, although many could agree that too much blood had been spilt, neither side was willing to admit defeat and few were interested in reconciliation. Interaction remained limited with both sides segregated into their respective regions, often with military units stationed in-between. The ongoing fighting in Ambon and

Poso where the Laskar Jihad remained active until 2002 also kept Christian communities on edge. Only over time did people begin to realize that further bloodshed on the scale of 1999–2000 was unlikely. Large-scale returns of IDPs began in 2001, but as late as 2008 some IDPs remained reluctant to return to their former homes. It was during this period, from roughly August 2000 through 2001 that Muslim and Christian communities began to cautiously interact again, and some individuals and organizations began to focus on reconciliation and the return of forced migrants.

Chapter 5

PEACE AND RECONCILIATION?

From Violence to Coexistence

After the declaration of emergency and the end of large-scale violence, local communities in North Maluku were inundated with calls for "reconciliation" (*rekonsiliasi*, Ind.) from a variety of sources. Trauma experts from Jakarta visited and lectured people on the importance of forgiveness and reconciliation as part of the healing process (Sitohang et al. 2003). Aid workers from international NGOs ran workshops for adults and funded "reconciliation parties" for schoolchildren. Finally, local politicians talked about the importance of reconciliation for the region's future in speeches at public ceremonies. In many of these events, the nature of reconciliation, and what was being asked of people, was left unstated other than a focus on preventing future violence. At times even the definition of the term remained unclear to those involved in seminars and workshops, since officials and practitioners largely conveyed the message using the English cognate. Regardless of the vague nature of what actually constituted rekonsiliasi (either for local people or practitioners), North Moluccans were continually reminded that it was necessary for the region's future stability and for the well-being of their children and grandchildren. Local communities, however, were more concerned with preserving the absence of violence, rather than with repairing or establishing interfaith links between communities, which may or may not, have existed before the conflict.

Despite the ambiguity of the idea of rekonsiliasi, postconflict analysis of Maluku and North Maluku has focused on the desire of local elites and particular communities for reconciliation.[1] Another way of looking at reconciliation, however, is to compare public rhetoric about reconciliation with "hidden transcripts" voiced in private.[2] The differences between these two discourses can be illuminating (Zorbas 2009). While the public discussion has focused on the importance of reconciliation and on everyone's apparent desire to repair relations, in private people remained more ambivalent, even those who voiced strong support in public. Another difference in these discourses focused on what reconciliation meant or entailed. Elite concerns with moving forward and forgetting were often at odds with local views on accountability, justice, and mistrust.

Negotiating the Peace in Tobelo and Galela: The View from the Top

In other conflict regions of Indonesia, the central government inserted itself directly into the local peace process. In Poso in Central Sulawesi, the minister of social affairs, Jusuf Kalla, convened and mediated a meeting between all sides in the southern Sulawesi town of Malino in December 2001. These discussions produced the Malino Declaration that laid the foundations for the end of that conflict. Jusuf Kalla oversaw a similar meeting, again in Malino, in which representatives from Muslim and Christian communities in Ambon agreed to peace (often referred to as Malino II).[3] Although violence continued in both locales after the Malino accords, the agreements did pave the way for the cessation of large-scale conflict in the two provinces. The Indonesian government made no such efforts in North Maluku, since the violence had largely ended of its own accord in July 2000. Vice President Megawati Sukarnoputri made a few visits to North Maluku during and after the violence, but these visits were largely symbolic.

Although the national government played no role in ending the conflict in North Maluku, some military commanders stationed in the province made efforts to stimulate peace by sponsoring communal meals between Muslims and Christians. These affairs were often little more than hastily organized "adat feasts" undertaken to meet the whims of military officers, rather than a reflection of any desire for reconciliation among the local population or any work by adat leaders. It appeared at times as though the armed forces thought that if people held communal meals and made a few speeches, they would be willing to put the past behind them. Officers seemed unaware, or unconcerned, that numerous communities had tried similar strategies in 1999 and failed. As a result, these military efforts had limited success, and in some cases people simply refused to take part.

The lack of serious government attempts to stop the violence in North Maluku or to foster reconciliation in its aftermath left it to NGOs and local communities to work on peace. International NGOs took some of the first steps. Their efforts usually took the form of interfaith meetings outside of North Maluku, often in Manado, with the goal of getting Muslims and Christians to sit down and talk in a neutral setting. For example, international NGOs held several seminars on peace journalism, or multiday workshops on reconciliation in Manado. Some people in North Maluku responded negatively to those who participated in these *ex situ* attempts at peace. They were shouted down and in some cases assaulted on their return home (*Ternate Pos* 2000e; Tindage 2006, 55n54). Furthermore, Muslims and Christians complained that these meetings were rather pointless since they preached only to the converted. Individuals who opposed reconciliation refused to attend, and in some cases, organizers did not invite them because their attitudes were not conducive to reconciliation.

In some parts of North Maluku, communities established local organizations to facilitate interfaith discussions, which occasionally led to formal declarations of reconciliation. In Jailolo in western Halmahera, local leaders formed a group called Team 30 to improve relations between Muslims and Christians. This team consisted of Muslim and Christian leaders chosen by their communities to work on conflict resolution. Eventually they signed a formal sixteen-point agreement to ensure the peace. This settlement created an opportunity for forced migrants from Jailolo, many of whom had fled to Ternate or Tobelo, to return home (Ngatomo 2006). Other communities throughout North Maluku made similar arrangements, for example there was a Team 25 in the subdistrict of Sahu (CPRU/UNDP 2004, 31).

In this chapter, I will focus on the peace and reconciliation process in northern Halmahera, in particular on relationships between Muslims and Christians in the former subdistricts of Tobelo and Galela. I concentrate on this part of the province because people in North Maluku considered those two subdistricts something of a linchpin for regional stability. If the people of Tobelo and Galela could achieve peace and the displaced could return to their homes in both places, some thought there would be a ripple effect throughout the province. Reconciliation in northern Halmahera would allow the large number of Christians from Galela in Tobelo to return to their villages and Muslims in Galela to return to Tobelo. Good relations in Tobelo would also permit Muslims from Tobelo in Ternate and Morotai to return and then Christians from those locales could return home as well. The interconnectedness of these returns, while rarely apparent to government officials charged with handling forced migrants, was quite evident to the IDPs. Christians from Morotai remained reluctant to return home due to the continuing presence of large numbers of Muslim IDPs from Tobelo in Morotai, the same people who had played a role in their expulsion from the region. Muslims IDPs in Morotai and Ternate remained wary of returning to Tobelo until some of the thousands of Christian IDPs from other regions had moved elsewhere. The high concentration of displaced people in Tobelo, or waiting to return there, made reconciliation in that particular locale central to the stability of the rest of the province.

The first serious in situ efforts at reconciliation in Tobelo and Galela began in October 2000 several months after large-scale hostilities had ceased. Two main considerations motivated this process, the desire of Tobelo Muslims to return home, and the desire of elites on both sides for Tobelo town to become the capital of the newly created district of North Halmahera. The initial meetings toward reconciliation took place in the village of Mamuya near the border between the subdistricts of Tobelo and Galela. Prior to the conflict Mamuya had been a religiously mixed village, but the violence had forced both Christians and Muslims to flee at various points, before it finally came under Christian control. Organizers chose this village primarily because it corresponded to the boundary between Muslim-controlled regions and Christian-controlled areas. Neither Muslim representatives nor their Christian counterparts would have to travel through any hostile population centers to attend the meetings. The village was also located only a few kilometers south of the main military checkpoint along the Trans-Halmahera highway between the two regions.

Organizers also chose this location for its historical significance as the border between Tobelo and Galela. I collected two different accounts of how Mamuya came to be the border between the regions. One version explains that the sultan of Ternate first established the border (*o tona ma langi,* Galela) between the subdistricts of Tobelo and Galela in the sixteenth century when he awarded several Galela villages south of Mamuya to the Tobelo as a reward for helping him defeat the Portuguese and their local allies. A large boulder near the spot still bears the footprint of the Tobelo leader and the imprint of his spear as he slammed it down to demarcate the edge of his new domains. The Dutch colonial government later reified this border in an effort to stop fighting between the Tobelo and the Galela, who still resented this loss of territory (Adeney-Risakotta 2005, 168). Another account claims the origins of the border existed prior to existence of the sultan of Ternate. In this version, in an effort to demarcate their borders the people of Tobelo and Galela agreed to start walking toward each other as soon as roosters announced the sunrise. They agreed that the spot where they met would become the border between the two regions. Unfortunately for the Tobelo, the Galela walked much faster and reached as far south as the village of Gorua before they met. The Tobelo were not happy with this decision and fought to have the border moved north. After many years of fighting, the two sides agreed that Mamuya would serve as the boundary. As evidence of both of these accounts, people point out that communities in the villages immediately north of Tobelo, such as Luari and Popilo, still speak Galela. In 2000, leaders on both sides thought the historical resonance of Mamuya would help bring legitimacy to any decisions they reached regarding peace in the northern Halmahera.

The first meeting, now referred to as Mamuya 1, took place on 11 October and consisted of a small contingent of Muslims and Christians and members of the armed forces. Tensions were still quite high on both sides at this time, since the massacre in Duma had taken place a mere four months earlier. Furthermore, large-scale violence was still occurring almost daily in Ambon and elsewhere in Central Maluku. Since organizers feared fighting might break out amongst participants during the gathering they limited the interaction between the two sides and soldiers "closely guarded" those who took part (Tindage 2006, 66). The organizers had decided beforehand that only two people would speak at this first meeting. The head of the Muslim delegation, Samsul Bahri Umar, a prominent member of the Muslim community in Galela and a leader of the Muslim militia during the conflict, spoke first:

> We, the Muslim community of the subdistricts of Galela and Tobelo, want to ask our brothers in Tobelo, if they would open themselves to receive us and to permit us to enter and fast [for Ramadan] in the land of our ancestors, where we were born, and where we grew up. Today our intention is only to convey our openheartedness and sincerity. (Tindage 2006, 67)

The head of the Christian delegation, Hein Namotemo from Tobelo, replied:

> From the bottom of our hearts, we apologize. We will go home first to discuss the good-intentioned request from our brothers at this beautiful meeting. The most important thing today is that we are sitting here together. The first step is to identify carefully the problems so we can, through stages, find agreement. Later, when it is time for IDPs to return, our leaders will sit down to talk about the returns. Let's not allow unauthorized returns to cause trouble. So we ask for patience, we should not be arrogant by saying this has to be so, or that has to be so, without trusting in God. Meetings like this are important and valuable, because if we do not have meetings like this our generation will be lost, and our future generations will be weakened, but we have to realize that thinking such as this [about reconciliation] is not yet shared by the masses. (Tindage 2006, 67–68)

According to local accounts from that time, Namotemo was justified in his caution. Talking about reconciliation and acting on those ideas still carried a risk to individuals from their own religious brethren. Many people were simply not ready or willing to consider allowing Muslims to return to Tobelo, or Christians to return to Galela. Leaders on the Christian side had so much concern about people's refusal to reconcile that when they sent the delegation to the first meeting in Mamuya, they left behind a separate delegation to handle any trouble that might arise in Tobelo town should news of the meeting leak out (Tindage 2006, 66–67).

Muslims also had to deal with a recalcitrant population. Opponents of reconciliation had displayed their opposition in August 2000 when members of the armed forces tried to facilitate the peace process in northern Halmahera. On 10 August the Indonesian Navy attempted to arrange a meeting between Muslim and Christian families from Tobelo and Galela. They planned for one ship to leave from the harbor in Tobelo town with Christians on board and another to leave from Soa-Sio, Galela with Muslims. The ships would rendezvous off the coast of Galela and the two sides could meet. They hoped that providing a neutral ground for the two factions to talk might help improve relations. Not everyone in Tobelo and Galela supported this plan. As the ship from Tobelo approached the prearranged meeting point, they received news that individuals opposed to reconciliation in Galela had refused to let the ship leave port and had thrown a bomb at the home of Samsul Bahri Umar in protest. The ship with the Christians from Tobelo tried to dock in Galela despite these developments, but people opposed to reconciliation turned it away.[4] Events such as this one in Galela left leaders wary of rushing any sort of meeting about reconciliation.

One topic not discussed at Mamuya 1, or any other meeting, was the issue of blame. Muslim and Christian leaders who took part in these talks realized that if they attempted to assign blame for the conflict, or ask for apologies, their task would be much harder, if not doomed, from the outset. As a result, participants at Mamuya 1 did not talk about responsibility or accountability. Subsequent meetings also avoided these topics and participants focused on reestablishing ties, opening communication, and discussing the return of IDPs. In interviews done in the years after the Mamuya meetings, organizers and participants answered questions of blame and culpability with a similar refrain: "We need to talk about the future, not the past. We need to forget who is right and who is wrong."

A series of other gatherings, each increasing in size and scope, followed this initial meeting. On 18 November, the two sides met again in Mamuya, a meeting now referred to as Mamuya 2. They continued their discussions from Mamuya 1 about the desire of Muslim IDPs to return to Tobelo and the Christian concerns that the time was not yet right for such a return due to the thousands of IDPs still in Tobelo. They agreed to let Muslims travel briefly to Tobelo to clean their ancestors' graves during Ramadan, and let Christians travel to Galela to do the same during Christmas (Tindage 2006, 71–73). In the aftermath of Mamuya 2, people slowly started to interact on an individual and more informal basis. As families visited their former homes to clean gravesites during the holiday season, they often met and talked to their neighbors, which helped lay the ground work for future returns. The formal Mamuya meetings ended with a significantly larger gathering on 24 December with approximately six hundred members of the Muslim and Christian elite in attendance. Also in attendance was Vice President Megawati Sukarnoputri who was touring the province to promote reconciliation. During this meeting, as opposed to earlier ones, the soldiers providing security allowed the attendees to mingle. Tindage (2006, 73–75) notes that this interaction paved the way for subsequent visits and discussions between the two communities. After Mamuya, similar meetings took place in Galela, Loloda, Morotai, and elsewhere in North Maluku as Christians and Muslims met to discuss the terms for the return of forced migrants.[5]

Despite the improved relations among the elite after the Mamuya meetings and the increased flow of Muslims and Christians between Galela and Tobelo, tensions continued and fears of renewed violence hampered efforts at reconstruction and impeded the return of the displaced. Influenced by ongoing violence in central Maluku and Poso, rumors of impending attacks still periodically swept the region. The end of 2000 and early 2001 was when outside militias began to play a significant role in the Poso and Maluku conflicts (Hasan 2002, 190–206). Newspaper headlines and radio reports focused on the intensified violence as the arrival of these extralocal militias escalated the fighting. For Christians in North Maluku the idea that the Laskar Jihad might eventually shift their attention north once they were finished in Ambon seemed like a distinct possibility.[6] Christians looked at the continuing violence and the quality and quantity of Laskar Jihad weapons and saw a sign of the government's continued unwillingness or inability to stop these militias. Muslim communities remained nervous about the intentions of their former Christian neighbors and how they might react to events elsewhere in eastern Indonesia. They wondered how Christians in North Maluku would respond to significant Muslim victories in Ambon or to a massacre of Christians. This mutual mistrust, anger, as well as feelings of revenge, permeated the region and continued to hamper any serious efforts to return IDPs to most parts of the province, particularly in Tobelo and Galela.[7]

The urgency of stabilizing the situation also had a political aspect. The provincial government had informed local politicians in Tobelo that if they did not calm the situation and facilitate the return of forced migrants,

the capital of a new district of North Halmahera would be placed somewhere other than Tobelo town. Several adat leaders in Tobelo, led by subdistrict head Hein Namotemo, decided that one way to ease tensions and to
facilitate IDP returns would be to hold an adat peace ceremony to ensure
that religious conflict did not break out again. This adat ceremony was the
initial step in local attempts to revitalize adat as a tool of reconciliation
and violence prevention (Duncan 2009a). Namotemo argued that agreements reached by government officials were no guarantee of peace. Furthermore, simply letting IDPs trickle back home ran the risk of future violence.
If Muslims and Christians took part in an adat ceremony and took an adat
oath (*o hahi*, Tobelo) to uphold the peace, the likelihood of future violence
would diminish. Adat leaders believed that although people were willing to
violate the law or flout the armed forces, they would be less prone to violate
an adat oath and suffer the consequences, which included illness and death.
They pointed to the success of an adat oath taken by the ethnic groups of
Kao in 1999 to guarantee their unity during the conflict. With these goals
in mind, the subdistrict head and his adat advisor organized a peace ceremony to take place in the center of Tobelo town, which would be accompanied by the formal signing of a declaration of peace between Muslims and
Christians.

The ceremony included Muslim and Christian participants, although
the latter contingent was much larger since most of the Muslim community
remained in Ternate. It began with prominent Muslim and Christian adat
leaders, a minister, an imam, and Benny Doro, a well known militia leader
on the Christian side, walking to the center of the field and standing behind
a table holding the Peace Declaration.[8] The religious professionals opened
with Christian and Muslim prayers. Traditional war leaders (*o kapita*, Tobelo) then marched onto the field, including Christian kapita from Tobelo
and Kao wearing red headbands, followed by Muslim kapita wearing white
bandanas. The two contingents stood facing each other in the center of the
field from a distance of about ten meters. After the kapita, a ritual leader
(*pemuka adat*, Ind.) and the adat secretary who had designed the ceremony
entered the field. Behind them were two young women carrying a set of
bowls. One woman carried a bowl of coconut oil and the other carried a
bowl of liquefied red sugar (*gula merah*, Ind.). Six Christian militia members followed bearing traditional Tobelo weapons of war: spears, dance
shields, and swords. Each warrior then handed Benny Doro their weapon,

which he then delivered to the kapita of Tobelo. The kapita of Tobelo stuck two spears into the ground a meter apart. He then leaned the dance shields against the inside of the spears. Finally, he stuck the two swords in the ground so they leaned against the outside of the spears.

The pemuka adat advanced to the center of the field and began speaking.[9] He explained that a year ago Muslims and Christians had been angry at each other to the point of spilling blood, to the point that people had died. Now they had to make peace. He then poured the bowl of red sugar over the weapons. The sugar symbolized the need to remove the bitterness from their relationship. He then did the same with the coconut oil, which symbolized the need to ease tensions by making relations between the two sides smoother. After the adat leader poured the sugar and oil on the weapons, the Christian kapita presented their Muslim counterparts with tobacco, betel nut, and betel leaf laid on the flat of a sword, a traditional sign of hospitably in Halmahera. The Muslim kapita reciprocated. After the exchange, a government announcer read the sixteen-point peace declaration in Indonesian. Representatives from both sides then signed the declaration along with a variety of government functionaries in attendance, including the governor of North Maluku.

The sixteen points of the Peace Declaration focused largely on agreements to stop religious harassment and provocation (See appendix B). Signatories would refrain from using the terms *red* and *white* that had come to signify Christian and Muslim during the conflict. They would also stop using the phrases *Laskar Kristus* and *Obet* to refer to Christians, as well as *Laskar Jihad* and *Acang"* to refer to Muslims.[10] The other focus of the declaration was an agreement to respect government authority in the region and to let the police, army, or courts handle any disturbances or violations of the law. The signatories also agreed to allow displaced communities to return and regain their property, but these returns would take place selectively and in stages to ensure a smooth transition. Despite the adat focus of the ceremony, the only reference to adat in the declaration was a brief note in article 1 on the fate of those who attempted to subvert the peace in Tobelo: "They will be victims and fail wherever they are for what they have done."

Both communities also agreed "not to bring up the past in order to justify or blame a particular party, but [only] to remember the past so it never repeats itself." Thus the Peace Declaration, much like the preconditions for the meetings in Mamuya, explicitly removed the issue of culpability from the discussion. The governor of North Maluku echoed these concerns in his speech at the ceremony:

> We have no need to look at the past; rather we should look to the future, if not for ourselves, then for the future of our children and grandchildren. For one year, our quarrels and our anger with each other led to many victims. It made some into orphans and widows. The saddest result was that our social institutions and solidarity were destroyed. Let each of us ask our conscience 'Why did we quarrel and what did we get?' Only destruction and decline. (Tindage 2001, 2)

His comments reflected standard government rhetoric about the need to forget what happened during the violence in order to build a better future.[11] Unfortunately, for the elite, their lack of concern with accountability or responsibility reified understandings among many in North Maluku that the government simply did not care about them or their suffering.[12] It did not care enough to stop it while it was happening, and it did not care enough to recognize it in the aftermath. When local officials in Galela told communities that they had to accept that the conflict was simply the work of God and move on, it was not well received:

> We are shocked that the government says we cannot blame anyone, and that we have to look at this as the work of God. You can call a famine, a drought, or a natural disaster the work of God, but social conflict is different. If a river turns to blood, you can say that is a curse sent by God, but the Muslims clearly invaded us. How can you say that is the work of God? Why do we have to share equal blame? (Galela subdistrict, May 2002)

Was It Really about Religion?

Government arguments that focusing on the violence would only foster animosity, which could then lead to future conflict, stemmed from a realization that the two sides could not agree on a single narrative of what had taken place. Muslim accounts of what happened were, and remain, largely irreconcilable with Christian ones. Rather than arguing over differing versions of the conflict by attempting to assign blame, official explanations often focused on the common Indonesian theme of outside provocateurs.

Officials hoped that blaming unknown agents and the shadowy hand of Jakarta would the shift the focus away from individuals accused of misdeeds and, just as important, from the religious differences between the antagonists. These attempts, however, have fallen largely on deaf ears. Too many people had been victims of violence committed by their neighbors, often in the name of religion. The religious overtones of these notions of victimhood and justifications for violence play into my larger argument about how the religious narrative of the conflict has solidified in its aftermath. Although people took part in the violence for a variety of reasons, in the postconflict period the polysemic nature of the violence has faded. Few people talked of motives that were not inflected with religion. Even when other motives were put forth for the action of a person or group, religion was almost inevitably brought forth to explain how an economic or political motive could turn violent. For example, I recorded an eyewitness account of a Muslim man singling out and killing a Chinese trader during the violence. For several years prior to the violence, the two had been involved in a land dispute, which the Chinese man was supposedly about to win in court. The wife of the Chinese trader in question surmised that this Muslim man had killed her husband to make the land dispute disappear and did so under the cover of the larger communal conflict. However, she explained it as a typical example of Muslim duplicity and sadism. So regardless of economic motive, she linked it back to religious differences.

Stanley Tambiah's (1996, 192) notions of transvaluation and focalization, which were helpful in understanding how the locus of the violence shifted from ethnicity to religion, remain important in looking at the aftermath of the conflict. Once again, focalization is a process that occurs among participants as they remove understandings of local conflicts from their particular contexts in time and space. Focalization occurred in North Maluku when the Bloody Sosol letter calling for Christians to cleanse the region of Muslims appeared. This letter and associated rumors led many local Muslims to set aside the particulars of the Kao-Malifut violence (border disputes, histories of migration, and feelings of disenfranchisement) and focus on the Muslim-Christian aspect of the conflict. Christians did the same after the riots in Ternate and Tidore. From that point on, both sides saw themselves in a religious war pitting Muslims against Christians. The second process, transvaluation, occurs as particular disputes are incorporated into a wider, extralocal context. Local conflicts expand to include a much larger number of adversaries involved in broader and larger conflicts only remotely connected to the original dispute. In North Maluku, participants began to see the struggle between local communities as part of a broader one between Muslims and Christians throughout the province and throughout Indonesia.

The understandings of the conflict created by these two processes have remained in force in its aftermath. Although individuals may have had a multiplicity of reasons for taking part in the violence (economic gain, boredom, revenge, religious zeal, or political goals), religion provided the filter to translate those motives into action and to explain or justify them after the fact. Even the December 1999 violence in Ternate City between the yellow troops of the sultan of Ternate and the white troops of his opponents, so often explained by outside observers through the lens of political rivalries, was usually framed on the ground in relation to religion. Members of the white troops often justified and explained their attacks on the supporters of the sultan of Ternate in terms of his ties to the Christian community. Although they complained about his political arrogance, they noted the large number of his traditional Christian subjects, and his support of the Kao, as evidence of his duplicity. A common theme in descriptions of the street fighting that December was the presence of Christian members of the sultan's troops. Members of the white troops noted that the head of the sultan's troops was supposedly a Christian man from Sahu, or that numerous members of his forces were Christians from Halmahera. Other opponents of the sultan described his actions at the end of December 1999 as attempts to prevent people in Ternate and Tidore from going to the aid of beleaguered Muslims in Tobelo in order to protect his Christian subjects.

As I discussed earlier, once the violence shifted to a focus on religious differences it changed the way people fought and the actions they were willing to take. The same holds true in the aftermath of the fighting. The master narrative of religion continued to dominate postconflict discussions, whether on the nature of intergroup relations, the creation of memorials to those who died, or efforts to prevent future conflict. When questioned about the political nature of the violence, people were quick to respond that although politics may have played a minor role, the true point of contention was, and long had been, religion. One man from Galela who was a member of Muhammadiyah noted:

> They [Christians] have long had a conspiracy to control Halmahera and North Maluku in general. Some people may say this is a political problem. I don't know about politics, but what I do know is that we Muslims know for certain that the Christians have always hated us. I am more inclined to think that Christians have long wanted to control us. A small example is the village of Salimule [in the Galela subdistrict]. . . . That village has only a few Christians, very few, maybe only fifty or sixty families out of approximately three hundred in the whole village. They already have a church there. But then all of the sudden there is another church built at the edge of the village, where there are no people. . . . That is evidence from the material side, from the nonmaterial side there is even more evidence. Lots of books were circulating among Muslims that smelled of Christianity. So if people say it is a problem of politics or borders, maybe that is true, but I think it is religion . . . according to me, this was a plan to control Islam, not about borders or politics. (Galela subdistrict, September 2002)

Thus, in contrast to the way outside observers are quick to minimize the role of religion as something being instrumentalized in the name of politics, people on the ground in North Maluku were equally quick to do the opposite. They explained away the political aspects of the violence as a façade for the religious nature of the conflict.

One of the more obvious examples of the association of the violence with religion could be seen in the way that North Moluccans labeled the conflict. While the elite consistently used the Indonesian word *kerusuhan,* which can be glossed as riot or communal conflict, outside of elite circles, or even among the elite in private, people referred to the violence in ways that called attention to its religious aspects. One example of this religious characterization can be seen in the equation of the conflict with the Muslim notion of jihad. One name that Muslims chose for their militia was Pasukan Jihad (Jihad Militia). Although the term *jihad* has a complex and multifaceted meaning in Islam, and one that is open to much dispute, Muslims in North Maluku generally used jihad when they described the war as one about religion. One Muslim man from Gorua explained it as follows:

Personally, I consider that [we fought] for the sake of the Muslim community, for the sake of religion, for the defense of religion. I am not hesitant to say that I personally think the conflict was definitely about religion. If it was a political problem I would not have gotten involved. . . . We opposed Christians and I consider it a jihad. (Gorua, September 2002)

Another man from the same village described it in a similar manner:

I do not know if the Synod was involved. I do not know that. . . . However, what I do know is that we still maintain that it was a religious war. Therefore, it was a jihad. (Gorua, September 2002)

Christians interpreted the violence in a similar way, although I rarely heard Christians use the Indonesian term *perang salib* (crusade) (I did hear it used by Muslims); they often used the term "war of religion" (*perang agama*, Ind.) and referred to their militia as Christ's Militia (Laskar Kristus, Ind.).[13]

Christians are not safe in Indonesia. . . . If they cannot kill us, they will kill our children. They want it make it a Muslim country, to implement the Jakarta Charter.[14] The Muslims know we can lead the country and that we are smarter than them. That is why they are scared, they have to kill us because of this. . . . Christians are different from the Muslims, and the difference is in our blood. If we are not careful all Christians will be finished in Indonesia. A religious war is never over. You can have peace between countries, but between religions, never. (Bitung, November 2001)

Ambivalence toward Reconciliation: The View from the Grassroots

INTERVIEWER: Before the violence, did you have Muslim friends?

CHRISTIAN MAN: I did.

INTERVIEWER: Do you have Muslim friends now?

CHRISTIAN MAN: No. If I see Muslims now I do not want to get close to them. I do not trust them. I know how they are. It's not the same as before.

(Tobelo, May 2002)

Although commentators have focused on those who want to reconcile (Sito-hang et al. 2003; Tindage 2006), there remain a large number of people and communities who have no desire to do so, and even more who remain deeply ambivalent. Despite official rhetoric concerning the need for recon-ciliation, little of this rhetoric appears to have seeped down to the grassroots in the decade since the conflict. Few in North Maluku desire a return to open conflict, but it appeared that people were primarily interested in non-violent coexistence rather than any broader understanding of peace and reconciliation that would include forgiveness or any sort of truth telling. Few people, however, saw forgetting what had happened and returning to the preconflict status quo, regardless of how idealized, as a viable option. The idea of returning to the peaceful coexistence that Muslims and Christians supposedly enjoyed prior to the outbreak of violence, what Zorbas (2009, 134), in her work on Rwanda, has called "the rosy past syndrome," was a frequent theme in discussions of reconciliation in North Maluku. When asked about the violence or reconciliation, Muslims and Christians through-out North Maluku would focus on the positive relations the two religions had prior to the outbreak of hostilities and express a hope that reconciliation would return them to this previous state of affairs, or as one Muslim man from Tobelo said: "Back then, before there was any of this [outside] influ-ence, our relationships were all very good. . . . For example, if there was a ceremony, we all showed up together. We helped each other. . . . What I mean is that our connections were very close." While these views focus on the positive aspects of intergroup relations such as family connections, mu-tual aid in building houses of worship and participation in festivals, they overlook the political and social tensions that existed prior to the outbreak of violence, which these same people noted in other conversations or other parts of their interviews.

Understandings of, and requirements for, reconciliation varied through-out North Maluku. Some thought achieving reconciliation would be easy and simply entailed the lack of violence. A leader of Muslim militia in Galela argued in 2004 that reconciliation had already occurred, but that peace (*per-damaian*, Ind.) was deeper (*lebih dalam*, Ind.) and required more intent (*lebih niat*, Ind.). Alternatively, others saw reconciliation as a much more difficult goal. In a discussion about the differences between peace and rec-onciliation in 2010, a Christian minister in Tobelo argued that peace was simple, while reconciliation was well nigh impossible. He used the analogy of a torn piece of tissue paper: "If you tear off a corner of tissue, it is easy enough to stick it back together. That is like peace. When you take two pieces and put them back together, however, the tear is still there. You can still see it. Reconciliation is what happens when you can no longer see the tear. That is very difficult."

Regardless of whether people used the term *peace* or *reconciliation*, the overriding idea was that they required serious effort and intent from everyone involved. The elite cannot simply declare that reconciliation has occurred or hold ceremonies and communal meals and point to their success. North Moluccans argued that any sort of reconciliation, beyond a mere façade, required intention, an intention that many simply did not have, or were not interested in cultivating. Many were simply ambivalent, but others maintained an active mistrust and dislike that no amount of "reconciliation talk" (*omong-omong rekonsiliasi*, Ind.), at least for the last decade, seems to have changed. Others simply had no interest in discussing the matter. These people were tired of the constant meetings and exhortations toward reconciliation. As one exasperated government official responded to my queries: "I am sick and tired of reconciliation. Enough already!" (*So pastiu deng rekonsiliasi. Cukup suda!* NMM).

A small number of people demanded that the government arrest certain individuals that they considered provocateurs. Unsurprisingly, these calls for arrest tended to follow religious lines with Muslims calling for the arrest of particular Christian leaders and Christians demanding the government prosecute certain Muslims. Christians, particularly those from Ternate and Tidore, wondered why the police had not detained those responsible for the fake letter that had sparked the riots in those towns, particularly since numerous people claimed to know who was responsible. A rare few called for the arrest of provocateurs on all sides. One Muslim IDP argued:

> From the Muslim side, in order to reach peace, we ask the government to move forward with the legal process and arrest provocateurs from the Muslim and Christian sides, because those people did not show responsibility to their religious brethren. Why hasn't the government used the legal process against the people intimately involved and who were particularly sadistic provocateurs? Don't just say their names all the time, and then never arrest them. They are just left alone in their homes. (Ternate, September 2002)

Despite these calls for prosecution, no one has been arrested for the violence in North Maluku, and it does not appear that anybody ever will be. Those individuals generally recognized as provocateurs have remained in or returned to their homes, and some have, at various points, achieved positions of prominence in the community. As a result, in postconflict North Maluku victims, perpetrators, and those who fall somewhere in between, are in many cases living side by side, or at least shopping in the same markets.

Some communities took part in "reconciliation" efforts that had little to do with a desire to improve intergroup relationships. The hardships of displacement led some IDPs to reconsider their public attitudes toward those of a different faith. Oftentimes, an effort at reconciliation was the only economically viable option available to displaced communities seeking to return to their places of origin. One Christian IDP explained it in the following way: "We still don't trust Muslims, but we have no choice. We have to go home; we have no work here [in North Sulawesi]." If that meant they had to live with Muslims or with Christians, it was a small price to pay for economic security. They needed to return to their old places of residence where they had gardens, or other means of pursuing a livelihood. Ambivalence toward reconciliation is evident throughout North Maluku in the return, or lack thereof, of forced migrants. IDPs have chosen not to return to a number of places. The reasons behind these decisions are numerous and complex, but IDPS often cited fears for their future safety if they returned to a region in which they were a religious minority. In several locations, returning IDPs have established new single faith villages within walking distance of their gardens rather than return to their homes and live as a minority in a larger multifaith community.

Participation in reconciliation activities also provided opportunities for profit. In some cases people who took part were genuinely interested in fostering reconciliation, but people who were not interested in reconciliation were not averse to using NGO interest in the topic to get funding, or to attend meetings on the subject in order to get the per diem money often handed out by NGOs. At times it appeared as though NGOs handed out money for "reconciliation activities" in order to show they were doing their job, not because they had designed a well-thought-out activity that might make a difference. As one NGO worker complained, "We have to provide our bosses and funders with photos of our activities, so it is easiest to do things we can take pictures of as proof to send them." Some IDPs often took part in reconciliation meetings simply because it was something to occupy their time. It was more interesting than sitting around an IDP camp, and if they were lucky they might get paid or get a free meal. I was often left with the impression that people were taking part in reconciliation activities in North Maluku in 2001 and 2002 because that was what they were told they were "supposed" to be doing in a postconflict situation.

I attended one reconciliation party (*pesta rekonsiliasi*, Ind.) at a junior high school in North Maluku in 2002 that exemplified this notion that people were simply going through the motions rather than making serious efforts at reconciliation. The organizer of this party was a Christian militia leader during the violence who consistently voiced his continuing mistrust and dislike of Muslims in private conversations. However, he had noticed that foreign NGOs were giving away money for reconciliation programs, as well as much larger contracts for development projects. He thought that if he made a name for himself as a proponent of reconciliation it might open the door to some of the larger more lucrative contracts. When I asked about the goal of his reconciliation party, he expressed his hope that the party would allow students to convey their desires for reconciliation and improve interfaith relations in the school. I thought it an odd choice of a venue since only a single Muslim student had returned.

Prior to the ceremony, I met with the school's principal to discuss his thoughts on the day's activities. He expounded for several minutes with the standard stock phrases about the importance of reconciliation for the region's future, and the need to forget the past and look forward. The conversation took an odd turn, however, once he finished his explanation. He asked me about the lack of support from the U.S. government for North Moluccan Christians and Indonesian Christians in general. He suggested that for every Christian killed anywhere in Indonesia, the United States government should kill a Muslim somewhere in the world in retaliation. He understood it might be difficult for them to go after Indonesian Muslims, but they could substitute American Muslims instead. He explained at length how this eye for an eye response to Muslim aggression would show the Indonesian Islamic community that they had to think twice before committing violence against Christians. Ironically, after explaining the importance of instilling fear in the Muslim community through arbitrary executions, he urged me to quickly finish my tea since he needed take part in the reconciliation ceremony.

Ambivalence toward reconciliation remained evident in the months and years after the conflict in the way communities claimed they would not allow IDPs to return. This rhetoric tended to mellow over time and in some cases it did so rather quickly. For example, in 2001 some Christians in Kao claimed that as soon as the armed forces guarding the Makianese returnees left, the Kao would attack and chase them out again. However, by 2004, the armed forces had left, most of the Makianese had returned to their villages, and talk of an attack had faded. Some individuals, however, put their rhetoric into action and changed the landscape to discourage returns. In Galela and Morotai, Muslim communities went to great lengths to remove evidence of the previous Christian presence from the landscape and in some cases systematically leveled entire villages. Others chose to destroy economic incentives for the displaced to return by cutting down people's clove and nutmeg trees. Sometimes these efforts worked. IDPs heard stories about the destruction of their valuable spice groves and decided to pursue a future elsewhere.

Lingering Mistrust and Reconciliation

Despite some of the positive developments associated with reconciliation and the beginning of IDP returns throughout North Maluku beginning in 2001, small skirmishes related to the conflict continued to take place across the region until at least 2002. Disgruntled Muslim IDPs who had recently returned to Tobelo attacked and destroyed parts of a village near Tobelo town in August 2002. In response, Christian mobs rioted through the mixed village of Gorua, burning Muslim homes and IDP barracks. Isolated shootings and beatings also took place in Galela and on Morotai as Christian IDPs started to return home in the second half of 2002. In September 2002, gunmen attacked three Christian villages in North Morotai that had weathered the communal violence unscathed, forcing thousands of residents to flee into the interior or to Tobelo (*Jawa Pos* 2002; *Kompas* 2002). These tensions persisted as late as 2012 when a drunken Muslim man from Tobelo mugged and killed a Christian man from the village of Wosia (*Malut Post* 2012a). In response, a large crowd from Wosia descended on the Tobelo neighborhood where the killer lived and only the intervention of the armed forces prevented violence. As news of the killing spread throughout Halmahera, so did fears of renewed violence (*Malut Post* 2012b).

In addition to actual violence, tensions persisted throughout the region due in large part to rumors that the other side was planning an attack and conflict could break out at any moment. People continued to pay attention to rumors, because their experiences during the conflict had shown that occasionally, no matter how outlandish, they could be true. Everyone seemed to know someone who had failed to heed earlier rumors and had paid with their life or had only narrowly escaped death. Rumors were so persistent that in some cases they had to be rebutted by government officials in regional newspapers (*Manado Post* 2002a, 2002b). People also worried that rumors of violence against returned IDPs in one part of the province could result in retaliatory violence in another.

I experienced the danger of dismissing rumors myself in August 2002. I was in a village south of Tobelo interviewing IDPs when a man rode up on a motorcycle to announce that Tobelo was in flames. He said that Muslim IDPs from the village of Gorua, where the army had recently found a weapons cache, had swept down into the northern parts of Tobelo and burned down several neighborhoods and the community college. My research assistant, an IDP from Ternate, was immediately on edge and said we needed to return at once to Tobelo town to assess the situation and see if we needed to flee to Manado. I dismissed his concerns, citing the numerous rumors that had scared him in recent months, all of which had proved untrue or at least extremely exaggerated. We finished the interview and then headed back to Tobelo town. He remained concerned, while I remained adamant that it was a rumor. However, as we passed the towns on the outskirts of Tobelo we noticed that the villages appeared eerily quiet. We started to see groups of armed men with traditional and homemade weapons patrolling the road, often with red headbands. The closer we got to Tobelo, the more armed men there were on the roads. As we neared the site of the supposed attack, we could see the plumes of smoke from the fires, as well as dozens of heavily armed Christian militia members gathered on the sides of the road. My assistant then pointed out the single file lines of armed men with red headbands disappearing into a coconut grove behind the village. It appears that an attack had indeed taken place. Some disenchanted Muslim IDPs had come down the coast from Gorua and then retreated back to their village burning homes and the parts of a college campus as they went. My research assistant was quick to point out my carelessness in disregarding the rumor, noting that his experience had shown him that one should listen to rumors, because they were often true.

One consistent rumor during my fieldwork in 2001–2 concerned the issue of certain communities stockpiling weapons in preparation for future violence. In the months after the conflict subsided, security forces made a big show of confiscating weapons from people throughout North Maluku. Oftentimes a few soldiers would simply show up in a village and demand that they turn over all of their weapons—both modern and traditional. Local communities did turn over a large number of bombs, spears, bows, arrows, and guns, both real and homemade, to the authorities, but they rarely surrendered all of their weapons. Often people made big productions over surrendering weapons that no longer functioned, or they quickly made inferior traditional weapons in order to have something to give the soldiers assigned to collect them. For example, army soldiers told one Forest Tobelo community that they would need to surrender all of their hunting weapons—all spears, bows, and arrows. Despite protests that as hunter-gatherers these "weapons" were in fact tools of their livelihood, the army insisted they comply and arranged a time for a pickup. Rather than surrender any of their weapons, they quickly made a large number of bamboo arrows, which they handed over to the soldiers when they came for the weapons. Some communities simply refused or threatened soldiers who demanded they surrender their firearms. Other people hid their quality firearms rather than turn them over to authorities, often burying them in their gardens. I knew one Christian man who traveled widely in northern Halmahera to advise people on how to prepare their firearms for burial. In several cases, the more foolhardy would bring out guns and bullets during interviews to show me that they still had them. Many communities kept traditional weapons, such as bows, arrows, spears, swords, and slingshots, in good supply and near at hand in case violence broke out again. The fear of new violence was particularly evident in mid-2002 when the provincial government began returning thousands of displaced Muslims from Ternate to the Tobelo region. In some cases, these rumors of communities actively stockpiling weapons turned out to be true. In Gorua in 2002 several arrests were made of people hoarding weapons and the police arrested others for attempting to purchase guns. Incidences such as this one, contributed to a continuing sense of wariness between religious communities. This ongoing mistrust of the religious other stemmed in part from North Moluccans own experiences during the conflict and the perception among many that their side was the primary victim of the conflict. These contrasting notions of victimhood have allowed mistrust to linger more than a decade after the conflict came to an end.

Chapter 6

Managing Memories of Violence

Competing Notions of Victimhood in North Maluku

It really happened, didn't it? If I look back at all that happened it is really incredible. Sometimes if I remember everything that happened then, I still don't believe it.

—A young woman from Central Halmahera, 2010

The ambivalence surrounding reconciliation and the reluctance of some communities to return to their homes were directly tied to the way North Moluccans were attempting to make sense of the violence and its aftermath. As I talked with people across the region, it was apparent that many were still trying to figure out why they had been singled out as victims of violence. Others sought to justify their actions during the conflict. As part of this process, they reappraised their experiences and those of others in an effort to confirm their versions of the communal violence and to vindicate their suffering. They were, in essence, "adapting memory to explanation" (Lemarchand 1996, 19), using memories of the violence and particular, albeit selective, understandings of preconflict relations to explain the origins of the violence and its course. Liisa Malkki's concept of mythico-history is helpful in looking at this process. In her analysis of how Burundian refugees in Tanzania talk about the past, Malkki put forward the idea of "mythico-history," which she describes as "not only a description of the past, nor even merely an evaluation of the past, but a subversive recasting and reinterpretation of it in fundamentally moral terms" (Malkki 1995, 54). These mythico-histories are concerned "with the ordering and reordering of social and political categories, with the defining of self in distinction to other" (Malkki 1995, 55). To create these mythico-histories they "seized historical events, processes and relationships and reinterpret them within a deeply moral scheme of good and evil" (Malkki 1995, 56). A similar reinterpretation of recent events was taking place in North Maluku. Motivated by their experiences of communal violence, North Moluccans were shaping mythico-histories that served their present interests: the justification of their violence and the validation of their suffering. They had a vested interest—whether emotional, moral, or political—in shaping perceptions of the conflict and laying the foundation for how its history would be told. As North Moluccans shared their experiences and situated them in a moral schema, certain themes about the violence emerged, and these often coalesced around the notions of victimhood and culpability.

Before exploring these themes, however, I want to also briefly consider what historian Steve Stern (2004) in his work on Pinochet's Chile calls "emblematic memory." He proposes the concept of emblematic memory as one way of understanding how people frame events and how they attach meaning to them. It "refers not to a single remembrance of a specific content, not to a concrete or substantive 'thing,' but to a framework that organizes meaning, selectivity, and countermemory" (Stern 2004, 105). Certain memories become emblematic because "they purport to capture an essential truth about the collective truth of a society" (Stern 2004, 68). These sorts of memories tell people not just what happened to them but what happened to their neighbors, their families, or their religious brethren: "People find in them an anchor that organizes and enhances the meaning of personal experiences and knowledge. . . . People find their anchor credible in part because of validation by similar memory echoes in a public cultural domain" (Stern 2004, 68). Emblematic memory refers to more than just how memories assume a certain level of uniformity within a group but also speaks to the hegemonic aspects of certain memories that replace or displace others (Stern 2004, 106). As I gathered stories about the violence in North Maluku, the organizing framework for these narratives, what Stern would call the emblematic memories about the conflict, focused on religion.

The political machinations of civil servants, the struggles over district boundaries, or personal quarrels between neighbors that also fed the conflict,

or created the conditions necessary for it to break out, were not what people emphasized in their postconflict narratives, discussions, or memorials
to victims. They highlighted the killing of their family members by militias wearing religious paraphernalia, or experiences of displacement at the
hands of their neighbors of a different faith. They focused on the atrocities
committed by Muslims or Christians and how the religion of the perpetra-
tor shaped these acts of violence. Muslims described the primitive savagery
that they considered emblematic of Christian violence. They focused on
incidences of cannibalism, the use of war magic and charms, or the indis-
criminate massacre of women and children as evidence of Christian bar-
barity. One Muslim woman summed it up after describing the killings in
Togoliua when she concluded that "those Christians are too barbaric. Just
imagine it; they kill small children. That is too much. That is barbarism
on top of barbarism." Christians, in turn, focused on the religious fanati-
cism of Muslims. They called particular attention to a perceived Muslim
concern, if not obsession, with martyrdom. They emphasized attacks on
minority communities, murdered children, abducted women, and forced
conversions to support their argument. These memories of how religion
was manifested in the violence continued to shape how Muslims and
Christians viewed each other in the aftermath of the conflict. People placed
a great deal of importance on these emblematic memories as they reassessed
past events to explain their present situation. Furthermore, they used these
understandings to make decisions about their future. Should they return
home? Could they trust their neighbors? What would happen if the violence broke out again? Could they rely on government guarantees for their
safety?

As should be evident by now, different social groups have different memories of the conflict. As a result, incompatible accounts of what happened
and conflicting notions of culpability pervaded the postconflict landscape.
Evidence of these different versions could be found in contrasting chronologies and the prevalent notion of victimhood on all sides. One GMIH minister noted these differences over dinner in Tobelo in June 2010 when she
asked me:

> You always ask about what happened and you have spent lots of time talking
> to Christians and Muslims. Do they agree? Which [version] is true? I was
> here when the conflict broke out. I saw it with my own eyes. I know what

happened. But I talk about it with Muslims and their version is different. But it is not true. I know that what they say happened, did not happen. But they say it did. So who is right? I am confused and I was here. (Tobelo, June 2010)

Although Muslim and Christian accounts differ significantly on issues of chronology or culpability, they do agree on two points, both of which are key elements in constructing notions of victimhood: the other side started it and it had something to do with religion.

Tales of Aggression

During my research visits to Tobelo town in 2001–2 I usually stayed in the home of one of my friend's nieces, a woman I will call Tujanga and her husband Lausu. Lausu and Tujanga were forced migrants from central Halmahera who ended up in Tobelo in early 2000 after fleeing the violence in their home village. In Tobelo they moved into the ruins of a small house abandoned by a Muslim family. The neighborhood where they lived had been completely destroyed at the end of 1999 by Christian militia, but in the subsequent months it had been repopulated by IDPs who moved into the burnt-out homes and patched them up as best they could with scavenged pieces of corrugated tin or plywood. Tujanga's immediate family did not live alone in their small three-room house. They shared it with several other members of her extended family who had fled fighting in Morotai, Ternate, and Obi. They often had other guests as well, since Lausu was prone to offer his guest room to IDPs passing through town. He would put them up for a few days and feed them while they waited for the next boat. It made the house a lively center of information as the constantly changing stream of guests sat out front at night and shared stories about the conflict.

During one visit, my research assistant brought an old friend, I'll call him Ansa, to Tujanga's house for an interview. Over the course of several hours, Ansa talked about the outbreak of violence in Tobelo and the destruction of neighboring Muslim villages. As we sat amidst the rubble of destroyed Muslim homes, he provided an extremely graphic and detailed account of the fighting and his role in it. He described how his first objective once the violence began was to find and kill his brother, a recent convert to Islam. Once he found some weapons he went looking for him and eventually joined in the larger conflict taking place around him. He expressed amazement at the chaos and the fury of the fighting. He described a scene in which people did not care what they did (*tara mau tau*, NMM.) and were killing who ever got in their way. The fighting was so intense that they spared no one: "Old ladies, we killed them. Children, we killed them. Why would we let them live? We searched through the fallen looking for people who were still alive and we killed them. Lots. Thousands." As Muslims emerged from hiding in the days that followed, they killed them as well. During our conversation, a small crowd had gathered to listen to the discussion and people periodically chimed in supporting Ansa's larger points or adding details from their own experiences. As we finished up, Ansa added, almost as an afterthought: "We had already eaten together [to prevent violence], but then it happened anyway. They said they would not attack us, but they did."

After Ansa left, I discussed the interview with some of the people staying in Lausu's house. As we went over the finer points of Ansa's story, I naively remarked that although North Moluccan Christians claimed to be different from Muslims, because their Christianity taught love and forgiveness, in fact they were the same. I pointed out how Ansa had described Christian atrocities similar to those that Christians attributed to their Muslim antagonists. Christians cited these sorts of atrocities as proof of Muslims' inherent violent nature and lack of compassion, yet Ansa had described comparable acts. As silence descended on the room in reaction to my ill-conceived comments, my host's nephew, an IDP from Morotai, looked at me incredulously and simply said: "They started it" (*Dorang kamuka*, NMM). Others in the room nodded and voiced their agreement. For them that simple fact, that "they started it," justified the actions that Christians had taken. Initially I was taken aback by the simplicity of the reaction, but as I heard similar refrains over the course of my fieldwork from both sides, this response started to make sense in terms of how people perceived the violence and their reactions to it. If the other side was the aggressor, their own reactions, no matter the violence involved, were justified. Since in most cases people saw the other side as the aggressor, there was little to regret.

An obvious example of these contradictory notions of aggression can be seen in the conflicting chronologies that people put forth when they explained the violence from beginning to end. The links in the causal chain varied depending on the religion of the teller. Each side had its focal points and used those incidents to justify their actions, while at the same time glossing over other incidents that may have influenced the larger course of events. Muslim versions highlighted atrocities committed by Christian communities and militias. Their explanations of the violence started with the expulsion of the Makianese from Malifut by the indigenous people of Kao and often jumped straight to the massacres in Tobelo, only briefly explaining events in Ternate and Tidore, but almost universally omitting the violence in central Halmahera. Christians began with the Makianese attacks on Kao villages, discussed the riots in Ternate and Tidore and the attacks in central Halmahera, but often glossed over the massacres in Tobelo, focusing more on the defensive nature of Christian actions there. They paid more attention to the violence against Christians on the islands of Obi, Bacan, Morotai, and the final expulsion of Christians from Galela.

When asked about particular incidents of violence, people focused on the ideas of instigation and revenge. Muslims pointed out that Christians were the instigators. A quote from a Muslim man in Popilo is emblematic of the response my research assistants and I gathered in interviews: "Muslims never attacked Christians first, it was always Christians first and then Muslims responded." Christians, unsurprisingly, often argued the reverse. As proof of the other side's aggression, people maintained that their community had been caught unaware and was thus unprepared for the attack. People maintained this claim despite their stories about the pervasiveness of rumors about impending violence and their knowledge that the religious other had been stockpiling weapons in preparation for the violence. These unsuspecting communities had only the most basic weapons to withstand a better organized, better armed, and numerically superior foe, all of which demonstrated that the other was the aggressor. Ansa, the man I quoted earlier, only had a kitchen knife when he headed off to battle. He had to beg, borrow, and scavenge other weapons as he went along. A Muslim man in Galela noted that his village had retreated into the forest rather than fight because they only had a few machetes to thwart attackers armed with bazookas, bows and arrows, and other weapons.

The preparation of the other side provided evidence that their enemies had been planning this violence for months, if not years. In accounts of the riots in Ternate, Christians noticed that the crowds that attacked their homes consisted of Muslims they did not know. Their neighbors took part in the riot in other parts of the city. This movement of people around the city showed a level of organization that belied Muslim and official claims of spontaneous rioting. On Halmahera, villagers told of thousands of enemy militia that attacked small numbers of resisters. A Christian man from the village of Kusu in Oba recounted: "When the invasion came, we were only twenty-five people. . . . We were attacked from the north, south, and west. We did not last long, we retreated behind the village. We fled. . . . There were about six thousand attackers." A man from the Muslim part of Gorua north of Tobelo town described the invasion of his village: "Two whole sub-districts attacked us, almost twenty-five thousand people. We were only a small village. They attacked at seven in the morning during Ramadan. We were still asleep. They attacked and attacked. We were confused. What could we do since we had no weapons?"

If we explore how the violence spread across the province, an argument could be made that large segments of it were fueled by revenge and retaliation.[1] The Kao chased the Makianese from Malifut in October 1999 in revenge for the destruction of the Pagu villages of Sosol and Wangeotak. These Makianese IDPs fled to Ternate where they instigated riots against Christians to seek vengeance for their defeat at the hands of the largely Christian Kao militia. Those riots and subsequent militia attacks on other Christian villages in central Halmahera created a large population of Christian forced migrants in Tobelo, where eventually Christians took part in several massacres of Muslims in retribution, some have argued, for the violence in Ternate, Tidore, and central Halmahera. Muslims who fled Tobelo to the neighboring island of Morotai joined forces with local Muslims and took revenge on Christian communities for the violence they suffered at the hands of Christians in Tobelo. This fighting on Morotai forced thousands of Christians to leave the island. Some of these IDPs fled to Tobelo where they joined Christian militia and exacted vengeance on Muslims on battle-fields throughout northern Halmahera. Finally, the killing or expulsion of the Christian community in the southern part of Galela, culminating in the massacre in the Christian village of Duma was considered by many as revenge for the killing of Muslims in Tobelo earlier that year, and for violence committed by Christian Galela militia in the early months of 2000. Although not all of the events that took place can be explained in this way, the flow of displaced populations and their subsequent actions certainly influenced the course of the conflict.

Christian narratives focused on Muslim aggression as the catalyst for the conflict. Christians argued that the Kao-Malifut violence had been a localized ethnic issue until the Muslims made it about religion. Christians pointed to the various ways the Makianese had switched the focus from ethnicity to religion in Ternate through the fabrication of a letter calling on Christians to cleanse the region of Muslims, the production of a fake Christian invasion map, and stories about the Christian nature of the violence in Kao-Malifut. These efforts constituted sufficient proof for many Christians that certain Muslims had made a concerted effort to expand the scope of the violence and deserved the blame. Furthermore, the riots in Ternate and Tidore and the militia attacks in central Halmahera pitted small Christian communities against overwhelming odds. For example, one Christian man refused to refer to the riots in Ternate as an example of communal conflict; he said instead that "Ternate was not communal conflict [*kerusuhan*, Ind.]. It was a massacre [*pembantaian*, Ind.]." These views of Muslims as aggressors were common throughout Christian communities in the province and remained an integral aspect of the way people retrospectively viewed the violence. It provided Christians with the rationale for preparations for violence in Tobelo and Galela and the atrocities committed there. Narratives about subsequent attacks on the islands of Morotai and Obi, where numerous Christian communities were forced to flee, repeated similar themes of Muslim belligerence and Christians battling overwhelming odds.

Unsurprisingly, Muslim narratives focused on Christian aggression. Makianese informants, who were involved in the initial ethnic-based conflict over redistricting, searched for religious elements in the violence in Kao-Malifut. They maintained that despite the ethnic basis of the conflict, the Christians in Kao had brought religion into the mix. Complaints over the redistricting issue were simply a ruse whereby the Christians sought to expel the Makianese, who they perceived as an obstacle to Christian expansionism, from the region. The Kao were able to overwhelm the Makianese only after they gathered Christian allies from other subdistricts. One Muslim man from Malifut explained, "When they invaded Malifut, the Christians gathered [other] Christians from all over the province of North Maluku. From each village there were twenty or thirty people, all gathered in Kao to invade Malifut. This means it was not a land problem, but definitely a crusade [*perang salib*, Ind.]." Following the violence in Malifut, fears of Christian aggression, whether manipulated or real, played a role in the outbreak of anti-Christian rioting in Ternate and Tidore and pogroms in central and southern Halmahera.

Muslim accounts of the violence in Tobelo and Galela in northern Halmahera also highlighted the instigating role of Christian communities. Almost unanimously, Muslims in Tobelo reported that they did not expect to be attacked in the final days of December 1999. One Muslim man from Tobelo explained:

> As a Muslim, if I look at the case of Tobelo, it is strange. We never did anything that was detrimental to them. I don't think so. Then suddenly our houses were burned, our mosques were burned. We never did anything like that. We never started anything like that, but then a conflict like Tobelo happened. Everyone knows that the Tobelo problem was not only a problem of the Tobelo people. The Tobelo problem was a religious problem. . . . It became the responsibility of all Muslims in North Maluku, in Indonesia even, to attack at once. (Ternate, September 2002)

This man's quote calls attention to both the culpability of Christian communities as the aggressors and to the religious nature of the conflict. The idea that Christians were the instigators, particularly in northern Halmahera, was a common theme in Muslim descriptions of the violence. They claimed to have made no preparations to defend themselves and remained unarmed. In their narratives, Muslims recalled how they were surprised at the outbreak of hostilities. A man from Gorua described the unanticipated nature of the initial Christian attacks in January 2000:

> At that time, the Muslim community was starting to fast when suddenly we were attacked by Christians. . . . At that point the Muslim community did not have any preparations at all. Suddenly we were attacked and we resisted. We held out with only a few machetes. Those who were more sophisticated had some rocks. In the end many Muslims were massacred because Christians had come from as far as Kao to join in and finish off the Muslims in the last two villages of Gorua and Popilo. (Tobelo subdistrict, September 2002)

Unlike their Christian neighbors, they had not stockpiled weapons. They had been lured into inaction by the communal meals and promises of peace.

Tales of Betrayal

Although willing to admit that both sides suffered to some degree, North Moluccans have created an imagined hierarchy of suffering that portrayed themselves as the primary victims of the conflict. Common themes in these accounts were ideas of betrayal and the violation of trust by neighboring communities, government officials, or the armed forces. As tensions mounted throughout the region after the initial bloodshed in late 1999, communities across the province tried to prevent the spread of violence through largely unsuccessful efforts at mediation. In retrospect, some saw these endeavors at conflict prevention as deliberate attempts to lull them into passivity and as evidence of treachery on the part of their Christian or Muslim neighbors (Oesman and Ahmad 2000). On both sides of the religious divide, vanquished communities shared stories about such betrayals. The communal feast that Ansa mentioned at the beginning of this chapter was one of many examples where communities took part in shared meals in ultimately unsuccessful attempts to prevent conflict. He justified the ferocity of the violence in Tobelo by noting that, despite participating in a communal feast to reaffirm their unity, Tobelo Muslims had still attacked their Christian neighbors. Over and over in narratives of the conflict Christians and Muslims focused on the surprise with which they met the violence. Common refrains included: "They said they would protect us"; "They told us we did not need to arm ourselves"; and "We had no weapons because we had agreed to peace." Let me use two examples from my field notes, one Muslim and one Christian, to highlight this idea of betrayal.

Marline was a young woman who lived in Ternate when the conflict began. A Christian from central Halmahera, she had been living there for several years to attend high school. As Makianese IDPs from Malifut streamed into the city she felt the tension rise, but thought nothing would come of it. She had close Muslim friends and Muslim family members, so she did not think the violence would spread to Ternate. The government kept telling everyone that it was safe and government cars with loudspeakers drove around town day after day proclaiming all was well. Unfortunately, all was not well. On the night of 6 November, Muslim mobs began rioting through the city attacking Christian homes and places of worship. Unlike most Christians, Marline was unable to get to an army base or police station, but she did manage to run to the nearby home of some Muslim friends who hid her in the ceiling of their house. Her friends waited by the front door and sent the rioters away when they came looking for her. The next day they dressed her in a Muslim outfit with a head scarf and put her on a public speed boat for the four-hour journey back to her village in the subdistrict of Oba in Central Halmahera.

She thought she would be safe in Oba since her family, including Muslim family members, lived there. When she arrived home, she learned that the local authorities had told everyone not to worry about the events in Tidore and Ternate and to ignore rumors of impending violence. They reassured Christians that they would be protected, just as the authorities had promised in Ternate. Once again, these proved to be empty promises. A few days after Marline arrived; several large groups of Muslim militia invaded the Christian part of the village. As Marline watched the attack, she saw policeman, soldiers, and some of her own relatives amongst the militia. She fled into the forest along with several hundred others and eventually crossed the interior of the peninsula to seek refuge on the other side of the island. The trip took almost two weeks and they were pursued by Muslim militia most of the way. Not everyone made it to the other side.

Eventually Marline and her family emerged from the forest near a transmigration settlement in the subdistrict of Weda where they were given food before traveling to the coastal village of Sosowomo. Unfortunately, after they arrived in Sosowomo, Muslim militia attacked the village, and they fled down to coast to the village of Lalubi. Once in Lalubi, government officials rounded up the IDPs and placed them on a ship. The officials told them that they would be taken back to safety in Oba. However, before the ship departed, one of Marline's younger brothers wandered off, so the entire family disembarked to find him and the ship left without them. They were lucky to be left behind, even though they subsequently had to flee from more militia attacks. The boat took the IDPs back to the Oba subdistrict and placed them in temporary barracks in the village of Siokona. Several weeks later Muslim militia attacked Siokona. Those who escaped this second attack crossed the island's forested interior once again. However this time, when they emerged from the forest in the subdistrict of Wasile, some of them were captured and killed by Muslims.

I recorded another story of betrayal from Muslim IDPs from the Tobelo village of Gamhoku, a mixed faith village about ten kilometers south of Tobelo town. As tensions rose in northern Halmahera in late 1999, Muslims and Christians in Gamhoku pledged to stay united. Muslims promised to protect their Christian neighbors if an outside force of Muslim militia attacked, and Christians would do the same if the large Christian community in the subdistrict decided to eliminate the Muslims. When violence broke out in Tobelo on 26 December the news quickly reached Gamhoku. The Muslims gathered in their mosque for protection. The Christian village head and the minister came to the mosque and asked the Muslims to relocate to the church so they would be more secure. They argued that the Christians would be able to defend them better in a church than they could in a mosque. One Muslim man explained: "They said they would protect us in the church in case a mob came from elsewhere to destroy the mosque. But actually it was not to protect us, but to deceive us into a massacre in the church. . . . As we entered the church they took all of our machetes. We were empty handed." Eventually a large group of people from neighboring villages arrived with the aim of killing the Muslims. In the end several dozen people were killed in and around the church. Of those who managed to escape, some were rescued by Christian relatives; others fled into the forest and traveled for up to six days through the island's interior before reaching safety.

The stories above highlight a number of types of betrayal that communities experienced during the conflict, including being betrayed or deceived by the government, by neighbors, or by family members. My field notes and interview transcripts are filled with dozens of similar stories. For example, in the village of Tile on Morotai, Christian IDPs said that their Muslim neighbors had told them not to run away even though the violence had spread to that island. A few days later their Muslim neighbors and some soldiers attacked them. In the village of Dokulamo in Galela, three days after the Christian community invited the local imam to a meeting where they pledged peace, they attacked their Muslim neighbors. IDPs from the island of Bacan recalled how the subdistrict head had visited them in the villages of Lola and Tuokoma to tell them Christians were safe. A day or two later they were invaded by Muslim militia. In the village of Dodaga in the Wasile subdistrict, Muslims and Christians held a peace ceremony with subdistrict leaders, and two weeks later Christians say they were attacked by Muslims.

In the aftermath of the conflict, these experiences left people reluctant to accept guarantees of safety from their former neighbors, as these had often proved baseless in the past. These betrayals demonstrated that Muslims or Christians could not be trusted. Although they may act friendly now and sign reconciliation agreements, their true nature had been on display during the conflict and could arise again. Some people admitted to actively teaching their children to distrust the religious other. One Christian man argued that it was his responsibility as a good father to cultivate a sense of distrust in his children so they would be prepared to deal with their future as a religious minority in Indonesia. This mistrust extended to government officials who in many cases had proven untrustworthy. For example, on several occasions local officials from the island of Bacan assured IDPs in North Sulawesi that it was safe for them to return in 2001. In response, the IDPs noted that the religious figures and government officials who were now telling them it was safe were the same ones who had signed statements prior to the conflict saying they would not take part in any violence, but they had all been seen either participating or simply standing by as their religious brethren attacked.

Stories of military involvement were also common and played a role in these narratives of victimization. These often focused on the failure of the police or the army to protect people, but a number also detailed the involvement of individual soldiers or in some cases entire units.[2] These stories usually involved Christian villagers describing how they were tricked into passivity by the armed forces. For example, on 2 February 2000, Muslim militia attacked and destroyed the Christian village of Raja on the island of Morotai. I interviewed two IDPs from Raja who described the attack in great detail. They said that on the morning of 2 February, nine soldiers arrived in the village and told them that they had nothing to fear. The soldiers said "You do not need to be scared with these issues. We are delivering these Indonesian flags for you to plant at each end of the village and at the harbor where boats enter." The soldiers explained that the flags demarcated a safe area, if Muslim militia attacked, it would be the same as if they were attacking Indonesia and the army would protect them. Immediately after this meeting, the villagers saw three boats approaching the village flying the flags of the jihad troops (*pasukan jihad*, Ind.) and quickly pointed it out to the soldiers. The soldiers told them not to worry about the attacking militia and that they would handle it. The soldiers then left in their boats to meet the militia and then all the boats headed to the south. The villagers thought the soldiers had arrested the militia members, but hours later the same three boats appeared again, this time accompanied by the soldiers. At the same time Muslim militia attacked Raja from the forest and from along the road. The villagers resisted for about an hour, but were heavily outnumbered and could not resist the modern automatic weapons being used by the soldiers. The villagers also saw the soldiers shooting at the church. They knew some of the attackers were soldiers because some of them had removed their jihad uniforms and people could see their military fatigues. Several villagers were killed in this attack, while the rest fled through the forest and crossed over to the island of Rau where they sought refuge.

The tale told by the Raja IDPs was not unique. Forced migrants from the village of Dodaga in Wasile told stories of being hunted through the swamps for a week by the Mobile Brigade police unit (Brimob, Ind.) that had been sent to protect them. Ironically the police demanded (via their bullhorns) that the people come out of hiding and be protected or the police would kill them. Members of the armed forces also shot at IDPs from Sabatai Baru on Morotai as they fled through the interior along logging roads. In general Christians believed that army and Brimob units sided with Muslim militia primarily due to their shared religious beliefs. During the conflict their distrust of the military stemmed more from the faith of the soldiers than from the military itself. When Christian soldiers or police were assigned to the area, which Christians argued rarely happened, they were known to help their religious brethren. One of the most telling examples was of the Christian Brimob police officers from Kalimantan who fled into the forest with IDPs from Siokona in the Oba subdistrict. Siokona was the location where the IDPs from Payahe had been resettled after they were rounded up in Lalubi as I mentioned earlier. The Christian Brimob were assigned to guard the barracks housing IDPs and protect them. Unfortunately, these barracks came under attack from Muslim militia. The outnumbered Brimob officers were forced to retreat into the forest with the IDPs they were guarding. The few IDPs I met from Siokona said they might not have made it without the aid from the Brimob officers.

Stories of military violence aimed directly at civilians were less prevalent among Muslims, but they complained about the reluctance of the armed forces to prevent particular incidents of violence. One Muslim man explained how he tried, and failed, to get help from the local army base as Christian militia overwhelmed the Muslim communities in Gorua and Popilo:

I ran to the army base and asked for help from the commander. I asked for help for people in Gorua. The commander said there was nothing he could do at the moment. "Later," he said, "later." However, by then Gorua was already destroyed. He would not provide any help at all. He just let it happen. This indirectly shows that those people [Christians and the armed forces] were working together. If they were not working together it is unlikely this would have happened. . . . That day extra troops actually came to Tobelo from Morotai. They wanted to send them to the south [of Tobelo]. What were they going to do in the south? The south is all Christian. Why not send them to the north to protect people? I was shocked by that. How could that happen? It was because the government was all Christian; there were no Muslims. . . . If there were Muslims in the government that would not have happened. (Ternate, September 2002)

In another example from Tobelo, several Muslims took shelter in the office of the Subdistrict Military Command (Koramil, Ind.) as Christian militias were cleansing that town of Muslims. The few military staff in the office quickly fled for their own safety, rather than defend those who had sought their protection. Most of the Muslims inside the office were subsequently killed. The army's inability to protect the people in the Koramil office was a frequently cited illustration of their failure (Oesman and Ahmad 2000, 73; Tomagola 2006, 67; Wilson 2008, 126). Muslims from Tobelo contrasted the army's failure to defend Muslims in Tobelo, with their ability to protect Christians in Ternate. Furthermore, on at least one occasion when Tobelo IDPs in Ternate attempted to travel to Halmahera during the conflict to retake their homes, they were stopped by the Indonesian army and several of them were killed. Muslims saw this violence as a further example of the army's lack of evenhandedness.[3]

The mistrust of the armed forces fostered by these incidents of betrayal or abuse extended into the postconflict period throughout North Maluku. In the years after the violence came to an end, people began to see the armed forces as part of the problem, rather than part of the solution. Some communities, particularly in northern Halmahera, believed that the armed forces wanted to maintain religious tensions even after the state of emergency was lifted, since it provided them with lucrative opportunities to make money.[4] If things remained unstable, the large businesses in the region, such as Barito Pacific and the Australian gold mine would continue to need their services. The longer Muslims and Christians were scared of each other, the longer they would pay the army for security to deliver them or their goods to the market. Many believed that members of the armed forces instigated, or least encouraged, the sporadic violence that broke out in North Halmahera in 2002 to maintain a certain level of tension and mistrust. After each incident, soldiers encouraged people to pay the military protection money if they wanted to move around. In some places reconciliation efforts were spurred by a desire to remove the armed forces, rather than a desire to reestablish interfaith ties.

Forgotten Saviors

Although I have concentrated on how people conceived of the violence and how they portrayed themselves as victims, my field notes are also filled with dozens of examples of people helping, rescuing, or protecting their supposed religious enemy. Oftentimes individuals did this at great peril to themselves. People would jump into the middle of massacres to rescue their relatives from execution by outsiders, or put themselves between rioters and their intended victims. For example, when a truckload of Muslim women and children was brought into the village of Kupa-Kupa from Togoliua in January 2000, enraged Christian militia wanted to kill all of them. However, a Christian militia leader stepped between the truck and the angry crowd and told them they would have to kill him first. Another Christian man from the village of Efe-Efe, on hearing that some of his Christian neighbors were in the forest hunting down the survivors from Togoliua with their dogs, quickly joined the hunt, but in an effort to rescue survivors rather than kill them. Among the IDPs from Ternate who fled to North Sulawesi were Muslim families who had tried to protect their Christian neighbors and as a result had to flee the island for their own safety. The adat troops of the sultan of Ternate, the pasukan kuning, took to the streets during the Ternate riots to protect their Christian neighbors and to stop their homes from being looted and destroyed when possible. Many Christian IDPs from Ternate were quick to point out that they would have perished in the riots if not for the protection granted by these troops. Christian Forest Tobelo in the Maba subdistrict seized Christian villagers who had looted an abandoned Muslim village, forced them to return the stolen goods, and then turned them over to the authorities.[5] Entire communities refused to attack their neighbors due to family or adat ties. Muslim Sawai in central Halmahera refused to join with outside militia in attacks on their Christian Sawai neighbors, largely sparing that ethnic group from the conflict. Christians on the island of Kakara off the coast of Tobelo protected their Muslim neighbors until they could be safely evacuated to Morotai.

Unfortunately the idea of saviors does not fit the narrative that either side is constructing, and thus they tend to be dismissed as immaterial to the larger picture. Examples that outside observers might point to as evidence that the conflict could not have been about religion—based on exceptions that disprove the thesis, whether that be a particular group's protection of their neighbors or their refusal to participate—are not seen to challenge the master narrative. These examples are considered largely irrelevant. The actions of those groups or individuals were not based on religion, but rather on ethnicity, friendship, or kin ties, and thus do not explain away the vast majority of actions taken in the name of religion. Saviors are remembered and praised individually, but their actions are set aside when considering the general stereotype of the religious other. Marline, a young Christian woman from Ternate, remains grateful to her Muslim saviors who hid her during the Ternate riots and then transported her to what they perceived would be safety—so much so that she zealously hides their identity for fear they still may be persecuted. The actions of that particular family, however, did nothing to change her understanding of the conflict as one based largely on religious differences, nor did it substantially change her opinion of Muslims in general. The exception proves the rule, people were capable of being decent if they could look past their Islamic or Christian identities, and thus it must be their religious ideologies that explain the violence.

The Instrumentalization of Victimhood

Whereas the management of memories within communities was focused more on explanation and validation of people's lived experiences of violence and suffering, narratives presented to outsiders (government officials, NGO representatives, or academics) were often shaped and managed with different goals in mind.[6] When North Moluccans shared accounts of the conflict with outsiders, they were working to convey a particular image to the outside world. In many cases the motives behind these accounts were not entirely cynical; they were looking to convince people about the legitimacy of their own interpretations and to find validation of their suffering. Oftentimes people were eager, in some cases insistent, to have their stories heard and recorded.[7]

People involved in the violence in North Maluku wanted their experiences to be included in my research to ensure that I got the "whole story." Although Muslims were reluctant to discuss the details of the violence with me personally, they were eager to share these stories with my Muslim research assistants. They wanted their voices to be heard and recorded as correctives to the facts put out by a government they mistrusted or biased media outlets. People passed on stories they thought I needed to hear or would insist I go and hear them myself. For them, the more gruesome the tale, the better. For example, when the wife of a minister who had been killed during the conflict was visiting Manado, a number of IDPs contacted me and insisted I talk to her. One friend argued: "You really need to talk to her for your research. They wrapped her husband up in a mattress and burned him alive. This is the important kind of information that you need." In another example a man from the island of Doi off the west coast of Halmahera sought me out in Tobelo because he had heard that I was interviewing people about the violence: "I heard you were recording people's stories from the conflict. They told me I could find you here. I came to explain to you what happened on Doi Island. So you can record it." At times it seemed as if people thought that the intensity of their own suffering would enhance their credibility as informants.[8]

A more cynical way of looking at this management of narratives of the violence is to explore how they were instrumentalized to convey a particular image to the outside world in an effort to access resources or support. In certain circumstances, Muslims and Christians presented purposively selective accounts of the violence to outsiders to shape their image. One of my more persistent encounters with this selectivity was in my interactions with a segment of the Christian elite in postconflict Tobelo town. They were well aware of the disconnect between their image of being a victimized minority and the various atrocities that Christians had committed during the conflict. As a result, they discouraged people from discussing the details of fighting that took place in Tobelo and at times confiscated photographs of atrocities from those who were prone to show them to visitors. When I first arrived in 2001, Christian leaders, including ministers, prominent traders, and others, assured me that the atrocities I had read about in the media or heard about from Muslims were nothing more than exaggerated stories. They explained away the images of burnt out mosques and mass graves that had circulated throughout Indonesia and internationally as examples of Muslim propaganda. On several occasions early in my field work, members of the Christian elite tried to convince me that no massacres had taken place in those mosques, but rather the bodies of the dead had been stored there after the violence and been burnt in a fire during subsequent rioting. Even after I had collected dozens of eyewitness accounts from people who had taken part in the attacks, the Christian elite continued to deny the validity of my data. Some dismissed the photographs of dead Muslim by explaining that the corpses were actually Christians who had been killed during the violence. When I noted that many of these wore white headbands signifying they belonged to Muslim militia, my interlocutors explained that the headbands had been switched for propaganda purposes, thus many of the photos of Muslim bodies were actually photos of dead Christians. When confronted with newspaper accounts of the violence, they explained that the atrocities described had actually been committed by Muslims, who now claimed to be the victims. Eventually, after long-term fieldwork in the region some of the Christian elite admitted that the massacres had taken place, but they argued that they could lose their status as victims if Westerners heard the graphic details or saw the photos. This instrumentalization of victimhood was just one more aspect of managing memories of the conflict and attempting to control or shape the interpretation of the violence.

Efforts to manage memories since the end of the conflict have focused largely on the justification of violence and the validation of victimhood. A significant aspect of these reinterpretations of the violence, as well as of the *longue durée* of North Moluccan history that preceded it, has been the focus on religion and the religious nature of the conflict. Although no single consensus exists over the cause, chronology, or meaning of the violence, competing accounts often call on religion as an explanatory framework. The religious nature of the violence has become an emblematic memory among both Christians and Muslims that provides a meaningful framework to understand a conflict that affected almost every family in North Maluku in some way. It explains why individuals or communities were targeted and why particular acts of violence were committed. The religious framework provides a moral scheme of good and evil for North Moluccans to reexamine past events and assess future relationships with the religious other.

Paul Brass (1996, 45) has argued that contests over controlling the interpretation of episodes of violence are "at least as important and probably more important than the outcome of specific violent struggles themselves." These contests help shape the reconstruction of society in the aftermath, as well as lay the groundwork for the interpretation of future conflicts and tensions. As North Maluku has recovered from conflict, maintaining certain interpretations of the violence, in essence reifying emblematic memories and essentializing certain versions of events, has become important for some communities. In the face of reconstruction and reconciliation efforts that have called on people to forget and move forward, or that have argued against religious interpretations of the violence, some communities have decided to move the discussions about memory from the realm of discourse to the material world through the construction of monuments commemorating certain aspects of the violence or memorials to those who died.

Chapter 7

MEMORIALIZING THE DEAD IN POSTCONFLICT NORTH MALUKU

As North Moluccans debated the issue of victimhood and started to re-build their lives much of the attention in the region shifted to postconflict recovery (CPRU/UNDP 2004; Tindage 2006). Local and regional government officials focused on returning forced migrants to their places of origin and shutting down camps for the displaced (Duncan 2008). International NGOs, such as the UN Development Program, World Vision, and International Medical Corps, worked to rebuild and expand infrastructure destroyed by the violence and to restore medical and educational services. Many of the problems created by communal violence could indeed be repaired: forced migrants could return home, churches and mosques could be rebuilt, gardens could be replanted. However, one of the biggest obstacles to recovery and reconciliation remained dealing with those who died and the memories of their deaths. Their absence served as a tangible reminder of the horrible events that took place and the societal divisions that caused them. Building on my discussion of memory in the last chapter, I now explore how some communities have dealt with the deceased in postconflict North Maluku and how efforts to memorialize the dead through martyr parks and other monuments are, in part, an attempt to solidify a particular narrative of the conflict and its religious points of contention.

The meanings behind these memorials are multifaceted. They are primarily about local desires to respect and remember those who were lost in the conflict and to recognize the sacrifices made in the name of religion and community. Thus in one sense they are about mourning and martyrdom. However, memorialization practices are part of the larger arena of postconflict politics and conflict resolution and cannot be seen independently from the way local communities experienced and perceived the conflict (Jelin 2007).[1] The notion of martyrdom highlighted in these memorials is tied to efforts by local communities in North Maluku to firmly articulate and entrench their version of events in the public memory. These are not incompatible goals. If those who died are martyrs, and have been interred in special martyr cemeteries or buried in extraordinary places in the village, these memorials serve as daily or weekly reminders of the conflict. The people who are honored were killed because of their religion, and these monuments have been established to highlight that point. Although government officials and regional scholars may argue that the conflict was actually about political corruption, or the spoils of decentralization, these monuments say otherwise.

These places represent what the Argentine sociologist Elizabeth Jelin (2007, 141) calls "vehicles of memory," attempts by communities to make certain historical meanings permanent and to stake a claim on the memory of what happened in the aftermath of conflict. Jelin (2003, 33–34) refers to the individuals or communities that build these sorts of memorials (or engage in similar practices) as "memory entrepreneurs," people "who seek social recognition and political legitimacy of *one* (their own) interpretation or narrative of the past" (Jelin 2003, 34, emphasis in the original).[2] Although the past cannot be changed, the meaning of the past is constantly malleable and subject to reevaluation and reinterpretation. In building these monuments and martyr cemeteries, North Moluccans were finalizing their version of events before official accounts (or denials) of what happened became hegemonic and paved over the violence and suffering that occurred with bland narratives of outside instigation or provocateurs.

Monuments and Graves in Indonesia

A number of scholars have explored how the Indonesian government has used memorials to boost nationalist fervor and to control interpretations of historical events (Wiener 1999; Schreiner 2002; Santikarma 2005). The New Order monument at Lubang Buaya for the seven generals killed in the purported communist coup of 30 September 1965 is the most prominent example. The myth of these men and the events surrounding their deaths represented one of the foundational texts of the Suharto regime (Schreiner 2005). North Moluccans are familiar with nationalist monuments and with the importance of memorials in defining historical narratives of past struggles. The Banau Heroes Cemetery (Taman Makam Pahlawan Banau, Ind.) in the provincial capital of Ternate is named after the leader of a 1914 rebellion against the Dutch in the subdistrict of Jailolo (*Organ der Nederlandsch-Indische Officiersvereeniging* 1930). In the town of Soa-sio, the capital of the Galela subdistrict, a small heroes cemetery commemorates seven people killed by the Dutch in the early days of the Indonesian revolution. Painted in red and white with a large flagpole, the nationalist aspects of this memorial are clear. In the village of Kao, a single grave commemorates the seven indigenous people killed in 1906 when the four ethnic groups of Kao (the Modole, Pagu, Tololiko, and Tobelo Boeng) joined to attack a Dutch barracks and chase off, albeit momentarily, the colonial power (*Indisch Militair Tijdschrift* 1907). This grave has come to symbolize the unity of those four ethnic groups and the importance of maintaining it. The power of the historical narrative associated with this particular gravesite became apparent in August 1999.

Other significant graves in Halmahera mark the resting place of people credited with bringing religion to the region. Hendrik van Dijken, the first Dutch Protestant missionary in North Maluku, is buried in Duma in Galela. The grave of Simon Vas, one of the first Catholic missionaries to Indonesia who died in 1534, can supposedly be found behind the village of Mamuya in Galela.[3] Finally, a grave near the village of Popon in Kao is said to be the burial place of Syekh Manysur, an Arab from Baghdad who locals believe introduced Islam to the Kao Islam. The indigenous Muslim communities of Kao commemorate his arrival with an annual pilgrimage to the grave and a communal meal. Thus the people of Halmahera are familiar with graves as historical artifacts and as commemorations of historical events.

They are aware that such places continue to define how the past is remembered and shape relationships in the present. It should come as no surprise that in the aftermath of the 1999–2000 conflict, there would be a desire to establish memorials to those who died in the fighting in an effort to solidify a particular narrative of that violence.

Martyrdom in North Maluku

The religious perceptions of the violence led many North Moluccans to consider those who died in the conflict, whether on the battlefield or in militia attacks, as martyrs. Many Christians believed they were fighting in the name of their God, for his glory, and with his support to maintain a Christian presence on Halmahera. Some Muslims believed they were fighting a holy war as well and that they were waging a jihad to protect Islam in North Maluku from the Christians. In the most obvious example, the local Muslim militia referred to itself as the Pasukan Jihad. Ja'far Umar Thalib, leader of the Laskar Jihad, declared that Christians in Maluku and North Maluku were "belligerent infidels" (*kafir harbi*, Ind.) who must be killed.[4] In some variants of Islamic discourse kafir harbi are considered one of the most dangerous categories of unbelievers and Islamic law obliges Muslims to wage war against them, and anyone who dies in this pursuit will achieve martyrdom.

Although a large number of people in Halmahera see those who died over the course of the violence as martyrs, religious authorities often voiced a different opinion. In line with their Calvinist doctrine, ministers and other officials from the GMIH argued that they have no way of knowing whether those who died in the name of Christianity had made it into heaven. This doctrine placed the church at odds with many of their parishioners whose family members perished during the conflict. These people saw their lost family members as martyrs and believed they had achieved eternal salvation. If possible, GMIH ministers avoided pointing out this doctrinal inconsistency to their congregation. As one minister said, "When they ask me if their family is in heaven because they are martyrs, I just nod my head and tell them they should pray." Muslim religious leaders gave an almost identical response as their Christian counterparts. They often answered that according to doctrine only Allah knows if a person will make it into heaven or not. As much as they would like to think that their loved ones were in heaven, and they believed they were, they have no way of knowing with certainty if that was the case. Despite these doubts among religious professionals, communities throughout North Maluku expressed a strong conviction that those who died were martyrs and had earned a place in heaven.

Preconflict Burial Practices in Tobelo and Galela

These notions of martyrdom and the importance that local communities place on remembering those who died during the conflict are evident when we compare these monuments and martyr cemeteries with the preconflict burial practices of Christian communities. The graveyards of many Christian communities in Tobelo and Galela are located on the outskirts of town. As you travel along the Trans-Halmahera highway, you often come across these cemeteries before entering or after exiting a village. In the twentieth century, graveyards were actively moved out of some villages.[5] Dutch missionaries and their successors in the GMIH wanted to create more distance between villages and graveyards as part of their efforts to sever relationships between the living and the dead.

Pre-Christian and pre-Muslim beliefs among the Galela and Tobelo focused largely on the veneration of ancestors (*o gomanga*, Tobelo; *o goma*, Galela). Although the Tobelo and Galela had a perception of a supreme being, he was largely seen as above human concerns; the ritual focus was on the ancestors.[6] Maintaining relations with these ancestors was important as some of them stayed within the community and could be either a benevolent force or a malevolent one. Strong ancestors were thought to protect the community from harm or aid its members in warfare and piracy. Failure to provide sustenance to these ancestors could result in illness and possibly death (Platenkamp 1988, 105). Dutch missionaries sought to sever these relationships between the living and the dead as part of their efforts to convert the Galela and the Tobelo. As early as 1874, less than a decade after his arrival, Hendrik van Dijken described Galela funerary practices, particularly their secondary mortuary rituals, as "one of the greatest transmitters of paganism" whose removal would help the Christianization of the region (1874, 157, as cited in Platenkamp 1988, 165).

Once communities converted to Christianity, the dead needed to be removed from the community and forgotten, because the dead were no longer to be thought of as social beings. Many Tobelo and Galela were reluctant to acquiesce to missionary demands to give up these relationships, and the issue remains a matter of concern for the church in the twenty-first century.[7] Some in the church now consider the spirits of the deceased as agents of Satan and something to be avoided. As GMIH ministers explained in 2010, the missionaries thought that moving the graveyards out of villages would limit people's contact with them. They hoped that decreased interaction would eventually remove the dead from the social community and put an end to associated beliefs.

In Christian villages today, when people die, their relations with the community are, at least according to the Christian church, supposed to be severed as they go either to heaven or to hell. The church actively discourages people from attempting to maintain relations with those who have died, beyond memorial services after their death and during annual visits to the cemetery at Christmas and New Year's. However, despite more than a century of these efforts to remove the ancestors and other spirits from the social world of the Tobelo and the Galela, people still interact with them in a variety of ways. Some continue to seek favors from their ancestors, a practice that while increasingly rare still occurs despite being frowned on by clergy and more devout Christians in the community.[8] Others rely on them for esoteric knowledge used in healing or magical practices, something that became popular during the conflict as people looked for talismans and charms to protect them. Some believed that the more prominent leaders in the fighting had received their superior fighting prowess and magical abilities to avoid harm directly from their ancestors.

Understanding the church's concerns with separating the living from the dead makes the postconflict burial practices of many Christian communities all the more significant, particularly when we consider that they were most often undertaken with the approval, and in some cases the encouragement, of the clergy. If one drove through Tobelo and Galela after the conflict, in addition to the graveyards located on the outskirts of town, one would also see graves of people who died during the violence prominently located in a number of churchyards. Since these people died defending their faith, their death has been treated differently. The placement of their graves in the churchyard, a place that is the center of village life and is associated with the vitality of the community, signals a different sort of death. These dead should be celebrated and remembered on a daily basis, rather than separated

(both literally and figuratively) from community life. It is not just these individuals who will be remembered, but the events that brought about their
deaths since they are often explicitly marked as martyrs. They will not be
set aside in a graveyard to be slowly forgotten; instead they will be interred
in the spiritual and social center of the community.

Christian villages take great pride in their churches and churchyards.
Communities expend vast amounts of effort and money to build large
churches with the latest styles. In some villages the construction and expansion of these churches seems to be a never-ending project. Although often
defended as a requirement for a growing congregation, there are other meanings inherent in these construction projects. The size and beauty of a church
reflects the wealth and vitality of the community, which some see as evidence
of God's approval and proof of their own sincerity. Just as the splendor of a
church represents the faith of the community, in smaller villages it is also a
symbol of the community itself and is often the focal point of a village.

It may seem that the GMIH has been placed in a slight predicament by
these new burial practices vis-à-vis their doctrine concerning salvation, as
well as their efforts to combat pre-Christian ideas. I would argue, however,
that the construction of these memorials has worked to their advantage.
The placement of graves and memorials at GMIH churches solidifies, if not
reifies, their dominance in the ever-expanding array of Christian denominations in Halmahera. It highlights the continuing importance of the GMIH
in those particular communities, as opposed to smaller non-GMIH congregations.[9] Thus the positive aspects of these memorials for the image and
position of the GMIH in North Moluccan society outweighs any ambivalence the church hierarchy may feel toward the various meanings attributed
to them. Furthermore, the GMIH has not objected to these memorials, because they were built while the church was directly involved in the conflict,
or dealing with its immediate aftermath, and to do so would not have sat
well with local communities.

Despite the iconoclastic reputation of the Dutch missionaries to the region,
who often demanded the communal destruction of ritual objects when local people were baptized, the colonial church maintained a rather ambivalent relationship with pre-Christian practices. Oftentimes this ambivalence
focused as much on co-opting them for church goals as it did on stopping
them.[10] As the postcolonial successor to the Dutch mission, the GMIH has
also had a rather ambivalent relationship with pre-Christian practices.

GMIH preachers often try to Christianize certain aspects of adat in an effort to supplant the pre-Christian ideas associated with them. One recent example would be the actions of certain GMIH ministers who ventured into the realm of fighting magic and protection during the conflict by baptizing warriors prior to battle and blessing magical charms to bestow them with the power of God, rather than the power of the ancestors or other magic. This flexibility continues in the aftermath of the conflict.

Although some clergy might struggle with the mutual exclusivity of the cosmological aspects of adat and Christianity, others in Halmahera see them as complementary realms of interaction and belief. People who regularly attend church, in some cases even those who serve as deacons (*anggota majelis*, Ind.), may also maintain relations with their ancestors, or with the Moro, the invisible beings who inhabit parts of the island's interior. They see nothing incompatible in working within both systems of thought. Thus, during the conflict, Christian fighters would adorn themselves with Bibles and posters of Jesus Christ while at the same time using magical practices and amulets for protection. They would call on Jesus and the Christian God for aid in battle, and also seek aid from the Moro. Battlefield accounts contain images of angels firing on attackers from up high, as well as ancestors and other spiritual beings appearing on the battlefield. The intermingling of pre-Christian ideas with church burial practices in the aftermath of the conflict, then, should not be too surprising.

Martyr Cemeteries in Galela

The most elaborate example of memorializing has been the creation of martyr cemeteries in several Christian villages in Galela.[11] The largest memorial is located in the village of Duma, the site of a church massacre that marked the end of large-scale violence in North Maluku in June 2000. More than 150 people, including many women and children, were killed in this final confrontation. After the survivors had surrendered, several army units arrived to protect the few remaining men and the large number of women and children who were still alive. Under the protection of the soldiers, the survivors quickly buried the bodies of those that had been killed, some in mass graves, and others in front of their destroyed homes. Before they left, they held a brief prayer ceremony during which they promised to return and rebury the dead in a more dignified manner. After the army evacuated the survivors to Tobelo, a large number decided to continue on to Manado in North Sulawesi. Unfortunately they boarded the ill-fated passenger ship *Cahaya Bahari* that left port from Tobelo on 28 June and was lost at sea.

For several years the people of Duma lived as IDPs in and around the town of Tobelo and in North Sulawesi. When they returned in 2003 after prolonged negotiations with their Muslim neighbors, one of their first tasks was to rebury the dead as they had promised. In fulfilling this vow, the community decided to separate them from the general graveyard in the village. The latter is seen as a place for those who died a natural death, while the new memorial is for those who died "too soon." As one woman said: "If I saw my daughter's grave in the general graveyard it would make me very sad because I know she died too soon. But when I see it in the martyr cemetery, it does not make me sad because I know that she is in heaven." This woman finds it relaxing to sit and chat with friends in the memorial, as it brings her a sense of peace.

The martyr cemetery is located next to the remnants of the now destroyed church where the killings took place. A sign with a large white cross marks the entrance to the memorial park and reads: Cemetery for the Beloved Martyrs of the Congregation in Duma (Taman Pusara Martir Jemaat "Dodara" di Duma, Ind.).[12] The site, designed by one of the war leaders from Duma, consists of twenty rows of ten identical graves (see figure 7.1). These graves are located on a large cement plaza of approximately 900 square meters. All of the tombstones are labeled with uniform metal plaques (see figure 7.2). In addition to identifying the occupant of each grave, these plaques have a picture of two angels blowing trumpets over a small Bible open to the inscription "Romans 14:8." This Bible verse, not written on the plaque, reads, "If we live, we live to honor the Lord; and if we die, we die to honor the Lord. So whether we live or die, we belong to the Lord." Each person is also referred to as a "martyr of the congregation" (*martir jemaat*, Ind.). Below the data that identifies the occupant of the grave is the inscription: "Don't let my struggle be in vain" (*Jangan sia-siakan perjuanganku*, Ind.). This graveyard includes everyone from Duma who was killed in the church on 19 June, as well as people from other villages who were killed that day. There are also a few graves of Duma residents who died elsewhere during the violence.

Once they had completed the construction of the graves, the village held a large ceremony to rebury the martyrs. Family members exhumed those who had died and the bodies were moved to their respective neighborhoods

Figure 7.1. The martyr cemetery in Duma, Galela subdistrict, North Maluku. July 2008.
Photo by Christopher R. Duncan.

Figure 7.2. Example of a tombstone from the martyr cemetery in Duma, Galela subdistrict, North Maluku. July 2008. Photo by Christopher R. Duncan.

where they were placed in new coffins. As two musicians played church hymns on the ruins of the former church, another parishioner rang a church bell. Each time the bell rang, all the coffins from a particular ministerial grouping (*lingkungan gereja*, Ind.) were brought to the new cemetery and placed inside a nearby tent. After a short service, in which one of the pastors referred to the new memorial as "historical proof" of what had taken place, the coffins were interred in the martyr cemetery to serve as a sign of respect (*tanda penghargaan*, Ind.) to those who died during the conflict.

The memorial eventually contained two hundred graves from more than eighty different families. After the martyr cemetery was finished, the man who played a prominent role in ensuring its construction passed away and was buried there as well. His grave was set off to the side at the front of the graveyard to symbolize his leadership role before and after the conflict. Thus, as he led the people of Duma during the fighting, he will lead them into the afterlife. With the exception of the person who designed it, only those who fell during the conflict were buried in the cemetery. Those who died after the conflict was over, or who will pass away in the future will be buried elsewhere regardless of the role they played. Thus, with the one exception, the cemetery has been set aside for martyrs rather than heroes. Those who distinguished themselves in the conflict, but survived, will have to be content with being buried in the general graveyard.

Through the construction of these memorials the people of Galela are underwriting a particular interpretation of the communal conflict. If the bodies had been buried in the regular cemetery, over the years people may have forgotten them, and they would fade from memory as they were just another grave among many. But by putting the graves all together in a single spot in the same place where many of the people fell defending their religion they have been marked out for special remembrance. Furthermore the monument was constructed in such a way as to effectively preclude any other interpretation of events. The signage leaves little to the imagination. It differs from regular graveyards in another crucial aspect: the entire cemetery is concrete. In the general cemetery the gravestones are made of poured concrete, but the cemetery itself consists of dirt, grass, weeds, and frangipani trees. Graves of those who are no longer remembered by their descendants often become overgrown with weeds and grass, eventually crumbling and disappearing. In contrast the martyr cemetery in Duma has been built with a more permanent aura, which informants cited as one aim of its construction.

One year after the formal opening of the martyr cemetery, the village built a monument to those lost on the *Cahaya Bahari* passenger ship (see figure 7.3). The plaque on the memorial reads: "Monument to the members of the Nita Congregation of the GMIH in Duma lost on the Motorship *Cahaya Bahari* on 29-06-2000."[13] Around the walls of the basin are plaques with the names of those who died when the ship sank. The community constructed the monument at the cost of 40,000,000 Indonesian rupiah (approximately four thousand U.S. dollars), but the plaques were paid for by the individual families and remain incomplete. The monument refers to those who died on the *Cahaya Bahari* as victims (*korban*, Ind.) rather than as martyrs (*martir*, Ind.), and whether this reflects how local people view their salvation remains unclear.

Once the people of Duma had finished their memorial, other nearby villages followed suit. Some communities, whose members had died in Duma on 19 June 2000 took their dead and built smaller memorials in their villages. The neighboring village of Makete built a martyr cemetery to hold the graves of those that died at Duma. In Makete the plaques on the tombstones

Figure 7.3. Monument to the victims of the *Cahaya Bahari* passenger ship in Duma, Galela, North Maluku. The large plaque on the monument reads, "Monument to the members of the Nita Congregation of GMIH in Duma lost on the Motorship *Cahaya Bahari* on 29-06-2000." The smaller plaques surrounding the monument contain some of the names of those who were lost when the ship sank. September 2004. Photo by Christopher R. Duncan.

are labeled with the phrase "martyr of the congregation" (martir jemaat, Ind.) written above a small Bible with a cross. The Bible verse written on the image of the book is Philippians 1:21, the text of which is written out below the identifying information on the plaque: "For to me, to live is Christ, and to die is gain."[14] A similar grouping of graves has been built in the Christian part of the village of Mamuya to house the graves of several people there who died during the conflict; however no signs explicitly mark this graveyard as a martyr park and the gravestones make no direct reference to the conflict, other than the dates when the people died.

Not everyone in northern Halmahera welcomed the idea of building a martyr cemetery in Duma or elsewhere. The armed forces initially discouraged the planning committee. They argued that building a monument to the dead would foster feelings of revenge and prevent the peaceful coexistence of Muslim and Christian communities. Neighboring Muslim communities were also wary of the martyr park for a variety of reasons. Their mistrust of Christian motives led to a rumor that the people in Duma were going to use the graveyard as a weapons cache, and the coffins would be filled with guns and bullets rather than bodies. One person even claimed that the Indonesian army sent someone from Jakarta to inspect the coffins before they were interred. Some Muslims wanted to duplicate the park, not for religious reasons, but to access the government funds they thought Duma had received for the park's construction. Once they realized that no such funds existed, the idea quickly faded. Muslims in Galela that I interviewed between 2006 and 2012 rarely mentioned any continuing discomfort with the park; they no longer considered it a potential source of conflict. Some even saw it as a point of reconciliation, they believed that the Christians in Duma would see the martyr cemetery and, rather than feeling a need for revenge, would be reminded on a daily basis of the suffering that comes with religious conflict.

Tobelo Churchyards

Christians in Galela were not the only ones who built memorials to those who perished in the fighting. In the subdistrict of Tobelo many of those who died in the conflict have been interred in churchyards (see figure 7.4). Those memorialized in Tobelo did not die in massacres, but as individuals

Figure 7.4. Monument for two Christian militia members in front of the GMIH church
in the village of Leleoto south of Tobelo town. Above the name of the deceased, it reads,
"Monument to Christ's Militia" (*Monumen Laskar Kristus*, Ind.). Below the name of
the deceased men is written Mark 8:35. This Bible verse reads, "For whoever wants to save
his life will lose it, but whoever loses his life for me and for the Gospel will save it."
The two men memorialized here were killed by the armed forces as they attempted to bring
explosives from the Wasile region to Tobelo. They were killed off the coast of Subaim and
their bodies disposed of at sea. May 2002. Photo by Christopher R. Duncan.

in the wider conflict. For example, the person buried in the churchyard in Paca was killed by the armed forces after attempting to buy bomb-making materials across the bay. The men buried in Pitu were shot by the army during a standoff at the main army blockade between Tobelo and Galela. Although considered martyrs by members of their communities, their martyrdom is less marked than it is in Galela. There are no explicit references to martyrdom on their gravestones, but the text often makes it clear that they died defending their faith. The epitaph on one of the graves next to the old church in the village of Pitu reads: "I struggled until the last drop of blood for Jesus who was insulted and the Christian community who was oppressed. Hey, my comrades keep going forward. No retreat."[15] The graves in the village of Kupa-Kupa refer to the deceased as "Christ's Troops" (Laskar Kristus, Ind.). In the village of Gura there are two graves of people who died in the conflict next to the church. Both tombstones refer to the deceased as a "Warrior of Christ" (Pejuang Kristus, Ind.) and, similar to the graves in Duma, have an image of the Bible with "Romans 14:8" written on it. The final line on each headstone differs, one reads, "Continue my struggle" (*Teruskan perjuanganku*, Ind.), and the other reads, "Don't let my struggle be in vain" (*Jangan sia-siakan perjuanganku*, Ind.). As noted above, these memorials generally consist of individual graves or at most a few graves placed near the village church. The placement of the graves in the churchyard, rather than in the general cemetary, has transformed them from relatively unimportant sites known only to the immediate family of the deceased into community memorials to glorify their struggle and that of their larger community to defend their faith.

Despite the prominent position given to these graves, not everyone in the Christian Tobelo community agrees with this practice. Some oppose it because they fear that the placement of graves near churches will be a constant reminder of the violence. Rather than seeing these graves as celebrations of those who died in the name of religion and community, critics see them as potential flashpoints that keep the community focused on interfaith conflict. They argued that people would see the graves and consistently be reminded of the violence done to their community by their Muslim neighbors, and it would hinder efforts at reconciliation. Others simply found the elevation of particular individuals in such a way to be improper. They argued that it gave too much attention to certain people who died in the conflict and ignored the suffering of the community at large.

Another interesting aspect of the graves in Tobelo is the similarity between the internment of people who died in battle and pre-Christian burial
practices. In pre-Christian Tobelo society, the Tobelo classified people who
died in two ways, either as *o heneoara* or as *o dilikine*. The first, o heneoara,
were those that died from old age and had exhausted all of their life force
(*o gurumini*, Tobelo). These were not seen as strong ancestors (Hueting 1922,
162). The second type of dead, o dilikine, are described as "strong spirit[s] of
those who died not a natural death but a violent death, particularly those
who died as a casualty of war, but also those that died from drowning, fall-
ing from a tree and the like" (Hueting 1922, 162). The Tobelo believed that
the spirits of these individuals, due to their unnatural deaths, retained some
of their life force and could serve as protective spirits. As one Tobelo informant told the Dutch missionary Hueting (1922, 163) in the early twentieth
century, the o dilikine "do not really belong to the dead, their place is
among the living." Tobelo believed that these particular ancestors stayed in
the community. Some Tobelo communities placed the bones of those deemed
o dilikine in small structures near their residences (*o gomanga ma tau / o
dodadi ma tau,* Tobelo) (Clercq 1889, 208–9; Platenkamp 1988, 179–80).[16]
Thus, one could see the treatment of those who died in the religious violence as, ironically, being connected with pre-Christian ritual practices.[17]
Just as the community remembered and honored the memory of powerful
ancestors through the construction of small ancestral houses, so have they
honored the martyrs of the 1999-2000 violence by interring them in socially
prominent places in the community, rather than placing them in the separate graveyard. When questioned about the similarities between these new
burials and pre-Christian practices ministers were quick to discount such
connections and focused instead on the Christian aspects of the burials and
their connection with the religious conflict.

Muslim Burial Practices

The Muslim community in North Maluku appears to be less interested in
building memorials for those who died in the conflict. The contrast in memorialization practices becomes readily apparent if we compare how Christians in Duma memorialized those who died in the church massacre, with
how the Muslim community of Popilo commemorated those who died in

the massacre in their mosque. The memorialization at Duma, as mentioned above, has been rather significant, and there is little subtlety in the public expression of martyrdom. The people of Popilo, also ethnic Galela and also the victims of a large-scale massacre, have responded in a different way. Popilo was the site of one of the largest massacres of the conflict when Christian militia killed several hundred people as they destroyed the last Muslim villages in the Tobelo subdistrict in early January 2000. Many from Popilo sought refuge in their mosque, but no quarter was given and almost everyone inside was killed. In the aftermath of the fighting, the armed forces buried the dead in a mass grave in front of the mosque.

After the people of Popilo returned to their village, the general consensus was to leave the mass grave unmarked. There appears to have been little interest in making any sort of memorial to those who died. Some disagreed with this decision and two families placed headstones on the spot to mark their lost family members. One gravestone notes the death of three members of a particular family and the other commemorates the death of a single individual (see figure 7.5). The latter does make a reference to martyrdom. Above the deceased's name (who actually appears to have been killed

Figure 7.5. Grave markers at the site of a mass grave in front of a mosque in Popilo, Tobelo subdistrict, North Maluku. July 2008. Photo by Christopher R. Duncan.

in the neighboring village of Gorua) is written "Wassuhada," a reference to the deceased's having died along the path to Allah.[18] Otherwise there is no mention of the dozens of other people interred there or their martyrdom.

Although the differences in memorialization practices between Duma and Popilo are obvious, there appears to be no single explanation for why this is the case. Many of the Muslims that I interviewed were at a loss to explain these differences. Some argued the lack of memorials stemmed from reformist Muslim concerns about graveyards. Certain Muslims in North Maluku, particularly those associated with Muhammadiyah, saw marking the graves of martyrs as unnecessary because Allah already recognized their sacrifice. Muhammadiyah has an antipathy toward gravestones and graveyards due in part to negative views on *ziarah*.[19] The head of the Indonesian Ulama Council in North Halmahera (Majelis Ulama Indonesia, Ind.) and principal of the Muhammadiyah school in Tobelo explained his views to me in 2010. He said it was permissible for people to visit the graves of their family after Ramadan as long as they only went to pray for the dead and to pay their respects. However, it would be a violation of the tenants of Islam if they took part in any other sort of ritual, such as leaving offerings, during these visits. Based on this view of graves, he argued that there was no need to build memorials to those who died during the conflict. Such monuments would only pose problems for future generations. They would serve as constant reminders of the violence perpetrated against Muslims and could provoke feelings of resentment and a desire for revenge. Another danger would be if the memorials contained the grave of a person who was particularly important to the local community, such as a traditional leader, or someone venerated as a martyr. Monuments to such individuals could lead people to start venerating or worshipping the dead, something that would, again, violate the tenants of Islam.

Not all Muslims agreed with these views held by Muhammadiyah. Interviews with individuals who had adat positions within the Muslim community provided different conclusions. The adat-based understanding of why monuments to martyrs were inappropriate was related to the special role of the sultan of Ternate in North Halmahera. The kapita of Galela, an adat leader of the Galela ethnic group appointed by the sultan of Ternate, dismissed the Muhammadiyah explanation. He said it was nonsense, and there were two reasons for not building monuments or burying people in front of mosques. Building a memorial was improper because monuments were reserved for sultans, not for ordinary people. Only sultans should have single graves where they can be revered, whereas ordinary people should be buried with their family in a cemetery. To build a monument to someone, or to place their grave alone in a significant place, would be akin to placing them on par with a sultan, which he considered inappropriate. As a result, he had argued against constructing any monuments or burying people deemed martyrs in prominent places in front of mosques.

Despite these differing opinions, some Muslim villages in northern Halmahera do contain graves with references to martyrdom, but none of them as elaborate or as well maintained as those found in Christian villages. In the center of Soa-sio, Galela a small cemetery holds the graves of a number of people who died during the conflict. Those buried here, however, are either people from outside of the region, or those who died during the height of the violence when people were too scared to travel to graveyards on the outskirts of town to bury the dead. The cemetery itself was not specifically constructed to valorize martyrs, and in fact it appears to be slowly disappearing as the tombstones disintegrate and are overgrown with vegetation. This decay should come as no surprise as the majority of the dead have no family in the region to maintain their graves. Some of these graves carry the inscription of "mujahidin" marking those that are buried there as individuals who died waging jihad and are thus, in the eyes of their loved ones, assured a place in heaven. However, Muslim leaders in Galela see this graveyard as an educational instrument to remind people of the cost of communal violence rather than as a monument to martyrdom. They argued the graveyard reminded everyone who passed it that conflict comes with a high price.[20]

The construction of these memorials to those who died in the religious conflict, whether the large-scale martyr park in Duma, or the more subtle references to martyrdom on isolated Muslim graves, are reminiscent of what anthropologist Laura Deeb (2008, 371), in her work on museum exhibitions and martyrdom in Lebanon, describes as "efforts to sediment the just-lived past into what is understood as 'history.'" Local communities constructed these sites as part of their efforts to actively define recent history and to gain control over the public narrative. As I have shown, they have focused on the religious aspects of these events. Those who died are memorialized as martyrs either explicitly as in the Galela case, or implicitly as in Tobelo. The monuments to the conflict highlight the religious dividing lines that communities have come to see as the defining factor in the conflict. No one has built memorials highlighting political differences or with references to the impact of decentralization and democratization on local communities. Although this may seem trivial, the various ways people remember a conflict, and, in the case of North Maluku, the way in which these memories have been literally set in stone or steel, will have ramifications for intergroup relations and other aspects of postconflict dynamics long after other visual reminders of the violence such as destroyed homes, IDP camps, and military checkpoints have disappeared. As the events recede in time and as official rhetoric attempts to paper over religious tensions, these monuments continue to highlight the religious aspects of the conflict. Denials of the role of religion will, at least in the near future, fall on deaf ears. Furthermore, appeals to forget the past and focus on the future could be met with skepticism in communities whose centerpieces, their churches, are surrounded by the graves of those who were killed based on their religious identities.

CONCLUSION

I began this book with an anecdote about a young woman named Marline who was frustrated by the way some people attempted to dismiss the religious nature of the conflict that had forced her from her home in North Maluku and killed dozens of her relatives. More than a decade later, Marline has not returned to Ternate and has no plans to do so. She visited a few times as part of reconciliation activities when she was an IDP in North Sulawesi but decided not to return. She lived in an IDP camp until 2004 when she moved to West Java where she had family, and where she found work managing a warehouse for a clothing store. She now lives in a Muslim majority region again but remains active in church and has become a prominent member of a Pentecostal congregation. Unfortunately, since her move to West Java religious tensions between segments of the Muslim community and Pentecostal churches have increased. Numerous churches have been shut down, and there have been threats of violence against others (International Crisis Group 2010). She has taken part in interfaith discussion groups aimed at preventing conflict but remains pessimistic about Muslim-Christian relations in general. The opinions she formed during the 1999–2000 conflict have changed little. She still argues that the violence in North Maluku was about religion. Like many North Moluccans in the decade after the end of hostilities, Marline remains unwilling to dismiss religion as simply a façade for politics or economics. She considers the politics surrounding the conflict largely irrelevant, and in fact knows very little about them.

Moving beyond Fears of Essentialism

Scholars of collective violence have rightly developed skepticism for explanations such as Marline's that appear to lean toward essentialism or primordialism in discussions of ethnic or religious-based violence.[1] We have long been told, correctly, that these clichéd descriptions of conflict and its inevitability fail to help us understand why collective violence takes place and ignores the political, economic, and social dynamics involved in such clashes. In our drive to remove the absolutes of essentialism, however, perhaps we have strayed a bit too far to the other side of the spectrum. While rejecting essentialist understandings of conflict as based on ancient hatreds has provided far more nuanced understandings of conflicts around the world and is something most anthropologists would embrace, I would argue it has also led to the dismissal of the role that such identities come to play in communal violence, what anthropologist Maja Povrzanović (1997, 162) has called "war-induced essentialism." One goal of this work has been to look at a particular example of religious violence in Indonesia, to talk about how participants perceived it as religious, and to highlight the importance of religious-based identities without getting bogged down by knee-jerk calls to avoid essentialism. Some colleagues have warned me of the dangers of seeing the violence in such a binary perspective of Muslim versus Christian, arguing that North Moluccans, like people anywhere, have multiple identities they can call on, including religion, ethnicity, gender, and class, depending on the context. This recognition of the multifaceted nature of identity, although an accurate description of North Maluku, fails to take into consideration a "war time politics of identity" (Povrzanović 1997, 153) that can occur in times of communal violence.

I would argue that productive studies of communal violence are those that rather than dismissing local perceptions about ethnicity and religion, explore how notions of primordialism and essentialism came to exist in certain contexts and how local communities understood and deployed them in times of crisis, or were the victims of such a process.[2] Throughout this book I have shown how the anticipation of violence, the experience of it, and the way people manage their memories in its aftermath served, in part, to essentialize these identities in the minds of those involved. Religious identities in North Maluku are no less constructed than any other form of identity in a globalized ever-changing world, but nonetheless, they came to be pivotal in people's understanding of the conflict. The factors that led to bloodshed in North Maluku were varied and included everything from recent politics to much deeper histories, from economic concerns to cultural ones. The reasons that religion came to the fore were just as varied and stemmed from many of the same sources—politics, economics, history, and local culture. In other cases of communal violence in Indonesia around the same time period, particularly where religion was not the most relevant aspect in local relations, ethnicity, class, or political affiliation were the main points of contention (Peluso and Harwell 2001; Bouvier and Smith 2008; Davidson 2008). Religious tensions were a long present aspect of North Moluccan society, just as they are in much of Indonesia. People may have mistrusted their Muslim or Christian neighbors, but that mistrust, or even disdain, was a far cry from the lethal animosity that came to characterize the conflict. This deadly hatred was a result of the communal conflict, not a causal factor.

Shifting Discourses of Violence

Once we realize that politics isn't everything and that there is more to understanding communal conflict than causation we can begin to explore how subjective perceptions shape violence and its aftermath. Although this will surely leave my political scientist colleagues unsatisfied, I have argued that while causation is an important aspect of studying communal violence in Indonesia and elsewhere, it is not the only facet of communal violence that demands our attention. Once conflicts have begun, participant understandings of it are subject to change, both during the fighting and afterward. Hence my larger concern with focusing on the religious aspects in order to explore how this discursive construction of the conflict made sense to participants, how it changed the violence itself, and how it continued to affect the region in the decade or so after the bloodshed stopped. Some participants were predisposed to see religion as the point of contention right from the outset, looking for and finding evidence of religious causal factors all around them, others changed their opinions over time, while some were never convinced.

I used Stanley Tambiah's notions of focalization and transvaluation to help explain how this discursive shift in the violence took place. In North Maluku, focalization occurred as Muslim communities began to set aside the particulars of the violence between the indigenous people of Kao and Makianese migrants and focused instead on the Muslim-Christian aspect of the conflict. Christians did the same after the anti-Christian riots in Ternate and Tidore. Both sides seemed to forget, or at least minimize, the importance of border disputes, histories of migration, ethnic animosity, local and regional politics, and feelings of disenfranchisement that might have been casual factors in the initial outbreak of conflict. Transvaluation occurred as North Moluccans, now perceiving themselves as part of a religious conflict, began to see their disputes as part of a much broader struggle, both current and historical, between Muslims and Christians throughout Indonesia. Just as Tambiah (1996, 192) suggests, these processes of focalization and transvaluation quickly turned the outbreak of violence into "self-fulfilling manifestations, incarnations, and reincarnations of allegedly irresolvable communal splits" that manifested themselves in a binary of war-induced essentialist identities. While understanding how the conflict narrative changed is helpful, I have also shown how this discursive shift changed the very nature of the violence and the course it took. North Moluccans began to call on a different set of terminology and a different set of ideas. They talked about jihad, wars of religion (*perang agama*, Ind.), and martyrdom rather than regional autonomy or redistricting. This religious language created new motivations, new targets, and new courses of action that subsequently altered the conflict. The framing of events in religious language essentially led people to create a new reality (Kippenberg 2011, 200). IDPs arrived in safe ports with tales about the desecration of corpses, the forced violation of religious taboos, and the forced conversions of those caught by the other side. What had previously been a localized land dispute became a struggle to protect the very existence of one religious community or another. Although religion might not have been a casual factor in the conflict, it became the defining one over time as the conflict narrative changed.[3]

Without taking into account the affect of this religious framing of events we cannot hope to understand, for example, the motives of Christians who remained in Duma to face near certain death to defend their church. They were given the opportunity to leave but chose martyrdom. Nor can we explain the willingness of Muslim men and women from Ternate, Tidore, or Sanana, places not directly affected by the violence, to join what many of them considered a jihad. Once religion became the accepted point of contention, the conflict became an existential one for many of those involved, reminiscent of what the sociologist of religion Mark Juergensmeyer (2008, 218) has termed a "cosmic war." Christians began to talk of Muslims' efforts to silence church bells forever on Halmahera, while Muslims discussed Christian plans for religious cleansing. Scholars of religion have observed that religious interpretations of violence can (but not always) increase its intensity (Lincoln 2006, 93-96; Jones 2008, 95-96; Kippenberg 2011, 200). For example, Juergensmeyer (2008, 219) notes that oftentimes religious-based violence can be directed at entire communities because "individuals are not important" in such conflicts, and in wars over religion "innocence is moot; all individuals are potentially soldiers." As a result, justice is meted out to all people of a particular religious identity, young and old, male or female. Other have noticed, in places as diverse as sixteenth-century France (Davis 1973, 165) and twentieth-century India (Kakar 1996, 194) that religious interpretations of violence often preclude feelings of guilt or regret among those who commit violent acts, thus heightening the potential for atrocities. Although some (cf. Cavanaugh 2009) have reacted to these arguments by claiming that religion is not inherently violent, neither I nor the aforementioned authors have made such a claim but rather explore how in certain cases religion can increase the intensity of particular conflicts or change the goals and objectives of participants. Religion does not necessarily make people more violent, but in some cases it can, and in North Maluku it did.

Memories and Conflict Narratives

My final goal in the book was to explore how North Moluccans were managing their memories of the violence once it ended. In particular I explored how the polysemic nature of the conflict has been homogenized and replaced with narratives of religious conflict. Rather than deconstruct this narrative and explain it away through anecdotal evidence of looters or individuals resolving grudges, I have investigated how this particular way of remembering the recent past came about and how it has influenced postconflict dynamics. In pursing this goal I demonstrated the usefulness of Steve Stern's (2004) concept of "emblematic memory," which refers to a framework that organizes and, perhaps more important, validates shared memories of the recent past. Certain understandings of events become hegemonic and replace or overshadow, other explanations. In North Maluku these emblematic memories have focused on religious points of contention. As a result, discussions of the violence, narratives of experience, or efforts to memorialize it often call attention to the religious facet of events, while marginalizing or dismissing other explanatory frameworks.

My exploration of how participants in communal violence seek to explain events after the fact also calls attention to the subjectivity and selectivity of conflict narratives. As my examination of North Maluku has shown, scholarly analyses of postconflict narratives need to pay attention not just to their content, but to their context, and to the intent of those who share them. This means more than triangulating differing accounts in an effort to discover the empirical truth. It requires that we examine these memories and the processes through which they were created for the anxieties and desires they communicate. As other scholars of communal violence have shown (Feldman 2003; Das 2006, 120), different versions of the past, both the recent and more distant, exist in the memories of different communities. Although reconciling these differences can prove difficult, understanding them, how they developed, and what they hold for the future is a crucial aspect in the study of communal conflict. In some cases these differences might simply be efforts to cover up atrocities in the face of persecution or shame, as in the case of Christian Tobelo elite attempting to deny the massacres that took place in Popilo and elsewhere. In other cases, however, particularly when we are exploring memories among nonelites, it can provide insight in how and why people responded to the violence the way they did.

My analysis of the tropes of betrayal and aggression prevalent in postconflict narratives in North Maluku, from victims and perpetrators (or those who played both roles), exemplified Liisa Malkki's idea of mythico-history, which Lemarchand (1996, 19) described as "the need to adapt memory to explanation." North Moluccans called on these shared narratives in efforts to explain why they were victimized and to justify their actions. As I gathered stories of the violence across North Maluku, these notions of betrayal and aggression permeated people's accounts. By shifting virtually all the blame to the other side, Muslims and Christians in North Maluku were able, at least in their own communities, to justify their actions during the conflict, as well as make claims on the present. The focus on betrayal and aggression exemplified the "subversive recasting and reinterpretation of [an event's] fundamentally moral terms" that Malkki argues are a significant aspect of mythico-history (Malkki 1995, 54). Again, my goal was not to disassemble these local ways of remembering or to distinguish truths from falsehoods. My aim was to explore how and why particular themes pervaded people's memories and why the discourse of religious violence has such staying power in North Moluccan communities. Any analysis of the conflict in North Maluku, or elsewhere, must take into consideration these mythicohistories and emblematic memories in order to understand how local communities experienced the violence and how they will rebuild their lives in its aftermath. Dismissing them as subjective accounts unworthy of serious scholarly attention does little to further analysis and serves only to reify the sense of victimhood inherent in those who created them.

The Value of Vernacular Understandings for Peace and Reconciliation

My exploration of local perceptions of the conflict as one based on religious differences is arguably more than an intellectual exercise, it points to issues that need to be taken into consideration in ongoing or future discussions about peace and reconciliation in the region. While scholars can argue over the "true" nature of the conflict, its causal mechanisms, and the importance of one chronology or another, for North Moluccans these discursive constructions of the conflict have ramifications for how communities recover. Religious differences continue to permeate North Moluccan society and they play an arguably even more important role in local identity than before the conflict. Future religious violence is not inevitable, but local and regional efforts to rebuild communities in postconflict North Maluku and to prevent future violence based on religious differences need to confront these understandings of the conflict rather than ignoring them as many officials in Indonesia have chosen to do. Communities and individuals, who see themselves as victims, often don't appreciate being told they that they don't understand their own experiences. In speaking of the importance of reconciliation, the theologian Nigel Biggar (2003, 8) observes that for victims of conflict "to suffer an injury and have it ignored is to be told effectively, 'What happens to you doesn't matter, because you don't matter.'" Any efforts to rebuild social relations in North Maluku must begin with a consideration of local notions of victimhood and perceptions of the conflict. I am not arguing for some sort of moral relativism that excuses human rights abuses or atrocities, but rather that a more sophisticated understanding about local perceptions of the conflict and what is was about be taken into consideration.

The peace-building work that has received the most attention in the region has dealt with these local perceptions of the violence as a religious conflict. I highlighted some of these efforts in chapter 5 when I discussed decisions by segments of the Tobelo community to use adat as a point of reconciliation.[4] Rather than dismiss understandings of the religious nature of violence as misguided, these people are seeking to change local discourses on identity by foregrounding cultural identity. It is too soon to tell if these proponents of adat will be successful, and they have had their critics, myself included (Duncan 2010). Tobelo is not the only place in North Maluku, or Indonesia for that matter, where this renewed interest in adat as a tool for conflict resolution and reconciliation has appeared. The sultan of Ternate has argued that strengthening adat is the only way to ensure future stability in the region (Sjah 1999) and has even made calls for turning North Maluku into a special administrative region (*daerah istimewa*, Ind.) subject to *Adat Moloko Kie Raha*.[5] In the early years of the twenty first century, numerous district capitals in North Maluku began holding annual cultural festivals that celebrated local traditions. A common feature of these festivals is an idealized notion of a peaceful North Maluku based on adat-mediated intergroup relationships (cf. Djafar and Taib 2011). Much as North Moluccans reinterpreted their past and their present to help them understand the conflict and its aftermath, proponents of this approach to peace-building are reinterpreting that same past in order to bring forth an idealized version that focuses on ethnic solidarity and interfaith harmony. This revitalization of adat will not necessarily prevent future conflict in the region, but it does provide one avenue for easing the current tensions present in North Maluku and elsewhere.[6] The strength of this approach is that while seeking to displace religious tensions, it does not deny or dismiss local understandings of religious violence. Any efforts to heal the rifts in North Moluccan society created by the communal conflict of 1999–2000 must pay attention to how local communities experienced and made sense of the conflict and its aftermath.

Appendix A

The Bloody Sosol Letter:
Indonesian Original and English Translation

Indonesian original

[Capitalization and typographical errors from the original have been left in this transcription; however, I have adjusted the spacing and removed hyphenation.][1]

Ambon, 29 July 1999

No: 028/SGT/CSIS/VII/99
Lamp: 1 (Satu) berkas
Sifat: Sangat Rahasia
Hal: Rencana serangan balik Sosol berdarah

Kepada Yth: Ketua Sinode Halmahera Di Tobelo

A.   PANDANGAN UMUM

Salam sejahtera dalam kasih Tuhan Yesus Kristus

   Surat Saudara telah kami terima, dan kami bersama Tim menanggapi serius. Mengantisipasi Program Otonomi Daerah maka perlu kiranya Sinode Halmahera dapat mengembangkan Program-Program kerja yang mandiri, dimana akan terpisah semua hubungan kerja baik secara interen maupun eksteren [*sic*] kita (Ambon dan Halmahera). Dengan demikian perlu adanya pemikiran-pemikiran yang lebih cemerlang sehubungan dengan peristiwa Sosol berdarah. Munculnya perang argumentasi diantara Pejabat Daerah Maluku Utara dan Halmahera Tengah dalam memasang Kerangka Dasar Ibukota Propinsi. Momen ini harus segera dimanfaatkan hingga dapat tercapai tujuan kita yakni:

- Mendiami/menduduki secara keseluruhan sekitar Kota Propinsi tersebut.

Dengan demikian Etnis Tobelo, Galela, Kao dan Sahu dapat mengambil alih sedikit demi sedikit melalui Program jangka Panjang dalam proses Pemerintahan, yang selama ini tidak pernah memperhatikan dan dianggap sebagai etnis yang sangat rendah oleh Etnis lainnya di Maluku Utara dan Halmahera Tengah.

   Bangkitkan Misi mulia Sang Gembala mendamaikan dunia dalam Kasih Tuhan-Yesus Kristus. Dilihat dari sisi Geografi Maluku Utara dan Halmahera Tengah diapit oleh Maluku Tengah (Ambon), Sulawesi Utara (Manado) dan Irian Jaya yang nota bene mayoritas Kristiani. Dengan demikian Program kita yang telah terencana untuk menyambut Propinsi baru ini akan lebih nyata dari tahun ketahun [*sic*]. Dalam proses pendekatan Gereja, tercatat Sulawesi Utara siap melepaskan Sanger-Talaut untuk Maluku Utara. Melalui pendekatan Sejarah, adat dan Budaya serta Kasih Tuhan Yesus, hal ini akan mendapat dukungan Pemda Maluku Utara.

   Dengan demikian Saudara-saudara kita dari Sanger Talaut akan mendapat tempat di daratan Halmahera dengan lebih leluasa, ini merupakan cikal bakal muncul laskar-laskar Kristus muda yang terampil menggunakan alat berburu / Prang [*sic*] dengan otak yang jernih penuh keberanian, bakal nanti akan dukung Etnis Tobelo, Galela, Kao dan Sahu. Bila tiba saatnya nanti akan muncul dua kekuatan besar yakni:

- Laskar Kristus Tuan Rumah
- Laskar Kristus Pendatang.

Kekuatan kedua diatas akan sulit ditandingi oleh etnis-etnis lainnya di Maluku—Utara/Halmahera Tengah (literatur Muslim plus Buton Bugis Makassar di Ambon). [end page 1]

B. STRATEGI SERANGAN BALIK SOSOL BERDARAH

Hasil rapat kami bersama Laskar Kristus asal Halmahera Utara yang sementara berada di Ambon memutuskan sebagai berikut:

1. Rangkul/himpun kekuatan besar dari berbagai Daerah Kristen pada tiap-tiap kecamatan sampai pada Desa-desa kecil termasuk Suku terasing melalui pendekatan Gereja dengan bahasa-bahasa Gerejani.
2. Peperangan harus diwarnai Etnis/perbatasan.
3. Rangkul Umat Muslim Kao dengan cara apapun dan sehalus-halusnya (ditopang dana).
4. Segera kabarkan biaya operasi perang (cadangan Dana Kira-kira Rp 4.00000000).
5. Dalam waktu dekat akan diberangatkan dua buah Landen (LST) ke teluk Kao dan dua buah motor ikan Cakalang di teluk Sidangoli.
6. Penyerangan dilakukan secara serempak sesuai petunjuk.
7. Mesjid, Rumah Sekolah, Kantor Pemerintah dijaga jangan sampai ikut terbakar.
8. Prinsip peperangan dengan metode pengusiran, lakukan pembunuhan sesadis mungkin bagi mereka yang melakukan perlawanan.
9. Himpun laskar elit pada Universitas Theologia Ternate untuk ikut berperang aktif.

C. TUJUAN

Suku Makian adalah salah satu etnis Maluku Utara asli yang paling banyak mendiami pesisir Halmahera dengan tingkat kebrutalan yang tinggi, pintar, pekerja keras, pemberani, dan sangat fanatik Islamic.

Tumpahkan seluruh kekuatan dengan cara apapun, laskar Kristus harus mampu mengalahkan mereka dengan cara pengusiran dan pembunuhan di Daratan Halmahera.

Lakukan peperangan dan pembunuhan sesadis-sadisnya agar terjadi Depresi mental dan Trauma terhadap prang [sic], jangan lakukan pembunuhan terhadap anak-anak kecil, ibu-ibu dan orang tua renta agar kita tidak kehilangan simpati. Lakukan pemeriksaan K.T.P. pada jalan Trans Tobelo sekarang juga dan tunjukkan kepada etnis lainnya dengan kata-kata simpati hingga terjadi pemisahan paham antara etnis dan SARA dapat lebih nyata dalam peperangan nanti.

Peperangan akan lebih akurat karena didukung dengan tenaga ahli Bom, ahli Strategi serta peralatan dan perlengkapan lainnya, yang akan tiba dengan Landen (LST) dengan berkedok menjual mobil bekas. Dua buah motor ikan cakalang yang telah disiapkan didepan kampung Gamdehe teluk Sidangoli beralasan rusak, sewaktu-waktu dapat digunakan untuk keperluan medadak.

Dengan berpegang pada poin-poin bab B (Strategi Perang) maka:

• Etnis Makian tidak mendapat dukungan dari umat Islam semaluku Utara / Halmahera Tengah
• Islam yang selama ini kita kenal dengan kekuatan utuh akan runtuh dicabik-cabik oleh kekuatan etnisnya sendiri.
• Etnis makian [sic] merupakan raksasa Islam Maluku Utara dan Halmahera Tengah bakalan tersungkur oleh multi etnis kita yang hakekatnya berariran [sic] Kristiani.

Proses ini akan merupakan raksasa baru yang akan muncul dengan wajah etnis asli Halmahera namun mengalir darah Yesus juru selamat yang datang pada milinium III [end page 2] untuk melengkapi segitiga emas yakni Maluku, Sulawesi Utara dan Irian Jaya, yang selama ini sudah kondusif dalam program Gerejani.

- Dengan tersungkurnya Raksasa Islam di Bumi Halmahera (Malifut) merupakan barometer bagi etnis lain untuk membuka Front peperangan baru, hal ini akan berefek:
  1. Etnis Ternate, Tidore, Bacan dan Sanana akan tercengan dan ketakutan melihat raksasa Kristus marajalela.
  2. Etnis lainnya yang beragama islam akan enggang [sic] dan takut masuk dalam wilayah Halmahera Utara.

Untuk itu yakin dan bulatkan tekad untuk menjalankan Misi mulia Ini. Yesus Kristus selalui menemani kita dalam menegakkan keadilan dan memperbesar Umatnya di bumi ini.
Salam Oikumene

A/n Dewan Pengurus S.G.T-C.S.I.S
Ketua Sinode Maluku
(SEMI TITALEY)

English Translation

No: 028/SGT/CSIS/VII/1999
Attachments: 1 (one) file
Nature: Very Secret
Re: Plan for the revenge invasion of Bloody Sosol

To the Honorable Head of the Halmaheran Synod in Tobelo

A.   GENERAL CONSIDERATIONS

Prosperous greetings in the love of our Lord Jesus Christ

We have received your letter, and we and the Team consider the situation serious. In anticipation of regional autonomy, it is essential that that Synod of Halmahera develop independent working programs, for when all working relationships, both internal and external between us (Ambon and

Halmahera) will be separated. Thus there is a need for more intelligent thinking in relation to the Bloody Sosol incident. There has arisen a war of words between regional officials from North Maluku and Central Halmahera over establishing the basic framework for the provincial capital. This moment must be used to achieve our objectives, namely:

- to inhabit / to occupy as a whole the area around the provincial capital.

Thus the Tobelo, Galela, Kao, and Sahu ethnic groups, which have long been ignored and regarded as the lowest ethnic groups by other ethnic groups in North Maluku and Central Halmahera, can, little by little through a long-term program, take over the governance process.

Awaken the noble mission of The Shepherd reconciling the world in the love of the Lord Jesus Christ. Seen from a geographical perspective, North Maluku and Central Halmahera are flanked by Central Maluku (Ambon), North Sulawesi (Manado), and Irian Jaya, which are generally known as majority Christian. Thus our plan to welcome the new province will become more real from year to year. Queries by the church have noted that North Sulawesi is ready to release Sangir-Talaud to North Maluku. Through traditional historic and cultural ties, as well as the love of Jesus Christ, this issue will find support from the regional government of North Maluku.

Thus our brothers and sisters from Sangir-Talaud will find space more easily on the mainland of Halmahera, this will be the root that gives rise to young warriors of Christ who are skilled in the use of the weapons of hunting and warfare and have pure minds and are full of bravery to support the Tobelo, Galela, Kao, and Sahu ethnic groups. When the time comes two major powers will arise, namely:

- The Indigenous Warriors of Christ
- The Migrant Warriors of Christ.

The other ethnic groups in North Maluku/Central Halmahera will have difficulty standing up to the strength of the two aforementioned groups. (According to Muslim sources and the Butonese, Bugis, and Makasarese in Ambon) [end page 1]

B.   STRATEGY FOR THE RETURN INVASION OF BLOODY SOSOL

In our meetings with the Warriors of Christ from North Halmahera that are currently in Ambon we decided the following:

1. To arm/gather great strength from Christian areas, from every subdistrict down to every small village, including the isolated tribes who should be approached by the church with biblical language.[2]
2. The war has to be framed as one about ethnicity/borders.
3. Arm the Kao Muslims in whatever way possible and as subtly as possible (to be supported with funds).
4. Immediately announce the cost of war operations (Reserve funds of approximately 400,000,000 rupiah).
5. In the near future two flat-bottomed transport ships will be dispatched to Kao Bay and two tuna fishing boats to Sidangoli Bay.
6. The attacks will be carried out simultaneously according to instructions.
7. Mosques, schools, and government offices should be guarded so they are not burnt down.
8. The war will be fought with methods aimed at expulsion, kill those who resist as sadistically as possible.
9. The elite warriors at the Theological University of Ternate will take an active role in the war.

C. GOALS

The Makian tribe is an indigenous North Moluccan ethnic group that mostly inhabits coastal parts of Halmahera, they have a high level of brutality, they are smart, hard workers, brave and very fanatic Muslims.

Concentrate all power in every way possible, the warriors of Christ must defeat them through expulsion and murder in mainland Halmahera.

Make war and kill them in the most sadistic ways possible in order to cause mental depression and war trauma, but do not kill small children, women, or the elderly so we do not lose sympathy. Start checking identity cards on the Trans-Tobelo highway and explain why with sympathetic language to other ethnic groups so they understand the difference between ethnicity and SARA (Tribe, Religion, Race and Class) so it will be clearer in the later wars.[3]

The attack will be accurate because it will be supported by bomb experts and strategic experts and tools and other equipment that will arrive with a flat-bottomed transport ship under the guise of selling used cars. Two tuna fishing boats are already prepared in front of Gamdehe village in Sidangoli Bay with the excuse that they are broken, at any time they can be used for unexpected needs.

By adhering to the pattern of war set out in the points of part B (War Strategy) then:

- The Makianese ethnic group will not find support from other Muslims in North Maluku / Central Halmahera
- The Muslim community that we have long known as a unified power will be torn asunder by the strength of its own ethnic groups.
- The Makianese ethnic group, the Islamic giant of North Maluku and Central Halmahera, will be defeated by our multiethnic coalition, tied together by our Christian faith. This process will create a new giant that will rise with the face of the indigenous ethnic groups of Halmahera with the blood of Jesus the Savior, who is coming at the third millennium [end page 2] to complete the golden triangle of Maluku, North Sulawesi, and Irian Jaya, which has always been conducive to the work of the Church.
- The defeat of the Islamic giant of the land of Halmahera (Malifut) will be a barometer for other ethnic groups to open a front in a new war, which will have these effects:
  1. The Ternatan, Tidorese, Bacan, and Sanana ethnic groups will be stunned and frightened by seeing the giant of Christ running rampant.
  2. Other Muslim ethnic groups will be reluctant and scared to enter North Halmahera.

Thus be confidant and commit to undertake this noble mission.

Jesus Christ is always with us as we enforce justice and enlarge his community of believers on earth.

Ecumenical greetings

In the name of the Governing
council of S.G.T-C.S.I.S.
Head of the Maluku Synod
(SEMI TITALEY)

APPENDIX B

Peace Declaration of the Tobelo Adat Community: Indonesian Original and English Translation

Indonesian original

[Capitalization and typographical errors from the original have been left in this transcription.]

DEKLARASI DAMAI MASYARAKAT ADAT TOBELO
PADA HARI KAMIS TANGGAL 19 APRIL TAHUN 2001
DI LAPANGAN HIBUA LAMO TOBELO

NASKAH DEKLARASI DAMAI

Atas berkat rahmat Tuhan Yang Maha Esa dan dengan didorongkan oleh keinginan yang tulus dari masing-masing pihak, maka kami masyarakat Adat Hibua Lamo Tobelo Islam-Kristen sepakat bahwa pada hari ini, Kamis Tanggal 10 April tahun 2001 Jam 10.00 WIT, setelah terjadi pertikaian yang telah mengakibatkan berbagai pengorbanan dan kerugian yang tidak

ternilai harganya baik harta maupun nyawa, serta penderitaan yang sung-
guh berat, di atas perkabungan dan kesedihan yang mendalam, maka kami
sepakat meletakkan senjata dan menghentikan permusuhan ini, serta mengadakan perdamaian sekali untuk selama-lamanya, dengan ketentuan-
ketentuan sebagai berikut:

Pasal 1

Kami semua sepakat dan berjanji tidak akan ada lagi permusuhan dan
pertikaian di Wilayah Adat Hibualamo khususnya kecamatan Tobelo.

Apabila ada orang atau kelompok orang yang merancang kejahatan
terhadap orang lain (kelompok agama lain) dan melakukannya, mereka
akan korban dan kalah di mana saja karena perbuatannya itu.

Pasal 2

Kami semua sepakat dan berjanji untuk tidak saling menghina, meleceh-
kan, dan mempermalukan orang lain atau kelompok agama lain, baik
langsung maupun tidak langsung. Kami juga sepakat untuk saling meng-
hormati dan menghargai orang lain, kelompok agama lain, untuk menjalankan ibadahnya, serta saling melindungi baik umatnya maupun tempat
ibadahnya masing-masing, dan hidup berdampingan secara harmonis,
aman dan utuh dalam persaudaraan sejati.

Pasal 3

Kedua belah pihak sepakat untuk tidak melakukan percakapan secara
rahasia atau sembunyi-sembunyi baik perorangan maupun kelompok, dan
tidak mengadakan pembicaraan jarak jauh dengan menggunakan alat
telepon, HT, SSB dan lainya untuk merencanakan dan membicarakan kejahatan terhadap pihak lain.

Apabila kedapatan ada yang melakukan hal ini, akan ditindak secara
tegas dan adil oleh pihak yang berkompeten, bahkan jika perbuatannya
itu dilakukan dua sampai tiga kali, maka orang tersebut harus keluar dari
wilayah Tobelo.

Pasal 4

Kami sepakat untuk tidak lagi mengungkit-ungkit masa lalu yang hanya
membenarkan dan/atau mempersalahkan pihak tertentu, tetapi perlu men-
genang masa lalu untuk tidak terulang lagi sampai selama-lamanya.

Pasal 5

Kedua belah pihak sepakat untuk pemulangan pengungsi dilakukan se-cara selektif dan bertahap.

Pasal 6

Setiap tamu dari luar atau pendatang yang bukan penduduk Tobelo, harus melapor kepada Kepala Desa atau Ketua Dusun atau Ketua Lingkungan setempat.

Pasal 7

Apabila terjadi perbedaan pendapat, baku marah atau berkelahi antar warga masyarakat, dilarang dan tidak dibenarkan mengikutsertakan golongan agama atau kelompok lain untuk terlibat dalam persoalan terse-but. Barang siapa yang menggunakan simbol agama dalam setiap persoa-lan yang terjadi, akan ditindak secara tegas oleh pihak yang berkompeten.

Pasal 8

Kedua belah pihak sepakat untuk saling menolong dan melakukan peker-jaan bersama, mencari nafkah bersama baik di darat maupun di laut, dan tidak saling mencelakakan satu dengan lainnya.

Pasal 9

Kedua belah pihak sepakat untuk tidak lagi menggunakan isitilah "merah" bagi umat Kristen dan "Putih" bagi umat Muslim, serta tidak menggu-nakan istilah atau ungkapan "laskar Kristen" bagi umat Kristen dan "las-kar Jihad" bagi umat Muslim, maupun "Acan" [*sic*] bagi warga Muslim dan "Obet" bagi warga Kristen.

Pasal 10

Kedua belah pihak sepakat bahwa Pemerintah dan Aparat Keamanan mau-pun POLRI adalah wakil-wakil Allah di dunia ini, untuk menjalankan dan menegakkan keadilan, kebenaran dan kejujuran dalam menjalankan tugas-nya sebagi pengayom dan pelindung rakyat, diberikan kepercayaan untuk melaksanakan tugasnya sesuai peraturan perundangan yang berlaku.

Karena itu maka setiap anggota Pemerintah, TNI dan POLRI, diminta dapat bersikap netral dan adil, berbicara, dan berperilaku secara santun, sopan dan berwibawa dalam menjalankan tugasnya.

Pasal 11

Kedua belah pihak juga sepakat untuk menghargai dan menjunjung tinggi Pemerintah, TNI dan POLRI, serta bersikap santun dan sopan kepada Pemerintah, Aparat Keamanan, maupun POLRI yang sedang menjalankan tugasnya.

Pasal 12

Kedua belah pihak sepakat untuk selalu bersatu dan bersama-sama dalam berbagai kegiatan baik menjaga kantibmas [sic] di desa masing-masing maupun menentang pengacau yang datang dari luar wilayah Tobelo.

Pasal 13

Kedua belah pihak juga sepakat, bahwa setelah penandatanganan surat kesepakatan ini, dan setelah pengungsi kembali ke desanya, maka semua harta benda dan kekayaan yang masih ada, tidak boleh diganggu gugat oleh siapapun yang bukan haknya.

Pasal 14

Apabila setelah Penandatanganan surat kesepakatan ini, lalu terjadi pelanggaran baik sengaja maupun tidak sengaja terhadap pasal-pasal kese-pakatan ini, harus bersedia mengganti seluruh kerugian yang ditimbul-kannya, serta harus mempertanggung jawabkan perbuatannya di hadapan Pengadilan sesuai hukum yang berlaku.

Pasal 15

Penandatanganan Kesepakatan ini, dilakukan secara sadar dan pikiran yang waras, tanpa ada paksaan dari pihak manapun

Pasal 16

Kesepakatan ini dinyatakan mulai berlaku pada saat ditandatangani oleh kedua belah pihak. Apabila di kemudian hari terdapat kekeliruan dalam kesepakatan ini, akan dilakukan perbaikan sebagaimana mestinya.

Demikian surat kesepakatan ini dibuat dan ditandatangani oleh kedua belah pihak, dan disaksikan oleh pejabat-pejabat Instansi terkait pada hari, tanggal, bulan dan tahun tersebut di bawah ini.

Dibuat dan Disepakati di Tobelo
Pada Hari Kamis Tanggal 19 April Tahun 2001

TOKOH MASYARAKAT KRISTEN	TOKOH MASYARAKAT MUSLIM
1. ZAKEUS ODARA	1. ABTAR SYAFEI
2. BERNARD BITJARA	2. JUSUP RACHMAD
3. ZADRAK TONGO TONGO	3. AMAN TARIMA
4. NAHOR LUTUNANI	4. MUCHLIS BABA
5. PDT. SS DUAN, MTH	5. M DJEN NURDIN
6. JOSEPH BARANI	6. RONO ETEKE[1]

SAKSI-SAKSI

CAMAT TOBELO	KETUA SINODE GMIH
IR. HEIN NAMOTEMO, MSP	PDT. AN AESH, MTH

KOMANDAN YON INFANTRI 742	KOMANDAN YON MARINIR
RULIANSYAH	B. HULIANTO
MAYOR INF. NRP. 30485	LETKOL MAR. NRP. 8557/P

GUBERNUR MALUKU UTARA	KOMANDAN SATPAM WIL II
	MALUKU UTARA
ABDUL MUHI EFFENDIE	M. ALFAN B
	KOLONEL MAR. NRP. 7873/P

English Translation

PEACE DECLARATION OF THE TOBELO ADAT COMMUNITY

THURSDAY 19 APRIL 2001

HIBUA LAMO FIELD IN TOBELO

PEACE DECLARATION TEXT

By the grace of God Almighty and motivated by the sincere desire of each party, we the Muslim and Christian Hibua Lamo Adat community of Tobelo agree that today, Thursday the 10th of April 2001 at 10:00 Eastern Indonesian Time, after a dispute that has caused sacrifice and the loss of priceless treasure and lives, and extreme suffering, as well as mourning and deep sorrow, we therefore agree to lay down our arms and cease these hostilities, as well as make peace once and for all with the following stipulations:

Article 1

We all agree and promise that there will be no more hostility or conflict in the Hibua Lamo Adat region, particularly the Tobelo subdistrict.

If any person or group of people plan evil against others (other religious groups) and carry it out, they will be victims and fail wherever they are because of what they have done.

Article 2

We all agree and promise not to insult, harass, or humiliate other people or other religious groups, either directly or indirectly. We also agree to mutually respect and appreciate other people, other religious groups, and their right to worship, and to mutually protect the followers of each religion and their places of worship, and to live harmonious, safe, and unified in true brotherhood.

Article 3

Both parties agree to not have secret or surreptitious conversations either as individuals or as groups, and to not hold long-distance conversations using telephones, walkie-talkies, CB radios, or other means of communication to plan and discuss crimes against another party.

If anyone is caught doing this, they will be dealt with firmly and fairly by the relevant authorities, and if they are caught a second or a third time these people will be expelled from the Tobelo region.

Article 4

We agree to not bring up the past only to justify and / or blame a particular party, but need to remember the past so it never repeats itself.

Article 5

Both parties agree that the return of IDPs will be done selectively and in stages.

Article 6

Every guest or migrant that is not a Tobelo resident has to report to the Village Head, Hamlet Head or local neighborhood head.

Article 7

If there is a disagreement, argument, or fight between members of the community, it is forbidden and prohibited to involve religious groups or other groups in these issues. Those who use religious symbols in any problem that occurs will be dealt with firmly by the relevant authorities.

Article 8

Both parties agree to help each other and work together, to make a living both on land and at sea, and not harm each other.

Article 9

Both parties agree to stop using the term *red* for Christians and *white* for Muslims, and to not use the term or phrase *Christian troops* for Christians or *Jihad troops* for Muslims, or *Acang* for Muslims or *Obet* Christians.

Article 10

Both parties agree that the government and the security forces, as well as the police, are the representatives of Allah in this world, and their duty is to implement and uphold justice, truth, and honesty as the protector and defender of the people, and they should be trusted to perform their duties in accordance with the prevailing laws and regulations.

Therefore, every member of the government, military, and police, are asked to be neutral and fair, to speak, and to behave in a polite, courteous, and dignified manner in carrying out their duty.

Article 11

Both parties also agree to honor and respect government officials, military and police personnel, and to be polite and courteous to government officials, military, and police personnel, who are performing their duty.

Article 12

Both sides agree to always be united and work together in various activities to maintain community safety and law and order in their respective villages, and to work against troublemakers who come from outside the Tobelo region.

Article 13

Both parties also agree that after signing this agreement, and after the IDPs have returned to their villages, all property and wealth that is still there, cannot be contested by anyone who is not entitled to it.

Article 14

If after signing this agreement there is a breach of the articles of this agreement, whether intentionally or unintentionally, those responsible must be ready to replace all of the losses that they cause, and must account for their actions before a court of law in accordance with applicable laws.

Article 15

This agreement has been signed with an understanding of its implications and without coercion from any party.

Article 16

This agreement shall come into force immediately after it is signed by both parties. If on a later date an error is found in this agreement it will be fixed accordingly.

Thus this agreement is made and signed by both parties, and witnessed by officials from relevant agencies on the day, date, month, and year mentioned below.

Made and Agreed to in Tobelo
On Thursday 19 April 2001

CHRISTIAN COMMUNITY LEADERS	MUSLIM COMMUNITY LEADERS
1. ZAKEUS ODARA	1. ABTAR SYAFEI
2. BERNARD BITJARA	2. JUSUP RACHMAD
3. ZADRAK TONGO TONGO	3. AMAN TARIMA
4. NAHOR LUTUNANI	4. MUCHLIS BABA
5. PDT. SS DUAN, MTH	5. M DJEN NURDIN
6. JOSEPH BARANI	6. RONO ETEKE

WITNESSES

SUBDISTRICT HEAD OF TOBELO   HEAD OF THE GMIH SYNOD
IR. HEIN NAMOTEMO, MSP   PDT. AN AESH, MTH

COMMANDER OF INFANTRY   MARINE COMMANDER
BATTALION 742
RULIANSYAH   B. HULIANTO
INFANTRY MAJOR NRP.[2] 30485   MARINE LT. COL. NRP. 8557/P

GOVERNOR OF NORTH MALUKU   SECURITY COMMANDER
AREA II NORTH MALUKU
ABDUL MUHI EFFENDIE   M. ALFAN B
MARINE COLONEL NRP. 7873/P

NOTES

1. Religious Violence?

1. I am not the only one to notice this predilection; Adam (2010, 44) writes in his research on postconflict Ambon that one Christian Moluccan woman complained: "Foreign researchers like you too easily downplay the central role played by religion in the conflict. I know it may be hard for western people to understand, but for me it was all about the preservation of my religion."
2. I refer to the conflict in North Maluku as the period "1999–2000" for the simple reason that the first major outbreak of violence occurred in 1999 and the last large-scale violence took place in June of 2000. This is a rather arbitrary set of boundaries; incidents of violence occurred well after June 2000, but these were more isolated events, in many cases tied to the armed forces.
3. Oftentimes these views of religion are based on Western conceptions that focus on belief and theology. Thus questions are raised about how the violence relates to the beliefs of certain religious traditions, or seek to find the theological content in peoples justifications—what chapter or sura are they citing in defending their actions.
4. We also need to recognize that although the definition or existence of something called "religion" may be a contentious topic in Western academe (Smith 1982; Asad 1983; Masuzawa 2005), this is not the case for most Indonesians.

5. Atkinson (1983) provides a detailed discussion of the construction of the category of religion in Indonesia. Kipp and Rodgers (1987) provide examples of how various groups in Indonesia dealt with this problem during the New Order period. Maarif (2012) explores how one group in Sulawesi, the Amma Toa, have dealt with these same policies in the post-Suharto period.

6. Although not related to communal violence, Richard Fox's (2010) comments on how scholars have periodized Balinese history provide a good example of this process.

7. Bourdieu (1977, 106, emphasis in the original) argues that "by cumulating information which is not and cannot always be mastered by any single informant—at any rate, never on the instant—the analyst wins the *privilege of totalization* (thanks to the power to *perpetuate* that writing and all the various techniques for recording give him, and also the abundant time he has for analysis)."

8. Along similar lines, Veena Das (2006, 123) has noted how in situations of communal violence it is hard to draw "a sharp distinction between that which happened (the brute fact) and that which was only alleged to have happened (the imaginary)" because "such distinctions can be seen with clarity only after the event."

9. For those looking for an extended analysis of the individuals involved or the organizational dynamics behind the conflict, I suggest Chris Wilson's book (2008) with his detailed account of violence along the Tidore-Galela axis in North Maluku.

10. Along these lines I agree with the anthropologist Liisa Malkki (1997, 96) who argues that anthropologists do not play the same role as the historian or the human rights researcher: "The anthropologist as witness is differently located. Here the injunction to know 'everything' and to find the key to unlock mysteries is not a central (or sometimes even meaningful) activity."

11. Some of these scholars include Feldman (1991), Malkki (1995), Lemarchand (1996), Brass (1997, 2003), Mironko (2004), and Trnka (2008).

12. Lambek (1996, 239) has noted how "the value of articulating a particular version of the past [is] explicitly connected to its moral ends and consequences for relations in the present."

13. I have provided a detailed account of my views on Gerry van Klinken's book on communal violence elsewhere (Duncan 2009b).

14. Space does not permit a complete list of these works, but a sampling of Indonesian language works on the violence in Maluku and North Maluku would include Hasan (2003), Sihbudi et al. (2001), Yanuarti et al. (2003), Pieris (2004), Yanuarti et al. (2004), and Waileruny (2011). A small sampling of particularly biased accounts on Maluku/ Ambon would include Putuhena (1999), Kastor (2000), and Shoelhi (2002).

15. For samplings of arguably biased accounts of the violence in North Maluku see Nanere (2000), Ahmad and Oesman (2000), Jati (2001), and Hoda (2000).

16. Contrary to recent calls for more rigorous survey methods in research on displaced populations (cf. Jacobsen and Landau 2003; for a different viewpoint see Rodgers 2004), I found that IDPs and others in the region were rather exasperated with formal questionnaires as they were constantly being surveyed by civil servants and NGOs. More important, they had come to see them as opportunities (albeit slim) to gain access to resources, particularly when the surveyor was not a government

official. They were often more concerned with providing the "correct" answer—correct being what they thought would get them money, food stuffs, etc.—than with providing information.

17. In addition to my two Muslim research assistants I also worked with a Galela research assistant, Freddy Salama, who carried out interviews that focused on the violence in Galela, and another, Fence Boroni, who interviewed Christian IDPs throughout North Sulawesi and North Maluku, with a focus on those from Morotai.

2. Historical Preludes to the 1999–2000 Conflict

1. Jamie Davidson (2008, 6) has aptly referred to these explanations as the "post-Suharto scramble approach."

2. A number of other scholars have argued that we need to take a more diachronic approach to understanding violence in Indonesia and look at deeper historical processes that might provide insight into the post-Suharto violence (Colombijn and Linblad 2002; Nordholt 2002).

3. Academic and media accounts share this clichéd tendency and frequently refer to Maluku and North Maluku as places known for interreligious harmony (Wilson 2008, 1, 11; Bräuchler 2010, 203; Crouch 2010, 242). These statements, however, are rarely backed up by significant evidence of this harmony, which was not always accurate in any case.

4. The impact of the violence of the mid-1960s following a purported communist coup on North Maluku remains undocumented.

5. For an example of missionaries exploiting these tensions see Hueting's (1907, 285–93) account of the initial conversions of some Tobelo to Christianity.

6. There is a significant amount of historical work on the Jesuit mission to the region in the sixteenth century (Jacobs 1974; Andaya 1993; Heuken 2002; Böhm and Pangemanan 2010) and the Dutch missionary period (Hueting 1934; Haire 1981; Magany 1984). The most recent missionary organization, the New Tribes Mission, has been the subject of an anthropological study (Duncan 1998, 2003). A number of local authors have written about the arrival of Islam to North Maluku (Amal 2002; Syamsuddin and Awal 2005).

7. Spanish priests tried several times to restart the Catholic mission in northern Halmahera and Morotai in the early 1600s after Spain conquered Ternate, but these efforts had limited success and were short lived (Heuken 2002, 103).

8. See Chauvel (1990) for an in-depth analysis of the RMS movement in Ambon.

9. The local media in North Maluku also speculated on the role of the RMS and may have influenced local opinions (*Ternate Pos* 2000b).

10. Followers of Buddhism and Hinduism initially struggled to be recognized as an acceptable religion and to bring themselves in line with the requirement of monotheism. Brown (1987) has written about Buddhism in Indonesia, while Picard (2011) and Geertz (1973), among others have written about the struggle of Hindus for state recognition. Confucianism was added to the list of official religions in 2000. Abalahin (2005) provides a good discussion of how this legal change took place.

11. For discussions of these church burnings see Tadjoeddin (2001) and Bertrand (2004, 90–113).

12. This rumor is reminiscent of a pamphlet that circulated in East Java in 1963 supposedly calling on Christian men to marry Muslim women as part of a larger Christianization strategy (Boland 1971, 227).

13. Fears and conspiracy theories regarding Islamization or Christianization are not unique to North Maluku but have a long history in Indonesia (Arifianto 2009). Schrauwers (2003) provides a detailed example of Christian fears of Islamization from Central Sulawesi.

14. The Indonesian transmigration program moves landless peasants and other impoverished rural and urban populations from the overcrowded islands of Java and Bali to the more sparsely populated parts of the archipelago. Begun during the colonial period, the program was initially aimed at relieving the perceived demographic stress on Java and Bali, and helping to incorporate the Outer Islands into the archipelago.

15. These regulations include Decree No. 70 of 1970 by the Minister of Religion on Guidelines for the Propagation of Religion (Keputusan Menteri Agama No. 70 Tahun 1978 Tentang Pedoman Penyiaran Agama, Ind.) and Decree No. 77 of 1978 by the Minister of Religion on Foreign Aid for Religious Organziations in Indonesia (Keputusan Menteri Agama No. 77 Tahun 1978 Tentang Bantuan Luar Negeri Kepada Lembaga Keagamaan di Indonesia, Ind.). Aritonang (2004, 430-35) provides an in-depth examination of these two pieces of legislation and their impact on Muslim-Christian relations in Indonesia during the New Order period. English translations of these decrees can be found in Husein (2005, 335–42).

16. To borrow a phrase that Wertheim (1980) used to describe these fears of Christianization throughout Indonesia, one could argue that Muslims in North Maluku were a "majority with a minority mentality."

17. Some of my Muslim informants in Ternate and Tidore considered the Indonesian translation of James Haire's (1998) history of the Protestant Church in Halmahera as evidence of plans to Christianize the region. The book's Indonesian title, *Sifat dan Pergumulan Gereja di Halmahera*, translates as The Nature and Struggle of the Church in Halmahera. They interpreted the "struggle" in the title as a struggle for control of Halmahera, rather than the theological struggle within the church that Haire was discussing.

18. Not all Muslims were receptive to modernist notions of a purified Islam cleansed of local practices. Local leaders who based their claims to power and status on local tradition and customary law (*adat*, Ind.), such as the sultan of Ternate, opposed or ignored these efforts.

19. Numerous authors have examined the impact of reform Islam on adat practices, as well as arguments about what counts as religion (*agama*, Ind.) and what counts as culture (*kebudayaan*, Ind.) in Indonesian Islamic societies (cf. Hefner 1985; Woodward 1989; Bowen 1993; Woodward 2011; Maarif 2012).

20. Danius (2012) provides an in-depth discussion of how this fatwa affected relationships between Muslims and Christians in Tobelo

21. Historian Richard Chauvel (1980, 78–79) made a similar observation when he noted that Muslim and Christians reformers in Ambon had shifted emphasis away

from earlier adat practices that had been part of the common heritage of Muslims and Christians.

22. In his analysis of religious violence in post-Suharto Indonesia, John Sidel (2006: 142) incorrectly argues that interdenominational conflict in Protestantism across the archipelago was caused by the same political and economic changes that lead to the large-scale religious violence in places such as Ambon and Poso. He fails to explore interdenominational conflicts outside of the immediate time period he sought to explain.

23. Several authors (Geertz 1959; Kahn 1978; Sidel 2006) have noted how Indonesian politics and society in the early postcolonial period were organized around certain groupings called *aliran*, which Sidel (2006) has glossed as "educational and associational currents." These groupings, which influenced what schools people attended, what political parties they joined, what places of worship they went to, were based to a certain degree on religious differences.

24. Bertrand (2002) and Klinken (2001) provide good overviews of the role of religion in these patronages networks in Ambon and Central Maluku, a topic beyond the scope of this book.

25. KTP is the acronym for the identity card, (*kartu tanda penduduk*, Ind.) that all Indonesians must have, which requires them to state their religion. The phrase *Islam KTP* or *Kristen KTP* refers to individuals who are not active or practicing members of the faith on their identity cards, but simply chose that faith for the sake of their identity card.

26. There is some disagreement in the literature over what constitutes the four ethnic groups of Kao. According to a recent local publication in Halmahera the four ethnic groups in Kao are the Modole, Pagu, Tobelo Boeng, and Toliliko (also Tololiko, or Towiliko) (Banari 2007). Fraassen's (1980, 134–38) analysis of the Dutch literature lists the four ethnic groups (which he refers to as "domains") as the Modole, Pagu, Tobelo Boeng, and Kao, with the Toliliko (he uses Tololiku) being included among the Kao, along with the Kao Islam. Although exact figures are unavailable, local people in Kao estimate that the Kao Islam make up approximately 10 percent of the indigenous population, while the other groups are predominately Protestant.

27. Struggles over control of the redistribution of wealth, the decentralization of political power, and the redrawing of district boundaries have been cited as a root cause of various conflicts in post-Suharto Indonesia (cf. Aragon 2001; Vel 2001; International Crisis Group 2003; Klinken 2007a).

3. From Ethnic Conflict to Holy War

1. There have been numerous accounts of the violence in Ambon, for scholarly examples see Aditjondro (2001), Klinken (2001), Bertrand (2002), Yanuarti et al. (2003).

2. Christians and Muslims from Ternate made similar accusations and argued that the increasing Makianese population in Ternate had changed the social fabric of that island in the last decades of the twentieth century.

3. Initial government reports about the resettlement of the Makianese in Malifut refer to it as part of the Makian subdistrict, which included the area around Malifut

(designated as Makian Daratan), and the islands of Makian and Moti (Lucardie 1985).

4. The six villages from Jailolo to be incorporated into the Makian Malifut subdistrict included Bobaneigo, Tetewang, Akelamo Kao, Gamsungi, Dum-Dum, and Pasir Putih (see Law 42/1999 Article 1[2] c). None of the people I interviewed from these villages in Jailolo mentioned concerns with their incorporation into the new subdistrict. According to their accounts, they were not swept up in the violence until after the riots in Ternate and Tidore.

5. Sangaji is a traditional honorific term from the Ternate language often applied to the leaders of ethnic groups who are appointed by, and supposedly answer to, the sultan of Ternate.

6. Current accounts (which vary) often describe the four non-Muslims as Christians. Some Tobelo Boeng communities on the coast converted to Christianity at the turn of the century, but most of the inland groups in Kao did not convert until after 1906 (Haire 1981, 183–84). For an historical account of the skirmish and the events leading up to it see (*Indisch Militair Tijdschrift* 1907).

7. Kayoa is an island to the south of Makian Island populated by migrants from the island of Makian.

8. See Law of the Republic of Indonesia Number 46/1999 about the creation of North Maluku Province, the Buru District, and the District of West Southwest Maluku (Undang-Undang Republik Indonesia Nomor 46 Tahun 1999 tentang Pembentukan Propinsi Maluku Utara, Kabupaten Buru, dan Kabupaten Maluku Tenggara Barat, Ind.).

9. Adeney-Risakotta (2005, 217–21) provides a detailed account of the struggles over the placement of the capital and the position of governor.

10. Benny Doro, one of the better-known leaders on the Kao side, told me that he placed an Indonesian flag and a guard at each mosque and ordered them to protect it, threatening: "If this mosque gets burned down, you [the guard] are responsible." He claims to have done this at every mosque in Malifut.

11. Wilson (2008, 56) reports that the mine had tried to allocate the same amount of jobs to both groups, but because the Makianese had higher levels of education, they got the majority of the jobs.

12. Wilson (2008, 81–83) documents the organized nature of these efforts by the Makianese to gain support from other segments of the Muslim community and to shift the focus from ethnicity to religion.

13. Bubandt (2008b, 2009) has written extensively about the Sosol Berdarah letter.

14. The role of rumors in the outbreak of violence has a long history in North Maluku particularly during the colonial period when rumors often led to rebellions (cf. Dijkstra 1915, 258).

15. Both the GPM and the GMIH letters are reproduced in Nanere (2000, 68–73).

16. Adeney-Risakotta (2005, 223) writes that prior to the riots in Tidore a radio announcement asked all Makianese to return to Malifut to help rebuild the mosques. This message would have been an obvious effort to switch the focus of the conflict from ethnicity to religion, as militia from Kao did not damage the mosques.

17. Wilson (2008, 91–92) writes that he could find no one who believed in the Sosol Berdarah letter during his research in 2004. Five years after the fact that should not be surprising, as almost everyone agrees that the letter itself was, retrospectively, a rather blatant and transparent act of provocation. To profess belief in the letter's authenticity in 2004 would have been an admission of gullibility that people would prefer to avoid. Other rumors that swept the region at the time, which have not been as thoroughly examined and debunked, yet which to an outside observer may appear just as unbelievable, remain well accepted as fact in many places. One must consider the atmospherics surrounding the reading of the letter in October 1999, as opposed to discussing it in 2004.

18. Wilson (2008, 83) discusses how the police were immobilized prior to the violence in Ternate and Tidore. Inaction in the face of violence was the norm throughout North Maluku during the period of the violence.

19. The GMIH also mentioned this massacre of children in a report released during the conflict. The report noted that "There were also dozens (*berpuluh-puluh*, Ind) of small children (below the age of five) that were wrapped alive in burlap tarps that this group of Muslims then tossed into the sea anchored with ballast" (Suara Peduli Halmahera 2000a).

20. Elsewhere in eastern Indonesia, the leader of the Laskar Jihad, Ja'far Umar Thalib, declared that Christians in Maluku were "belligerent infidels" who must be killed. Anyone who died fighting them would die a martyr. Thalib (2000) made this declaration based on various fatwas he had requested from Islamic scholars in Saudi Arabia and Yemen (Hasan 2005).

21. Drexler (2007) and Spyer (2002a) have both noted similar examples elsewhere in Indonesia.

4. Massacres, Militias, and Forced Conversions

1. North Moluccans frequently used the Indonesian word (and English loan word) *trauma* in their discussions of the violence and its impact on individuals and communities, a topic explored by Bubandt (2008a). Numerous anthropologists have explored how the Western discourse of trauma has taken root in non-Western contexts (Zarowsky 2000; James 2010).

2. The government of North Sulawesi appeared to be the only one that learned from the failure of the local government in Ternate to properly handle forced migrants. When the first IDPs from Ternate and Tidore arrived in that province they were housed in a central location and not allowed to leave the camp at will, but had to sign in and out. The government hoped that this would limit the spread of rumors and minimize the possibility of violence breaking out in North Sulawesi (Duncan 2005a).

3. Adeney-Risakotta (2005, 261, 265) notes similar developments in Galela.

4. The Indonesian original read "Orang Islam adalah saudara kami tapi ethnis Makian, Kayoa dan Tidore adalah perusuh, 'angkat kaki' dari Tobelo."

5. Detailed local accounts of the fighting in Tobelo are available from both a Muslim perspective (Ahmad and Oesman 2000, 54–87) and a Christian one (Nanere 2000, 94–102).

6. Contrary to many news reports, the village of Togoliua is not a Javanese transmigration site. The village of Togoliua consisted largely of Muslim Tobelo from Tobelo town who moved to the south to be closer to their gardens and other North Moluccan Muslims. There is a transmigration site named UPT Togoliua several kilometers to the east, but the transmigrants at that site, like the others in Kao and Tobelo, were forcibly removed by the army before the violence could reach them.

7. Soa-Sio is the name of the subdistrict capital in Galela, and is also the name of the main city on the island of Tidore.

8. For various estimates ranging from 771 to 3,000 victims, see *Suara Pembaruan* (2000), *Kompas* (2000c), and *Republika* (2000d).

9. The term *kapita* is used by some groups in Halmahera (such as Modole, Pagu, Tobelo and Galela) to refer to war leaders. Villages usually have a kapita chosen by the community (such as in Tobelo) or the position is hereditary (such as among the Modole). There are also kapita for entire ethnic groups, such as the kapita of Tobelo, or the kapita of Galela. The latter became rather controversial in the early years of the twenty-first century as some argued they had to be appointed by the sultan of Ternate, while others thought otherwise.

10. In an earlier publication (Duncan 2005a, 56), I noted the "the virtual absence of violence directed against Javanese transmigrants." In retrospect that was an overstatement as I explain in the main text.

11. See Wilson (2008, 130–46) and Klinken (2007a, 109–22) for more detailed accounts of the politics and politicians involved in the conflict on the streets of Ternate.

12. I heard similar stories from Christians in Tobelo who said that Muslims in Tobelo believed that reinforcements were on the way from Ternate to help them in their struggle there.

13. Villages and hamlets destroyed in South Morotai included Tutuhu, Wayabula, Raja, Baringin, Tile, Pilowo, Pandanga, Juanga, Daruba, Daeo, Sambiki, Sabatai Baru, and Sangowo. In North Morotai the hamlets and villages destroyed included Buho-Buho and Bere-Bere.

14. The village head of Posi-Posi Rao insisted that no one launch attacks on Morotai from his village for fear of retribution. Those who wished to take part in the fighting had to travel to Halmahera and join red forces there. These efforts ensured that Posi-Posi Rao remained peaceful throughout the conflict.

15. The villages attacked on Obi and surrounding islands included Tapa on Tapa Island, Galala on Bisa Island, and Anggai, Kampung Baru, Kawasi, and Bobo on Obi. I also gathered accounts of Muslims on Obi being killed for refusing to take part in the violence.

16. Violence broke out again on Obi in late May and early June of 2001 in the villages of Bobo and Woi.

17. Other news sources cited this article in their descriptions of events (*Sydney Morning Herald* 2000; *Jakarta Post* 2000b). Church-based reports also mention its role in inciting the violence (GMIH 2000). *Republika* frequently ran stories about the conflict

with provocative headlines, such as "Christian IDPs protected in pesantren on Seram Island; Hundreds of corpses start to rot in Tobelo" (*Republika* 2000c). Fealy (2003) has explored *Republika's* penchant for provocative journalism.

18. The report is incorrect in claiming that a large number of people were killed in the Muslim village of Luari in the northern Tobelo subdistrict. The people of Luari fled to the nearby army base or the island of Morotai before the village was attacked. Thus while the village itself was entirely destroyed by Christian militia, the people of Luari escaped relatively unharmed that day.

19. This gathering was not the first call for a jihad in support of Muslims in Maluku. Other Muslim leaders had begun calling for a jihad in 1999. Muhammad Anis Matta, the general secretary of the Islamic political party, Partai Keadilan, called for a jihad in a sermon he delivered on Idul Fitri in 1999 (Matta 1999 as cited in Riddell 2002, 81). Other organizations had been recruiting volunteers to go to central Maluku since the outbreak of violence in March 1999 in Ambon (Hasan 2006, 109).

20. Rais subsequently denied that he supported the jihad (Dateline 2000). Despite these denials, Christians from North Maluku did not like Amien Rais. At one point he had to cancel a visit to an IDP camp in North Sulawesi after IDPs made it known that he would not be received well (*Manado Post* 2000).

21. Hasan (2006) provides an in-depth history of the creation of the Laskar Jihad and its ideology.

22. The International Crisis Group (2000a, 7n46) reported that the Laskar Jihad sent a team to Ternate and Tidore in February 2000 after which they decided that local forces were adequate and they should concentrate on Ambon and Maluku. In contrast, Wilson (2008, 156-57) says that the Laskar Jihad did offer aid to North Moluccan Muslims, and even sent a number to Ternate, but local leadership declined their help for a variety of reasons.

23. The Laskar Jihad was only one of several national militant Muslim groups involved in the various religious conflicts in Indonesia at the turn of the century; others included Laskar Jundullah, Jemaah Islamiyah, and Laskar Mujahidin. A source for the International Crisis Group (2002, 20) reported that Laskar Mujahidin had a "strong presence" in North Maluku.

24. The Laskar Jihad's high media profile and overstated claims led many outside observers to give them credit for the work of local Muslim militia in North Maluku. Both Aragon (2005, 44) and the International Crisis Group (2004, 14) note a similar process in Central Sulawesi where the Laskar Jihad's media operations had a predilection for claiming, or receiving, credit for the successes of other, more secretive, militias in the region. These media operations included a website (discussed by Bräuchler [2004]), a newspaper, and frequent interviews with the national press in both mainstream publications such as *Tempo* and *Gatra*, as well as more radical publications such as *Sabili*.

25. Forced conversions were also reported from the conflict in central Maluku (*Harian Umum Siwalima* 2000; *Jakarta Post* 2000a; Masariku Network 2001a; Woodward 2007, 99–100).

26. The Masariku Network (2001c), a Protestant group that published Christian accounts of the conflict on the internet, published a list of examples of forced conversions to

Islam. They also published an account of forced conversions to Christianity from Halmahera, albeit based on information provided by the GMIH (Masariku Network 2001b). Birgit Bräuchler (2003) has written extensively about the Masariku Network and other aspects of the Maluku conflict on the internet.

27. The Indonesian press covered the forced conversions in Lata-Lata (*Gamma* 2000; *Republika* 2000a), although they received less press than those in Central Maluku. They were also mentioned in publications by the Laskar Jihad (Thalib 2001). The global Christian community, particularly that segment focused on the persecution of Christians, took a special interest in Lata-Lata (Flinchbaugh 2001; International Christian Concern 2001; Compass Direct 2002; International Friends of Compassion 2002).

28. Since the end of the conflict, 117 of them have them have returned to Islam, while the others have remained Christian.

29. There is not space here to go into an in-depth discussion of the concept of agency, but when discussing the term, I am relying on Ahearn's (2001) definition of agency as the "socio culturally mediated capacity to act." Lubkemann (2008) provides a good discussion of the issue of agency in wartime in his analysis of war as a social condition in Mozambique.

30. Outside of North Maluku, Clarke (2006) provides examples of individuals who chose nonviolent resistance over violence in the Poso, Maluku, and West Kalimantan conflicts.

31. Wilson (2008, 124) incorrectly writes that "Weda Bay" in the District of Central Halmahera was "the one area in North Maluku in which violence did not occur." Although the area immediately surrounding the Weda Bay Nickel mining operation may have remained violence free, Weda Bay as a geographical entity did not. Muslim militias attacked a number of villages in the bay, such as Tilope and Goen, and forced the Christian populations of these villages, consisting largely of Tobelo and Sangirese migrants, to flee. The subdistrict escaped the violence (primarily because it is almost 100 percent Muslim), as did large parts of northern Morotai, the island of Gebe, and the Sula Archipelago with the exception of the one small incident mentioned earlier.

32. Duma had also been the field site for a Summer Institute of Linguistics field team in the 1980s and early 1990s that translated portions of the Bible into the Galela language. Although this fact received some attention on the internet in a Jemaah Islamiyah magazine (*Al-Bunyan* 2000), it never came up in interviews conducted by me or my research assistants.

5. Peace and Reconciliation?

1. A number of scholars and NGOs have published research on reconciliation in eastern Indonesia. Tindage (2006), Sitohang et al. (2003), Lakawa (2008, 2011), and the Crisis Prevention and Recovery Unit of the United Nations Development Programme (CPRU/UNDP 2004) have written about North Maluku. Bräuchler (2009a), Muluk and Malik (2009), Hohe and Remijsen (2003) and Batmomolin (2000) have

looked at Maluku, while Braithwaite et al (2010, 147–242) and Bräuchler (2009b) have explored the topic of reconciliation throughout Indonesia.

2. For more on the idea of hidden transcripts versus public transcripts see Scott (1990).

3. Malik (2005) and Cunliffe et al. (2009) provide in-depth analyses of the Malino agreements.

4. Tindage (2006, 62–64) presents a similar account of these events.

5. Tindage (2006) and Nanere (2000) present partial lists of these meetings. The peace agreements signed in these cases often mirrored the one signed in Tobelo discussed below. The now defunct Manado-based newspaper *Berita Telegraf* (2001) described an example from Morotai. Hontong (2012, 165–66) provides a copy of the peace agreement reached in Galela.

6. Fears of the Laskar Jihad were not limited to North Maluku. Neighboring provinces with large Christian populations, such as North Sulawesi (Duncan 2005b, 35) and Papua (Bubandt 2009, 574-75) were also inundated with rumors of impending Laskar Jihad attacks.

7. Malifut was one exception. The Makianese IDPs from Malifut were some of the first IDPs to return to their homes. In large part, their early return was facilitated by the lack of other IDPs living in their homes. Muslim homes in Tobelo were often occupied by forced migrants from elsewhere, and the same could be said for Ternate.

8. One challenge to the organizers was how to incorporate the well-known militia leader Benny Doro who did not have any status under customary law. They decided to give him a supporting role in the ceremony nonetheless, since they acknowledged he had played a major role in the conflict, and any peace ceremony without him could be open to question.

9. I was unable to re-create the complete text of this speech. It apparently had never been written down, and video recordings of the event were subsequently edited leading to the loss of several parts of the larger speech.

10. Acang, short for Hasan, and Obet, short for Robert, were the names of the Muslim and Christian children in a televised public service announcement in Ambon aimed at stopping the violence in Maluku (Spyer 2006a). Rather than put a stop to the violence, the public service announcement provided derisive monikers for both sides in the conflict.

11. The governor repeated these concerns several days later in a ceremony for returning IDPs in North Maluku when he asked them to "forget the past, because the past will not solve your problems. The past is destroyed homes, orphans, widows, and widowers" (Tindage 2001, 3).

12. The national government did form a commission in 2002 to investigate human rights violations in Maluku (but not North Maluku) as stipulated in the Malino agreement. However, their final report has not been released due to fears it could spark further violence (Cunliffe et al. 2009, 14–16).

13. Woodward (2010) provides a good exploration of how tropes of the Crusades have become popular in Indonesian Islamic discourse in recent years and how this ties into Muslim views of colonial history and globalization.

14. The Jakarta Charter (Piagam Jakarta, Ind.) refers to the draft preamble of the Indonesian Constitution that was written in the early days of Indonesia's independence.

It included a statement that all Muslims would be subject to Islamic law. This idea was a hotly contested one in the debates that surrounded Indonesia's independence, and although initially in the preamble, it was eventually removed. It has, however, resurfaced periodically in Indonesian politics as certain Muslim politicians have tried to reinsert the idea back into the Indonesian Constitution. See Elson (2009) for an in-depth discussion of the Jakarta Charter.

Chapter 6 Managing Memories of Violence

1. Paul Brass (2006) has noted that this "situating" of events is part of the revenge and retaliation theme common in various forms of collective violence.
2. A large amount has been written about the role of the armed forces in the violence in central Maluku in Ambon (Suadey 2000; Aditjondro 2001; Azca 2005, 2006) but less has been written about their role in the conflict in North Maluku.
3. The shootings in Ternate were widely covered in the national (*Indonesian Observer* 2000; *Forum Keadilan* 2000b) and local media (*Ternate Pos* 2000a, 2000f, 2000g).
4. The government lifted the state of civil emergency in North Maluku in March 2003.
5. This is the same Forest Tobelo group that Sidel (2006, 256n184) incorrectly blames for the large-scale violence in parts of northern Halmahera in early 2000. However, rather than massacring Muslims, they were working alongside them to protect their property from marauding Christians. Sidel makes a number of factual mistakes in his argument that newly converted Forest Tobelo groups played a prominent role in the violence in northern Halmahera. He incorrectly writes that the New Tribes Mission was "based in the northeastern [sic] district of Tobelo" (Sidel 2006, 181). The New Tribes Mission was not based in Tobelo but has worked on the northeastern peninsula of the island in the subdistrict of Maba since the early 1980s, a location that is rather distant and isolated from Tobelo. He also fails to consider that there are a number of different Forest Tobelo groups on Halmahera and not all of them have been the focus of the New Tribes Mission. In particular, the few family groups that took part in the violence in Togoliua were from the Kao subdistrict, alongside a few individuals from the Wasile subdistrict, none of whom were either "new converts" or from groups that were connected to the New Tribes Mission. Furthermore, Sidel (2006, 256n184) cites my own work out of context. In an earlier work I wrote that as Forest Tobelo "attitudes towards Christianity have changed since their conversion, their attitudes towards Islam have solidified. Instead of seeing Islam in terms of pork taboos and funny prayer positions, they now view it as the wrong choice made by a misguided people who have not been informed about Jesus Christ" (Duncan 1998, 170). Sidel uses this quote to argue that newly converted Forest Tobelo would appear to be inclined to take part in massacres of Muslims. If he had continued reading, however, he would have noted that rather than despise Muslims, my point was that while some newly converted Forest Tobelo "had a desire to scoff at Muslims," in much the same way they derided the practices of coastal Christian villagers, others wanted to share the Gospel with them and bring them salvation (Duncan 1998, 170–71).

Based on multiple visits and numerous interviews with Forest Tobelo from the Maba subdistrict between 2001 and 2013, it is clear that only one Forest Tobelo who converted to Christianity under the aegis of the New Tribes Mission in the 1990s took part in the conflict, and he took part in the fighting in Mamuya and in efforts to rescue Duma, not in the massacres in Tobelo.

6. Theidon (2003) makes this point in her discussion of highland Peru when she notes that each narrative that is shared in postviolence discussions has "a political intent and assumes both an internal and an external audience."

7. My experiences were similar to those of Veena Das (1985, 5) who noted that survivors of communal violence in South Asia "wanted their suffering to become known as if the reality of it could only be reclaimed after it had become part of a public discourse."

8. Robben (1995, 83) notes one problem inherent in this type of fieldwork interaction when he warns of the "dangers of seduction" that ethnographers face when gathering accounts of violence from both victims and perpetrators. People involved in communal conflict have a great stake in ensuring that the anthropologist adopts their point of view and reiterates it in her publications. Thus informants must persuade (or "seduce" to use Robben's phrase) the anthropologist into accepting their accounts of the violence as the "correct" ones that supersede those recorded from the other side.

7. Memorializing the Dead in Postconflict North Maluku

1. A number of anthropologists have explored the construction of memorials (Verdery 1999; Coombes 2003; Jelin 2003, 2007; Deeb 2008), or even cemeteries (Scheele 2006), in postconflict dynamics and processes of reconciliation and their relationship to people's experiences and understandings of a particular conflict. In her analysis of Algerian graveyards, Scheele (2006, 860) perceptively notes that while local political discourse can ignore the reality of conflicts and their official resolutions (or lack thereof), the bodies of those who died in the conflict are a palpable reality that local communities must face.

2. Along similar lines, these monuments also resemble Pierre Nora's "places of memory" (*lieux de mémoire*, French). Nora (1989, 19) writes that the "most fundamental purpose of lieux de mémoire is to stop time, to block the work of forgetting, to establish a state of things, to immortalize death, to materialize the immaterial . . . all of this in order to capture a maximum of meaning in the fewest signs, it is also clear that lieux de mémoire only exist because of their capacity for metamorphous, an endless recycling of their meaning in an unpredictable proliferation of their ramifications."

3. The supposed presence of the grave of the Catholic missionary Simon Vas has become a contentious issue since the 1999–2000 conflict ended. Prior to the conflict, regional Catholics made annual pilgrimages to the grave for prayer and to clean it. Since the end of the conflict, Muslims in Mamuya have contested the claim that the grave belongs to Simon Vas, and argue instead that it belongs to the ancestors of a local Muslim family. In 2009, the Vatican's ambassador to Indonesia visited Mamuya to celebrate the 475th anniversary of the arrival of Catholicism in

North Maluku, during which he signed a commemorative plaque (Böhm and Pangemanan, 2010, 294–97). According to Christians I interviewed in Mamuya in October 2012, local Muslims prevented the Catholic church and the district tourist board from subsequently erecting this plaque to mark the location and designate it a tourist attraction. During that same visit, I had a lengthy discussion on the provenance of the grave with a group of Muslim men working the garden in which it was located, they took issue with the claim the grave belonged to Simon Vas.

4. Although the Laskar Jihad had a minimal presence in North Maluku, declarations such as these filtered down to the region and often confirmed what those involved in local Muslim militia believed about the nature of the conflict.

5. There are exceptions: some people inter their loved ones next to their homes, but villagers tend to frown on this practice, and it is discouraged by the church.

6. Space does not permit an in-depth examination of Tobelo or Galela pre-Christian funeral practices. Hueting (1922, 137–82) and Platenkamp (1988, 152–89; 1994) provide in-depth discussions of Tobelo pre-Christian cosmology and funeral practices, while Ajawaila (1990) and Baarda (1914) discuss pre-Christian Galela funeral rituals.

7. People's attachments to their ancestors were so strong that in some cases the requirements that they dissolve these relationships was an obstacle to conversion to Christianity or Islam. Although the Christian missionaries were firm in their call to sever these ties, Muslim preachers showed some flexibility. In the village of Seki in Galela, for example, the Muslim teacher who converted the population also converted their ancestors by rearranging their graves to face Mecca and performing a short prayer service (Amal 2000, 28–29).

8. Platenkamp (1988), during his fieldwork with the Tobelo in the 1980s, noted a gradual decline in the maintenance of relations with the dead.

9. All of the examples of monuments discussed here, both in Tobelo and Galela, have been built at GMIH churches. I am unaware of any such monument at a non-GMIH church anywhere in Halmahera.

10. In one of the better-known examples, Dutch missionaries tried to reshape Tobelo adat to make it more compatible with Christianity (Hueting 1910; Haire 1981, 182)

11. Hontong (2012, 54–55) provides a complete list of martyr cemeteries and monuments at Christian churches in Galela.

12. *Dodara* is the Galela word for love / affection (*kasih / kasih sayang*, Ind.).

13. Indonesian original: Monumen Korban Anggota Jemaat GMIH "Nita" Duma Tanggal 29-06-2000 di KM Cahaya Bahari.

14. Indonesian original: Karna bagiku hidup adalah Kritus [sic] dan mati adalah keuntungan.

15. Indonesian original: Aku telah berjuang hingga titik darah terakhir justru Yesus yang di nista dan umat Kristiani yang di tindas. Hai Rekan Ku maju terus pantang mundur.

16. Hueting (1922, 163) writes that a Tobelo who has a *dilikini* in their immediate family treats them as precious relics and they are carried around in an ornate box in order to access their power.

17. Platenkamp (1990) has made similar comparisons between Christian practices and pre-Christian Tobelo rituals in relation to both death and marriage. Hotong (2012) has made a similar argument for the construction of martyr cemeteries in Galela.

18. The phrase *wassuhada* appears to be a variant of the plural of the Arabic term for martyrs (*shuhada*, Arabic); however only one name is on the tombstone. The family that placed the tombstone on the mass grave was unavailable for comment.

19. Ziarah is an Arabic-derived Indonesian term used to refer to a pilgrimage to a holy place, often a grave or shrine (Doorn-Harder and Jong 2001).

20. A few graves are located next to the mosque in the Galela village of Soakonora, but these individuals were buried there during the conflict because people were too scared to travel to regular graveyards at that time. None of them refer to martyrdom.

Conclusion

1. The most frequently cited example is the former Yugoslavia about which there has been an at times rather contentious debate among scholars (Hayden 1996; Sells 1996; Povrzanović 1997, 2000; Hayden 2007).

2. A short, and by no means inclusive list of such works would include Sells's (1996) and Hayden's (1996), albeit contradictory, analyses of the former Yugoslavia, Nussbaum's (2007) exploration of Hindu nationalism in India, and Mamdani's (2001) study of ethnicity in the Hutu-Tutsi conflict in Rwanda.

3. James Hughes (2007) provides an interesting account of a similar transition in the discursive construction of violence in his analysis of how the conflict in Chechnya transformed from a separatist struggle focused on Chechen nationalism to jihad.

4. I have explored efforts to use adat as a tool for reconciliation in Tobelo elsewhere in an extended analysis of the notion of hibualamo (Duncan 2009a).

5. One of the more discussed attempts to use adat to prevent future conflict in North Maluku has been the resurgence of the four sultanates (Ternate, Tidore, Bacan, and Jailolo) of North Maluku (Klinken 2007b). Scholars working in Maluku have noticed similar developments (Bräuchler 2009a).

6. There have been a few political clashes in the years since the communal violence ended, particularly the protracted contestation of the 2007 gubernatorial elections (International Crisis Group 2009). At no point did these conflicts become entangled in issues of religious differences.

A. The Bloody Sosol Letter

1. Previously published versions of the letter (Nanere 2000, 71–73; Sitohang et al. 2003) transcribed the letter incorrectly.

2. The term *isolated tribes* refers to the Forest Tobelo, the forest-dwelling foragers that live throughout Halmahera's interior. They have a violent reputation throughout the province and are widely feared (Duncan 2001).

3. SARA is an Indonesian acronym that stands for Tribe, Religion, Race, and Class (*Suku, Agama, Ras, dan Antar-Golongan*, Ind.). It refers to aspects of Indonesian society that the state thought could pose a threat to national unity. During the New Order, the Indonesian government eventually banned any public discussions of these issues (Emmerson 1976, 274, as cited in Kipp 1993, 109).

B. Peace Declaration of the Tobelo Adat Community

1. The name Rono Eteke was handwritten on the original document. The place for a name after the number six had been left blank.
2. NRP is an acronym for Personnel Registration Number (Nomor Registrasi Personil, Ind.), which refers to the serial numbers used for armed forces officers.

References

Abalahin, Andrew J. 2005. "A sixth religion? Confucianism and the negotiation of Indonesian-Chinese identity under the Pancasila state." In *Spirited politics: Religion and public life in contemporary Southeast Asia*, edited by Andrew C. Willford and Kenneth M. George, 119–42. Ithaca, Cornell Southeast Asia Program.

Abdullah, Muskin H. 2003. "Kerusuhan Maluku Utara dalam perspektif sosial budaya." In *Memikirkan kembali "Maluku dan Maluku Utara,"* edited by Imron Hasan, 129–38. Makassar, Lembaga Penerbitan Universitas Hasanuddin.

Adam, Jeroen. 2010. How ordinary folk became involved in the Ambonese conflict: Understanding private opportunities during communal violence. *Bijdragen tot de Taal-, Land- en Volkenkunde* 166(1): 25–48.

Adeney-Risakotta, Farsijana. 2005. "Politics, ritual and identity in Indonesia: A Moluccan history of religion and social conflict." Ph.D. diss., Radboud Universiteit Nijmegen.

Aditjondro, George Junus. 2001. "Guns, pamphlets, and handie-talkies: How the military exploited local religious tensions in Maluku to preserve their political and economic privileges." In *Violence in Indonesia*, edited by Ingrid Wessel and Georgia Wimhöfer, 100–28. Hamburg, Abera.

Ahearn, Laura M. 2001. Language and agency. *Annual Review of Anthropology*. 30: 109–37.

Ahmad, Kasman Hi, and Herman Oesman, eds. 2000. *Damai yang terkoyak: Catatan kelam dari bumi Halmahera*. Ternate, Kelompok Studi Podium, LPAM Pemuda Muhammadiyah Maluku Utara and Madani Press.

Ajawaila, Jacob W. 1990. *"Sasao* and *boroka*: Exchange in the Galela death ritual." Paper presented at "Halmahera Research and Its Consequences for the Study of Eastern Indonesia, in particular the Moluccas," Royal Institute of Linguistics and Anthropology, Leiden, October 7–12.

Alfatah, M. Nur. 2003. "Konflik Maluku Utara, berkaca pada heroisme Babullah." In *Memikirkan kembali "Maluku dan Maluku Utara,"* edited by Imron Hasan, 113–16. Makassar, Lembaga Penerbitan Universitas Hasanuddin.

Algadri, Hamid. 1994. *Dutch policy against Islam and Indonesians of Arab descent in Indonesia*. Jakarta, LP3ES.

Alhadar, Smith. 2000. The forgotten war in North Maluku. *Inside Indonesia* 63(July–September): 15–16.

Amal, M. Adnan. 2000. "Sejarah Islam dan Kristen di Galela & Tobelo." In *Damai yang terkoyak: Catatan kelam dari bumi Halmahera*, edited by Kasman Ahmad and Herman Oesman, 15–47. Ternate, Podium.

———. 2002. *Maluku Utara: Perjalanan sejarah 1250–1800 (jilid I)*. Ternate, Universitas Khairun.

Andaya, Leonard Y. 1993. *The world of Maluku: Eastern Indonesia in the early modern period*. Honolulu, University of Hawai'i Press.

Aragon, Lorraine. 2001. Communal violence in Poso, Central Sulawesi: Where people eat fish and fish eat people. *Indonesia* 72: 45–79.

———. 2005. Mass media fragmentation and narratives of violent action in Sulawesi's Poso conflict. *Indonesia* 79: 1–55.

Arifianto, Alexander R. 2009. Explaining the cause of Muslim-Christian conflicts in Indonesia: Tracing the origins of Kristenisasi and Islamisasi. *Islam and Christian-Muslim Relations* 20(1): 73–89.

Aritonang, Jan S. 2004. *Sejarah perjumpaan Kristen dan Islam di Indonesia*. Jakarta, BPK Gunung Mulia.

Asad, Talal. 1983. Anthropological conceptions of religion: Reflections on Geertz. *Man* 18(2): 237–59.

Atkinson, Jane Monnig. 1983. Religions in dialogue: The construction of an Indonesian minority religion. *American Ethnologist* 10(4): 684–96.

Azca, M. Najib. 2005. "Security forces in Ambon: From the national to the local." In *Violence in between: Conflict and security in archipelagic Southeast Asia*, edited by Damien Kingsbury, 231–54. Clayton, Monash Asia Institute.

———. 2006. In between military and militia: The dynamics of the security forces in the communal conflict in Ambon. *Asian Journal of Social Science* 34(3): 431–55.

Baarda, M. J. van. 1914. Een apologie voor de dooden. Bijdrage tot de kennis van het Galelareesche volk. *Bijdragen tot de Taal-, Land- en Volkenkunde* 69(1): 52–89.

Banari, Jesaya. 2007. Pertemuan masyarakat adat Hibualamo (Hoana Modole, Boeng, Pagu, Towiliko). Tobelo, North Halmahera, North Maluku.

Bartels, Dieter. 1977. "Guarding the invisible mountain: Intervillage alliances, religious syncretism and ethnic identity among Ambonese Christians and Moslems in the Moluccas." Ph.D. diss., Cornell University.

———. 2003. "Your god is no longer mine: Moslem-Christian fratricide in the central Moluccas (Indonesia) after a half-millennium of tolerant co-existence and ethnic unity." In *A state of emergency: Violence, society and the state in Eastern Indonesia*, edited by Sandra Pannell, 128–53. Darwin, Northern Territory University Press.

———. 2010. "The evolution of God in the Spice Islands: The converging and diverging of Protestant Christianity and Islam in the colonial and post-colonial periods." In *Christianity in Indonesia: Perspectives of Power*, edited by Susanne Schröter, 225-58. Berlin, Lit.

Batmomolin, Lukas. 2000. "Religious conflict in Ambon, Indonesia: Reconciliation through the *pela gandong* system." Master's thesis, American University.

Berita Telegraf. 2001. "Warga Kristen-Islam Morotai berdamai." *Berita Telegraf*. 30 June.

Bertrand, Jacques. 2002. Legacies of the authoritarian past: Religious violence in Indonesia's Moluccan islands. *Pacific Affairs* 75(1): 57–85.

———. 2004. *Nationalism and ethnic conflict in Indonesia*. Cambridge, Cambridge University Press.

Biggar, Nigel. 2003. "Making peace or making justice: Must we choose?" In *Burying the past: Making peace and doing justice after civil conflict*, edited by Nigel Biggar, 6–22. Washington, DC, Georgetown University Press.

Böhm, C. J., and Frits Pangemanan. 2010. *Sejarah gereja Katolik Maluku Utara, 1534–2009*. Yogyakarta, Kansius.

Boland, B. J. 1971. *The struggle of Islam in modern Indonesia*. Hague, Martinus Nijhoff.

Bourdieu, Pierre. 1977. *Outline of a theory of practice*. Cambridge, Cambridge University Press.

Bouvier, Hélène, and Glenn Smith. 2008. "Spontaneity, conspiracy, and rumor: The politics of framing violence in Central Kalimantan." In *Conflict, violence, and displacement in Indonesia*, edited by Eva-Lotta Hedman, 231–48. Ithaca, Cornell Southeast Asia Program.

Bowen, John R. 1993. *Muslims through discourse: Religion and ritual in Gayo society*. Princeton, Princeton University Press.

———. 1996. The myth of global ethnic conflict. *Journal of Democracy* 7(4): 3–14.

Braithwaite, John, et al. 2010. *Anomie and violence: Non-truth and reconciliation in Indonesian peacebuilding*. Canberra, Australian National University Press.

Brass, Paul R. 1996. "Introduction: Discourses of ethnicity, communalism, and violence." In *Riots and pogroms*, edited by Paul R. Brass, 1–55. Basingstoke, Hampshire, Macmillan.

———. 1997. *Theft of an idol: Text and context in the representation of collective violence*. Princeton, Princeton University Press.

———. 2003. *The production of Hindu-Muslim violence in contemporary India*. Seattle, University of Washington Press.

———. 2006. Victims, heroes or martyrs? Partition and the problem of memorialization in contemporary Sikh history. *Sikh Formations* 2(1): 17–31.

Bräuchler, Birgit. 2003. Cyberidentities at war: Religion, identity, and the internet in the Moluccan conflict. *Indonesia* 75: 123–51.

———. 2004. Islamic radicalism online: The Moluccan mission of the Laskar Jihad in cyberspace. *The Australian Journal of Anthropology* 15(3): 267–85.

———. 2009a. "Mobilizing culture and tradition for peace: Reconciliation in the Moluccas." In *Reconciling Indonesia: Grassroots agency for peace*, edited by Birgit Bräuchler, 97–118. New York, Routledge.

———, ed. 2009b. *Reconciling Indonesia: Grassroots agency for peace*. New York, Routledge.

———. 2010. "Religions online: Christian and Muslim (re)presentations in the Moluccan conflict." In *Christianity in Indonesia: Perspectives of power*, edited by Susanne Schröter, 203–24. Berlin, Lit.

Brown, Iem. 1987. Contemporary Indonesian Buddhism and monotheism. *Journal of Southeast Asian Studies.* 18(1): 108–17.

Bruinessen, Martin van. 2002. Genealogies of Islamic radicalism in post-Suharto Indonesia. *South East Asia Research* 10(2): 117–54.

———. 2003. "Post-Suharto Muslim engagements with civil society and democracy." Paper presented at Third International Conference and Workshop "Indonesia in Transition," organized by Koninklijke Nederlandse Akademie van Wetenschappen and Labsosio, Universitas Indonesia, Depok, August 24–28.

Bubandt, Nils. 2000a. Conspiracy theories, apocalyptic narratives, and the discursive construction of 'the violence in Indonesia.' *Antropologi Indonesia* 24(63): 15–32.

———. 2000b. "Malukan apocalypse: Themes in the dynamics of violence in Eastern Indonesia." In *Violence in Indonesia*, edited by Ingrid Wessel and Georgia Wimhöfer, 228–53. Hamburg, Abera.

———. 2004. "Violence and millenarian modernity in Eastern Indonesia." In *Cargo, cult, and culture critique*, edited by Holger Jebens, 92–116. Honolulu, University of Hawai'i Press.

———. 2005. "On the genealogy of *sasi*: Transformations of an imagined tradition in Eastern Indonesia." In *Tradition and agency: Tracing cultural continuity and invention*, edited by Ton Otto and Poul Pederson, 193–232. Aarhus, Aarhus University Press.

———. 2008a. "Ghosts with trauma: Global imaginaries and the politics of post-conflict memory in Indonesia." In *Conflict, violence, and displacement in Indonesia*, edited by Eva-Lotta Hedman, 275–302. Ithaca, Cornell Southeast Asia Program.

———. 2008b. Rumors, pamphlets, and the politics of paranoia in Indonesia. *Journal of Asian Studies* 67(3): 789–817.

———. 2009. From the enemy's point of view: Violence, empathy, and the ethnography of fakes. *Cultural Anthropology* 24(3): 553–88.

Al-Bunyan. 2000. "Howard, peneliti atau provokator?" *Al-Bunyan.* 14 August.

Cavanaugh, William T. 2009. *The myth of religious violence: Secular ideology and the roots of modern conflict*. New York, Oxford University Press.

Chauvel, Richard. 1980. Ambon's other half: Some preliminary observations on Ambonese Moslem society and history. *Review of Indonesian and Malaysian Affairs* 14(1): 40–80.

———. 1990. *Nationalists, soldiers, and separatists: The Ambonese islands from colonialism to revolt, 1880–1950.* Leiden, KITLV.

Clarke, Helen Jenks, ed. 2006. *Nonviolent resistance: People's stories from Indonesian conflicts.* Yogyakarta, CSPS Books.

Clercq, F. S. A. de. 1889. Dodadi ma-taoe en goma ma-taoe of zielenhuisjes in het district Tobélo op Noord-Halmahera. *Internationales Archiv für Ethnographie* 2: 204–12.

Colombijn, Freek, and J. Thomas Linblad, eds. 2002. *Roots of violence in Indonesia: Contemporary violence in historical perspective.* Leiden, KITLV.

Compass Direct. 2002. "Snapshots of suffering from Indonesia's trouble spots." *Compass Direct: Global News from the Frontlines.* Accessed February 2002. Available at http:// old.lff.net/resources/compass/feb152002.txt.

Coombes, Annie E. 2003. *History after apartheid: Visual culture and public memory in a democratic South Africa.* Durham, Duke University Press.

CPRU/UNDP. 2004. Towards peaceful development: Rebuilding social cohesion and reconciliation; Central Sulawesi and North Maluku. Jakarta, Crisis Prevention and Recovery Unit of the United Nations Development Programme.

Crouch, Harold. 2010. *Political reform in Indonesia after Soeharto.* Singapore, Institute of Southeast Asian Studies.

Cunliffe, Scott, et al. 2009. Negotiating peace in Indonesia: Prospects for building peace and upholding justice in Maluku and Aceh. Brussels, International Center for Transitional Justice and Elsam.

Danius, Ebin E. 2012. Hubungan Kristen-Islam pasca konflik di Tobelo Halmahera Utara. *Uniera: Jurnal Ilmiah Lintas Ilmu* 1(1): 28–43.

Das, Veena. 1985. Anthropological knowledge and collective violence: The riots in Delhi, November 1984. *Anthropology Today* 1(3): 4–6.

———. 2006. *Life and words: Violence and the descent into the ordinary.* Berkeley, University of California Press.

Dateline. 2000. "Indonesia's leadership struggle." Accessed February 2006, http://news .sbs.com.au/dateline/indonesias_leadership_struggle_129781 (site discontinued).

Davidson, Jamie S. 2008. *From rebellion to riots: Collective violence on Indonesian Borneo.* Madison, University of Wisconsin Press.

Davis, Natalie Zemon. 1973. The rites of violence: Religious riot in sixteenth century France. *Past and Present* 59(1): 51–91.

Deeb, Lara. 2008. Exhibiting the "just-lived past": Hizbullah's nationalist narratives in transnational political context. *Comparative Studies in Society and History* 50(2): 369–99.

D'Hondt, Laura. 2010. Seeking environmental justice in North Maluku: How transformed injustices and big interests get in the way. *Law, Social Justice & Global Development Journal (1).* Accessed August 27, 2012. Available at http://www2.warwick.ac .uk/fac/soc/law/elj/lgd/2010_1/dhondt.

DHV Consulting. 1982. Engineers reconnaissance survey report, feasibility for transmigration settlements development. Jakarta, DHV Consulting.

Dijk, Cornelis van. 1981. *Rebellion under the banner of Islam: The Darul Islam in Indonesia*. The Hague, Martinus Nijhoff.

Dijk, Kees van. 2001. *A country in despair: Indonesia between 1997–2000*. Jakarta, KITLV.

Dijken, Hendrik van. 1874. Almaheira. *Berigten van de Utrechtsche Zendingsvereeniging* 15(9): 149–63.

Dijkstra, H. 1915. Opstand en bekeering. *De Macedonier* 19: 257–65.

Djaafar, Irza Arnyta. 2005. *Dari Moloku Kie Raha hingga negara federal: Biografi politik Sultan Ternate Iskandar Muhammad Djahir Sjah*. Yogyakarta, Bio Pustaka.

Djafar, Arifin, and Rinto Taib. 2011. *Geliat Legu Gam Moluku Kie Raha: Pesona Kie Raha, pesona Nusantara*. Ternate, Dewan Pakar Kesultanan Ternate.

Djahir, M. S. 1966. Maluku Utara; bahan-bahan keterangan, data-data dan fakta-fakta guna pembentukan daerah tingkat 1 Maluku Utara dengan daerah-daerah tingkat 2. Ternate, Badan Perantjang Pemekaran Daerah-Daerah Tingkat 2 Menudju Daerah Tingkat 1 Maluku Utara (BAPERAN MALUT).

Doorn-Harder, Nelly van, and Kees de Jong. 2001. The pilgrimage to Tembayat: Tradition and revival in Indonesian Islam. *Muslim World* 91(3–4): 325–54.

Drexler, Elizabeth F. 2007. The social life of conflict narratives: Violent antagonists, imagined histories, and foreclosed futures in Aceh, Indonesia. *Anthropological Quarterly* 80(4): 961–95.

——. 2008. *Aceh, Indonesia: Securing the insecure state*. Philadelphia, University of Pennsylvania Press.

——. 2009. "Impunity and paranoia: Writing histories of Indonesian violence." In *Mirrors of justice: Law, power in the post-Cold War era*, edited by Kamari Clarke and Mark Goodale, 229–47. Cambridge, Cambridge University Press.

Duncan, Christopher R. 1998. "Ethnic identity, Christian conversion and resettlement among the Forest Tobelo of northeastern Halmahera, Indonesia." Ph.D. diss., Yale University.

——. 2001. Savage imagery: (Mis)representations of the Forest Tobelo of Indonesia. *Asia Pacific Journal of Anthropology* 2(1): 45–62.

——. 2002. "Resettlement and natural resources in Indonesia: A case study." In *Conservation and mobile indigenous people: Displacement, forced settlement and sustainable development*, edited by Dawn Chatty and Marcus Colchester, 347-61. Oxford, Berghahn Books.

——. 2003. Untangling conversion: Religious change and identity among the Forest Tobelo of Halmahera, Indonesia. *Ethnology* 42(4): 307–22.

——. 2005a. The other Maluku: Chronologies of conflict in North Maluku. *Indonesia* 80: 53–80.

——. 2005b. Unwelcome guests: Relations between internally displaced persons and their hosts in North Sulawesi, Indonesia. *Journal of Refugee Studies* 18(1): 25–46.

——. 2008. "Where do we go from here? The politics of ending displacement in post-conflict North Maluku." In *Conflict, violence, and displacement in Indonesia*, edited by Eva-Lotta Hedman, 207–30. Ithaca, Cornell Southeast Asia Program.

——. 2009a. Reconciliation and reinvention: The resurgence of tradition in postconflict Tobelo, North Maluku, Eastern Indonesia. *Journal of Asian Studies* 68(4): 1077–104.

———. 2009b. Review of "Communal violence and democratization in Indonesia: Small town wars." *Indonesia* 87(April): 125–28.

———. 2010. "The use and abuse of customary law in a North Moluccan town." Paper presented at In Search of Middle Indonesia, Final Research Conference, Koninklijk Instituut voor Taal-, Land- en Volkenkunde, Leiden, Netherlands, September 27–29.

Eklöf, Stefan. 1999. *Indonesian politics in crisis: The long fall of Suharto, 1996–98.* Copenhagen, NIAS.

Ellen, N. A. 1906. Uit eenen brief van mevrouw N. A. Ellen. *De Haagsche Zendingsbode* 9(11): 78–79.

Elson, R. E. 2009. Another look at the Jakarta Charter controversy of 1945. *Indonesia*(88): 105-30.

Emmerson, Donald K. 1976. *Indonesia's elite: Political culture and cultural politics.* Ithaca, Cornell University Press.

Evans-Pritchard, E. E. 1937. *Witchcraft, oracles, and magic among the Azande.* Oxford, Clarendon Press.

Fealy, Greg. 2003. Tall tales: Conspiracy theories in post-bomb Indonesia. *Inside Indonesia* 74 (April–June 2003): 6–8.

Feldman, Allen. 1991. *Formations of violence: The narrative of the body and political terror in Northern Ireland.* Chicago, University of Chicago Press.

———. 2003. Political terror and the technologies of memory: Excuse, sacrifice, commodification, and actuarial moralities. *Radical History Review* 85: 58–73.

Fitzgerald, Tim. 2006. Bruce Lincoln's "Theses on Method": Anthitheses. *Method and Theory in the Study of Religion* 18: 392–423.

Flinchbaugh, C. Hope. 2001. "Indonesia: The horrors of jihad." *Charisma.* Accessed May 2006. Available at http://www.charismamag.com/spirit/world-religions/366-indonesia-the-horrors-of-jihad.

Fortgens, J. 1904. Onder de Tobaru van het landschap Ibu. *Berichten van de Utrechtsche Zendingsvereeniging.* n.s. 17(5): 65–76.

Forum Keadilan. 2000a. "Amien Rais: 'Saya akan menyerukan jihad'." *Forum Keadilan* 8(41): 80–81.

———. 2000b. "Halmahera masih membara." *Forum Keadilan* 9(6): 70–71.

———. 2000c. "Laskar menggertak, Gus Dur terancam." *Forum Keadilan* 9(3): 76–77.

Forum Komunikasi Masyarakat Propinsi Maluku Utara Makassar. 2000. Bantahan terhadap pernyataan Sultan Ternate (Drs. Mudafar Syah) dalam pemberitaan tgl 21 & 22 Januari 2000 melalui siaran SCTV dan TPI serta media cetak di Indonesia. Makassar, Forum Komunikasi Masyarakat Propinsi Maluku Utara Makassar.

Fox, Richard. 2010. Why media matter: Critical reflections on religion and the recent history of "the Balinese." *History of Religions* 49(4): 354–92.

Fraassen, Ch. F. van. 1980. "Types of sociopolitical structure in North-Halmaheran history." In *Halmahera dan Raja Ampat: Konsep dan strategi penelitian*, edited by E. K. M. Masinambow, 87–150. Jakarta, LEKNAS-LIPI.

Fransz, A. L. 1976. Gereja Masehi Injili Halmahera. *Peninjau* 3: 3–76.

Gamma. 2000. "Pindah agama: Ikrar syahadat di Lata-Lata." *Gamma* 2(6): 81.

Gatra. 1999. "Persaingan dua Sultan." *Gatra* 6(2): 44.

Geertz, Clifford. 1959. "The Javanese village." In *Local, ethnic, and national loyalties in village Indonesia: A Symposium*, edited by G. William Skinner, 34–41. New Haven, Yale University, Southeast Asia Studies.

———. 1973. "'Internal conversion' in contemporary Bali." In *The interpretation of culture*, edited by Clifford Geertz, 170–89. New York, Basic Books.

GMIH. 2000. Halmahera report 3: Peta kerusakan wilayah jemaat-jemaat Kristen di Halmahera. Tobelo, GMIH.

Hagen, James M. 2006. *Community in the balance: Morality and social change in an Indonesian society*. Boulder, Paradigm Publishers.

Haire, James. 1981. *The character and theological struggle of the church in Halmahera, Indonesia, 1941–1979*. Frankfurt am Main, Peter D. Lang.

———. 1998. *Sifat dan pergumulan gereja di Halmahera, 1941–1979*. Jakarta, BPK Gunung Mulia.

Hakiem, Lukman, ed. 1991. *Fakta dan data usaha-usaha Kristenisasi di Indonesia*. Jakarta, Majalah Media Dakwah.

Harian Umum Siwalima. 2000. "Matheus "Mansyur" Masan: Saya dipaksa masuk Islam." *Harian Umum Siwalima*. 9 December.

Hasan, Imron, ed. 2003. *Memikirkan kembali "Maluku dan Maluku Utara."* Makassar, Lembaga Penerbitan Universitas Hasanuddin.

Hasan, Noorhaidi. 2002. Faith and politics: The rise of the Laskar Jihad in the era of transition in Indonesia. *Indonesia*. 73: 145–69.

———. 2005. Between transnational interest and domestic politics: Understanding Middle Eastern fatwas on jihad in the Moluccas. *Islamic Law and Society* 12(1): 73–92.

———. 2006. *Laskar Jihad: Islam, militancy, and the quest for identity in post-New Order Indonesia*. Ithaca, Cornell Southeast Asia Program.

Hasani, Yusuf, and Rusmin Effendy. 2011. *Mengurai konflik pilkada Maluku Utara*. Jakarta, Candi Cipta Paramuda.

Hayden, Robert M. 1996. Imagined communities and real victims: Self-determination and ethnic cleansing in Yugoslavia. *American Ethnologist* 23(4): 783–801.

———. 2007. Moral vision and impaired insight: The imagining of other peoples' communities in Bosnia. *Current Anthropology* 48(1): 105–31.

Hefner, Robert W. 1985. *Hindu Javanese: Tengger tradition and Islam*. Princeton, Princeton University Press.

———. 2000. *Civil Islam: Muslims and democratization in Indonesia*. Princeton, Princeton University Press.

Henley, David. 2007. The fate of federalism: North Sulawesi from Persatuan Minahasa to Permesta. *Moussons* 11: 89–105.

Herriman, Nicholas. 2006. Fear and uncertainty: Local perceptions of the sorcerer and the state in an Indonesian witch-hunt. *Asian Journal of Social Science* 34(3): 360–87.

Heuken, Adolf. 2002. *'Be my witness to the ends of the earth!': The Catholic Church in Indonesia before the 19th century*. Jakarta, Cipta Loka Caraka.

Hoda, A. 2000. *Tragedi kemanusiaan di Jazirah Halmahera: Retaknya sebuah nilai*. Ternate.

Hoffman, Daniel. 2005. Violent events as narrative blocs: The disarmament at Bo, Sierra Leone. *Anthropological Quarterly* 78(2): 328–53

Hohe, Tanja, and Bert Remijsen. 2003. "Peacemaker for religious conflicts? The value of *pela* relationships in Ambon." In *Hinduism in modern Indonesia: Between local, national, and global interests*, edited by Martin Ramstedt, 126–43. New York, RoutledgeCurzon.

Hontong, Sefnat. 2012. *Eksistensi pusara dodara: Upaya hermeneutika etis-sosiologis bagi pengembangan budaya damai di Halmahera*. Yogyakarta, Kanisius.

Hueting, Anton. 1907. Referaat op de algemeene vergadering der Utrechtsche Zendingsvereeniging, gehouden in 1907. *Mededeelingen van wege het Nederlandsche Zendelinggeenootschaap* 51: 285–304.

———. 1910. Verordeningen aangaande de adat der inlandsche christenen op het eiland Halmahera (zoaals die vastgesteld zijn door de christen-hoofden en oudsten der districten Tobèlo, Galéla. Kau, Sidangoli, en Loda). *Bijdragen tot de Taal-, Land- en Volkenkunde* 63(1): 33–92.

———. 1921. De Toboloreezen in hun denken en doen. *Bijdragen tot de Taal-, Land- en Volkenkunde* 77(1): 217–357.

———. 1922. De Toboloreezen in hun denken en doen (tweede gedeelte). *Bijdragen tot de Taal-, Land- en Volkenkunde* 78(1): 137–342.

———. 1934. *Geschiedenis der zending op het eiland Halmahera*. Oegstgeest, Zendingsbureau.

Hughes, James. 2007. *Chechnya: From nationalism to jihad*. Philadelphia, University of Pennsylvania Press.

Husein, Fatimah. 2005. *Muslim-Christian relations in the New Order Indonesia: The exclusivist and inclusivist Muslims' perspectives*. Jakarta, Mizan.

Indisch Militair Tijdschrift. 1907. Kort overzicht van de ongeregeldheden op Halmahera. *Indisch Militair Tijdschrift* 38: 328–31.

Indonesian Observer. 2000. "Four killed in battle between army, jihad forces in Ternate." *Indonesian Observer*. 5 May.

International Christian Concern. 2001. The untold tragedies of Maluku: Press release. 9 March. Accessed July 2012. Available at http://www.persecution.org/2001/03/09/the-untold-tragedies-of-maluku/.

International Crisis Group. 2000a. Indonesia's Maluku crisis: The issues. Jakarta, International Crisis Group.

———. 2000b. Indonesia: Overcoming murder and chaos in Maluku. Jakarta, International Crisis Group.

———. 2002. Indonesia backgrounder: How the Jemaah Islamiyah terrorist network operates. Jakarta, International Crisis Group.

———. 2003. Indonesia: Managing decentralisation and conflict in South Sulawesi. Jakarta, International Crisis Group.

———. 2004. Indonesia backgrounder: Jihad in Central Sulawesi. Jakarta, International Crisis Group.

———. 2009. Local election disputes in Indonesia: The case of North Maluku. Jakarta, International Crisis Group.

———. 2010. Indonesia: "Christianisation" and intolerance. Jakarta, International Crisis Group.

International Friends of Compassion. 2002. "Report from Indonesia IFC director: Carl Cady February 15, 2002." Accessed December 2002, http://www.ifcus.org/pages /newsletter216.htm (site discontinued).

Jacobs, Hubert, ed. 1974. *Documenta Malucensia*. Vol. 1. *1542–1577*. Rome, Institutum Historicum Societatis Iesu.

Jacobsen, Karen, and Loren B. Landau. 2003. The dual imperative in refugee research: Some methodological and ethical considerations in social science research on forced migration. *Disasters* 27(3): 185-206.

Jakarta Post. 2000a. "Reports of forced conversion in Maluku confirmed: Governor." *Jakarta Post*. 21 December.

———. 2000b. "Troops evacuate Maluku refugees." *Jakarta Post*. 5 January.

James, Eric. C. 2010. *Democratic insecurities: Violence, trauma, and intervention in Haiti*. Berkeley, University of California Press.

Jati, Heru. 2001?. *Dan bunda pun menangis: Kisah tragis korban kerusuhan Maluku Utara*. Tangerang, Visimedia.

Jawa Pos. 2000. "Kesultanan Tidore desak Polri tangkap Sultan Ternate." *Jawa Pos*. 24 June.

———. 2002. "Bentrok lagi, warga resah di Morotai, 300 rumah dibakar." *Jawa Pos*. 17 September.

Jelin, Elizabeth. 2003. *State repression and the struggles for memory*. Minneapolis, University of Minnesota Press.

———. 2007. Public memorialization in perspective: Truth, justice and memory of past repression in the southern cone of South America. *International Journal of Transitional Justice* 1(1): 138–56.

Jones, James W. 2008. *Blood that cries out from the earth: The psychology of religious terrorism*. Oxford, Oxford University Press.

Juergensmeyer, Mark. 2008. *Global rebellion: Religious challenges to the secular state, from Christian militias to al Qaeda*. Berkeley, University of California Press.

Kahn, Joel S. 1978. Ideology and social structure in Indonesia. *Comparative Studies in Society and History* 20(1): 103–22.

Kakar, Sudhir. 1996. *The colors of violence: Cultural identities, religion, and conflict*. Chicago, University of Chicago Press.

Kastor, Rustam. 2000. *Konspirasi politik RMS dan Kristen menghancurkan ummat Islam di Ambon Maluku*. Yogyakarta, Wihdah Press.

Kelabora, Lambert. 1976. Religious instruction policy in Indonesia. *Asian Survey* 16(3): 230–48.

Kiem, Christian G. 1993. *Growing up in Indonesia: Youth and social change in a Moluccan town*. Saarbrucken, Breitenbach.

———. 1995. Re-Islamization among Muslim youth in Ternate town, Eastern Indonesia. *Sojourn* 8(1): 92–127.

Kipp, Rita. 1993. *Dissociated identities: Ethnicity, religion, and class in an Indonesian society*. Ann Arbor, University of Michigan Press.

———. 2000. 'Bangsa goes above *agama*': The nationalist credentials of Christian Indonesians. *Documentatieblad voor de Geschiedenis van de Nederlandse Zending en Overzeese Kerken*. 7(2): 2–25.

Kipp, Rita Smith, and Susan Rodgers, eds. 1987. *Indonesian religions in transition.* Tucson, University of Arizona Press.

Kippenberg, Hans G. 2011. *Violence as worship: Religious wars in the age of globalization.* Stanford, Stanford University Press.

Klinken, Gerry van. 2001. The Maluku wars: Bringing society back in. *Indonesia* 71: 1–26.

———. 2007a. *Communal violence and democratization in Indonesia: Small town wars.* London, Routledge.

———. 2007b. "Return of the sultans: The communitarian turn in local politics." In *The revival of tradition in Indonesian politics: The deployment of adat from colonialism to indigenism,* edited by Jamie S. Davidson and David Henley, 149–69. London, Routledge.

Kompak-Dewan Dakwah. 2000. "Peduli Ambon / Maluku." *Media Dakwah.* 308: Special insert.

Kompas. 2000a. "11 penumpang KM Cahaya Bahari yang hilang ditemukan satu tewas, 10 selamat." *Kompas.* 3 July.

———. 2000b. "Enam wakil Laskar Jihad Maluku bertemu presiden." *Kompas.* 6 April.

———. 2000c. "Pangdam XVI/Pattimura: Kerusuhan Maluku Utara tewaskan 771 jiwa." *Kompas.* 17 January.

———. 2002. "Pulau Morotai pulih kembali." *Kompas.* 19 September.

KWPMDTPPH. 1995. Penyelenggaraan transmigrasi dan pemukiman perambah hutan di Propinsi Maluku: Sebegai laporan dalam rangka kunjungan kerja Menteri Transmigrasi dan Pemukiman Perambah Hutan di Propinsi Maluku. Ambon, Departemen Transmigrasi dan Pemukiman Perambah Hutan, Kantor Wilayah Propinsi Maluku.

Lakawa, Septemmy E. 2008. Women, theology and testimony of peace. *Women's Letter* 1: 15–19.

———. 2011. "Risky hospitality: Mission in the aftermath of religious communal violence in Indonesia." Ph.D. diss., Boston University.

Lambek, Michael. 1996. "The past imperfect: Remembering as moral practice." In *Tense past: Cultural essays in trauma and memory,* edited by Paul Antze and Michael Lambek, 235–54. New York, Routledge.

Leith, Jennifer G. 2001. "Representation, resources and resettlement as development in Eastern Indonesia." Ph.D. diss., University of East Anglia.

Lemarchand, René. 1996. *Burundi: Ethnic conflict and genocide.* Cambridge, Cambridge University Press.

———. 1998. Genocide in the Great Lakes: Which genocide? Whose genocide? *African Studies Review* 41(1): 3–16.

Lincoln, Bruce. 2006. *Holy terrors: Thinking about religion after September 11.* Chicago, University of Chicago Press.

Lubkemann, Stephen C. 2008. *Culture in chaos: An anthropology of the social condition in war.* Chicago, University of Chicago Press.

Lucardie, G. R. E. 1984. "The geographical mobility of the Makianese: Migratory traditions and resettlement patterns." In *Halmahera dan Raja Ampat sebegai kesatuan majemuk,* edited by E. K. M. Masinambow, 333–45. Jakarta, LEKNAS-LIPI.

——. 1985. Spontaneous and planned movements among the Makianese of Eastern Indonesia. *Pacific Viewpoint* 26(1): 63–78.

Maarif, Samsul. 2012. "Dimensions of religious practice: The Ammatoans of South Sulawesi." Ph.D. diss., Arizona State University.

Magany, M. Th. 1984. *Bahtera injil di Halmahera*. Ambon, GMIH.

Malik, Ichsan. 2005. "The Malino peace process in conflict resolution in Poso and Maluku." In *Violent internal conflicts in Asia Pacific: Histories, political economies, and policies*, edited by Dewi Fortuna Anwar, Hélène Bouvier, Glenn Smith, and Roger Tol, 276–81. Jakarta, Yayasan Obor.

Malkki, Liisa H. 1995. *Purity and exile: Violence, memory, and national cosmology among Hutu refugees in Tanzania*. Chicago, University of Chicago Press.

——. 1997. "News and culture: Transitory phenomena and the fieldwork tradition." In *Anthropological locations: Boundaries and grounds of a field science*, edited by Akhil Gupta and James Ferguson, 86–101. Berkeley, University of California Press.

Malut Post. 2012a. "2 desa di Tobelo memanas." *Malut Post*. 31 August.

——. 2012b. "Masyarakat Halsel diminta tak terpancing." *Malut Pos*. 1 September.

Mamdani, Mahmood. 2001. *When victims become killers: Colonialism, nativism, and the genocide in Rwanda*. Princeton, Princeton University Press.

Manado Post. 1999a. "Bursa figur gubernur mulai hangat." *Manado Post*. 20 September.

——. 1999b. "Ribuan warga Ternate unjuk rasa." *Manado Post*. 1 September.

——. 2000. "Kuatir dilempar telur busuk, Amien batal temui pengungsi Malut." *Manado Post*. 21 December.

——. 2002a. "Sarundajang: Tak benar ada kerusuhan di Tobelo." *Manado Post*. 15 July.

——. 2002b. "Tobelo aman, jangan tanggapi SMS berantai." *Manado Post*. 20 July.

Masariku Network. 2001a. Masariku Report 131: Peralihan agama secara paksa sebagai dampak kerusuhan Maluku. Ambon, Masariku Network.

——. 2001b. Masariku Report 142: Kasus Islamisasi paksa di Halmahera. Ambon, Masariku Network.

——. 2001c. Masariku Report 143: Jumlah kasus dan wilayah penyebaran penduduk korban Islamisasi paksa di provinsi Maluku dan Maluku Utara. Ambon, Masariku Network.

Masuzawa, Tomoko. 2005. *The invention of world religions: Or, how European universalism was preserved in the language of pluralism*. Chicago, University of Chicago Press.

Matta, H. M. A. 1999. "Khutbah Idhul Fithri 1420h: Pelajaran dari jihad Maluku." Accessed December 2000, http:// www.keadilan.or.id/Seruan/SpecRamadhan1420H /KutbahIed7/kutbah ied7.html (site discontinued).

Media Dakwah. 1999a. "Umat Islam Talaga diserang." *Media Dakwah* 302: 28.

——. 1999b. "RMS ingin hancurkan Ambon." *Media Dakwah* 306: 48–49.

——. 2000. "Politik belah bambu rezim paranoid." *Media Dakwah* 308: 42–45.

Mironko, Charles. 2004. "Social and political mechanisms of mass murder: An analysis of perpetrators of the Rwandan genocide." Ph.D. diss., Yale University.

Mujiburrahman. 2006. "Feeling threatened: Muslim-Christian relations in Indonesia's New Order." Ph.D. diss., Universiteit Utrecht.

Muluk, Hamdi, and Ichsan Malik. 2009. "Peace psychology of grassroots reconciliation: Lessons learned from the "Baku Bae" peace movement." In *Peace psychology in Asia*, edited by Cristina J. Montiel and Noraini M. Noor, 85–103. New York, Springer.

Nanere, Jan, ed. 2000. *Halmahera berdarah: Suatu upaya mengungkap kebenaran*. Ambon, Yayasan Bina Masyarakat Sejahtera dan Pelestarian Alam.

Ngatomo, Purwanto. 2006. "Sejarah perjuangan tim rekonsiliasi konflik komunal di Halbar." *Jurnalis Maluku Utara*, Accessed March 2006. Available at http://purwanto -malutpost.blogspot.com/2006/03/sejarah-perjuangan-tim-rekonsiliasi.html.

Nora, Pierre. 1989. Between memory and history: *Les lieux de mémoire. Representations* 26(1): 7–24.

Nordholt, Henk Schulte. 2002. "A genealogy of violence." In *Roots of violence in Indonesia: Contemporary violence in historical perspective*, edited by Freek Colombijn and J. Thomas Linblad, 33–61. Leiden, KITLV.

Nussbaum, Martha C. 2007. *The clash within: Democracy, religious violence, and India's future*. Cambridge, Belknap Press of Harvard University Press.

Oesman, Herman, and Kasman Hi. Ahmad. 2000. "Retaknya mozaik kerukunan." In *Damai yang terkoyak: Catatan kelam dari bumi Halmahera*, edited by Kasman Ahmad and Herman Oesman, 139–43. Ternate, Kelompok Studi Podium, LPAM Pemuda Muhammadiyah Maluku Utara and Madani Press.

Orgaan der Nederlandsch-Indische Officiersvereeniging. 1930. Het verzet op Halmaheira in 1914. *Orgaan der Nederlandsch-Indische Officiersvereeniging* 15(12): 529–31.

Peluso, Nancy Lee, and Emily Harwell. 2001. "Territory, custom, and the cultural politics of ethnic war in West Kalimantan, Indonesia." In *Violent environments*, edited by Nancy Lee Peluso and Michael Watts, 83–116. Ithaca, Cornell University Press.

Pemerintah Daerah Halmahera Utara and Dinas Pariwisata Halmahera Utara. n.d. *Hibua Lamo: Memehami eksistensi serta mendalami filosofi kaum Hibua Lamo di jasirah Halmahera*. Tobelo, Pemerintah Daerah Halmahera Utara and Dinas Pariwisata Halmahera Utara.

Permana, Nurhayat Arif. 2002. Revitalisasi lembaga adat dalam menyelesaikan konflik etnis menghadapi otonomi daerah: Studi kasus Pulau Bangka. *Antropologi Indonesia* 26(68): 74–85.

Picard, Michel. 2011. Balinese religion in search of recognition: From *Agama Hindu Bali* to *Agama Hindu* (1945–1965). *Bijdragen tot de Taal, Land- en Volkenkunde* 167(4): 482–510.

Pieris, John. 2004. *Tragedi Maluku: Sebuah krisis peradaban: analisis kritis aspek politik, ekonomi, sosial budaya, dan keamanan*. Jakarta, Yayasan Obor Indonesia.

Platenkamp, J. D. M. 1988. "Tobelo: Ideas and values of a North Moluccan society." Ph.D. diss., Leiden University.

——. 1990. "Transforming Tobelo ritual." In *Understanding rituals*, edited by Daniel de Coppet, 74–96. London, Routledge.

——. 1994. "Marriage and death: Social change in Tobelo." In *Maluku dan Irian Jaya*, edited by E. K. M. Masinambow, 105–18. Jakarta, LEKNAS-LIPI.

——. 2012. Sovereignty in the North Moluccas: Historical transformations. *History and Anthropology*. DOI: 10.1080/02757206.2012.697062

Povrzanović, Maja. 1997. Identities in war. Embodiments of violence and places of belonging. *Ethnologia Europaea* 27:153–62.

———. 2000. The imposed and the imagined as encountered by Croatian war ethnographers. *Current Anthropology* 41(2): 151–62.

Probojo, Lany. 1998. *Tradition und moderne in Tidore, Indonesien: Die instrumentalisierung islamischer rituale und ihre politische relevanz.* Münster, Lit.

———. 2010. Ritual guardians versus civil servants as cultural brokers in the New Order era. *Indonesia and the Malay World* 38(110): 95–107.

Pudja, I. G. N. Arinton, ed. 1989. *Adaptasi masyarakat Makian di tempat yang baru (Malifut).* Jakarta, Departemen Pendidikan dan Kebudayaan, Direktorat Jenderal Kebudayaan, Direktorat Sejarah dan Nilai Tradisional, Proyek Inventarisasi dan Pembinaan Nilai-Nilai Budaya.

Purdey, Jemma. 2006. *Anti-Chinese violence in Indonesia, 1996–1999.* Honolulu, University of Hawai'i Press.

Putuhena, M. Husni. 1999. *Buku putih tragedi kemanusian dalam kerusuhan di Maluku: sebuah prosesi ulang sejarah masa lalu.* Ambon, Lembaga Penerbit Eksistensi Muslim Maluku.

Raharto, Aswatini. 1995. *Migrasi kembali orang Sangir-Talaud dari pulau-pulau di wilayah Filipina.* Jakarta, Puslitbang Kependudukan dan Ketenagakerjaan, Lembaga Ilmu Pengetahuan Indonesia.

———. 2000. "Return migration among the Sangirese: Life and adjustment in the homeland." In *Population movement in Southeast Asia: Changing identities and strategies for survival*, edited by Abe Ken-ichi and Ishii Masako, 239–53. Osaka, National Museum of Ethnology.

Reid, Anthony. 1993. *Southeast Asia in the age of commerce, 1450–1680.* Vol. 2. *Expansion and crisis.* New Haven, Yale University Press.

Republika. 2000a. "Fajar Islam bersinar di desa Lata-Lata, Bacan." *Republika.* 26 May.

———. 2000b. "Konflik Maluku mulai reda, Gus Dur: Korban Galela hanya lima." *Republika.* 14 January.

———. 2000c. "Pengungsi Kristen Pulau Seram berlindung di pesantren, ratusan jenazah di Tobelo mulai membusuk." *Republika.* 15 January.

———. 2000d. "Tiga desa diserbu, wanita diperkosa di Halmahera dalam semalam 800 Muslim dibantai." *Republika.* 4 January.

Riddell, Peter G. 2002. The diverse voices of political Islam in post-Suharto Indonesia. *Islam and Christian-Muslim Relations* 13(1): 65–84.

Risakotta, Farsijana. 1995. "Etalase modernisasi pembangunan pedesaan: Suatu analisis social dan tinjuan etis terhadap cerita transformasi usaha perkebunan di Galela." Master's thesis, Universitas Kristan Satya Wacana.

Robben, Antonius C. G. M. 1995. "The politics of truth and emotion among victims and perpetrators of violence." In *Fieldwork under fire: Contemporary studies of violence and survival*, edited by Carolyn Nordstrom and Antonius C. G. M. Robben, 81–103. Berkeley, University of California Press.

Rodgers, Graeme. 2004. 'Hanging out' with forced migrants: Methodological and ethical challenges. *Forced Migration Review* 21: 48–49.

Roest, J. L. D. van der. 1914. *Herinneringen uit den zendingsarbeid op Halmahera*. Rotterdam, J. M. Bredée.

Sabili. 2000a. "Kesaksian korban kebiadaban kaum kafir di Maluku." *Sabili* 7(16): 32–35.

———. 2000b. "Thamrin Amal Tomagola, sosiolog: 'Perebutan wilayah agama'." *Sabili* 7(19): 30.

Salim, Makmum. 1995. *Sejarah operasi-operasi gabungan terhadap PRRI-Permesta*. Jakarta, Pusat Sejarah dan Tradisi ABRI, Markas Besar Angkatan Bersenjata Republik Indonesia.

Santikarma, Degung. 2005. "Monument, document and mass grave: The politics of representing violence in Bali." In *Beginning to remember: The past in the Indonesian present*, edited by Mary S. Zurbuchen, 312–23. Singapore, Singapore University Press.

Scheele, Judith. 2006. Algerian graveyard stories. *Journal of the Royal Anthropological Institute* 12(4): 859–79.

Schrauwers, Albert. 2003. "Through a glass darkly: Charity, conspiracy, and power in New Order Indonesia." In *Transparency and conspiracy: Ethnographies of suspicion in the new world order*, edited by Harry G. West and Todd Sanders, 125–47. Durham, Duke University Press.

Schreiner, Klaus H. 2002. "'National ancestors': The ritual construction of nationhood." In *The potent dead: Ancestors, saints and heroes in contemporary Indonesia*, edited by Henri Chambert-Loir and Anthony Reid, 183–204. Honolulu, University of Hawai'i Press.

———. 2005. "*Lubang Buaya*: Histories of trauma and sites of memory." In *Beginning to remember: The past in the Indonesian present*, edited by Mary S. Zurbuchen, 261–77. Singapore, Singapore University Press.

Scott, James. 1990. *Domination and the arts of resistance: Hidden transcripts*. New Haven, Yale University Press.

Sells, Michael A. 1996. *The bridge betrayed: Religion and genocide in Bosnia*. Berkeley, University of California Press.

Shoelhi, Mohammad. 2002. *Laskar jihad: Kambing hitam konflik Maluku*. Jakarta, Pustaka Zaman.

Sidel, John T. 2006. *Riots, pogroms, jihad: Religious violence in Indonesia*. Ithaca, Cornell University Press.

Sihbudi, Riza, et al., eds. 2001. *Bara dalam sekam: Identifikasi akar masalah dan solusi atas konflik-konflik lokal di Aceh, Maluku, Papua dan Riau*. Bandung, LIPI-Mizan Pustaka - Kantor Menristek RI.

Sitohang, Henry H., et al. 2003. *Menuju rekonsiliasi di Halmahera*. Jakarta, Pusat Pemberdayaan untuk Rekonsiliasi dan Perdamaian.

Sjah, Mudaffar. 1999. Solusi kultural dalam konflik Maluku Utara. Ternate, Kesultanan Ternate.

Smith, Jonathan Z. 1982. *Imagining religion: From Babylon to Jonestown*. Chicago, University of Chicago Press.

Sorabji, Cornelia. 2006. Managing memories in post-war Sarajevo: Individuals, bad memories, and new wars. *Journal of the Royal Anthropological Institute* 12(1): 1–18.

Spyer, Patricia. 2002a. Fire without smoke and other phantoms of Ambon's violence: Media effects, agency, and the work of imagination. *Indonesia* 74: 21–36.

———. 2002b. "One slip of the pen: Some notes on writing violence in Maluku." In *Indonesia in transition: Work in progress*, edited by G. Asnan and Henk. Schulte Nordholt, 181-200. Yogyakarta, Pustaka Pelajar.

———. 2002c. "Shadow media and Moluccan Muslim VCDs." In *9/11 and After: A Virtual Casebook*, edited by Barbara Abrash and Faye Ginsburg. New York: Center for Media, Culture, and History Virtual Casebook Series. Accessed January 2007. Available at http://www.nyu.edu/fas/projects/vcb/case_911/fieldreports/spyer.html.

———. 2006a. "Media and violence in an age of transparency: Journalistic writing on war-torn Maluku." In *Religion, media, and the public sphere*, edited by Birgit Meyer and Annelies Moors, 152–65. Bloomington, Indiana University Press.

———. 2006b. "Some notes on disorder in the Indonesian postcolony." In *Law and disorder in the postcolony*, edited by Jean Comaroff and John Comaroff, 188–218. Chicago, University of Chicago Press.

———. 2007. "Christ at large: Iconography and territoriality in postwar Ambon." In *Religion: Beyond a concept*, edited by Hent de Vries, 534-89. Bronx, NY, Fordham University Press.

———. 2008. Blind faith: Painting Christianity in postconflict Ambon. *Social Text* 26(3): 11–37.

Steenbrink, Karel A. 1993. *Dutch colonialism and Indonesian Islam: Contacts and conflicts, 1596–1950*. Amsterdam, Rodopi.

———. 2004. Christianity and Islam: Civilizations or religions? Contemporary Indonesian discussions. *Exchange* 33(3): 223–43.

Stern, Steve J. 2004. *Remembering Pinochet's Chile: On the eve of London, 1998*. Durham, Duke University Press.

———. 2006. *Battling for hearts and minds: Memory struggles in Pinochet's Chile, 1973–1988*. Durham, Duke University Press.

———. 2010. *Reckoning with Pinochet: The memory question in democratic Chile, 1989–2006*. Durham, Duke University Press.

Strenski, Ivan. 2010. *Why politics can't be freed from religion*. Chichester, U.K., Wiley-Blackwell.

Suadey, Ahmad, et al. 2000. *Luka Maluku: Militer terlibat*. Jakarta, Institut Studi Arus Informasi.

Suara Hidayatullah 2000. "Di atas saya ada enam lapis mayat." *Suara Hidayatullah.* 13(3): 66–68.

Suara Peduli Halmahera. 2000a. Data Peristiwa Kerusuhan Payahe – Bagian I. Pitu, Tobelo, Suara Peduli Halmahera.

———. 2000b. Laporan kejadian-kejadian yang berhubungan dengan konflik-konflik yang bernuansa SARA di Maluku-Utara (khususnya di Ternate, Tidore, dan di Halmahera). Pitu, Tobelo, Suara Peduli Halmahera.

Suara Pembaruan. 2000. "FJP jelaskan 3.000-an orang tewas di Halmahera." *Suara Pembaruan.* 8 January.

Suryadinata, Leo, et al. 2003. *Indonesia's population: Ethnicity and religion in a changing political landscape*. Singapore, Institute of Southeast Asian Studies.

Syamsuddin, Sukari, and Basir Awal, eds. 2005. *Moloku Kie Raha dalam perspektif budaya dan sejarah masuknya Islam*. Ternate, Himpunan Pelajar Mahasiswa Ternate.

Sydney Morning Herald. 2000. "Indonesia powerless in face of islands at war." *Sydney Morning Herald*. 5 January.

Tadjoeddin, Mohammad Zulfan. 2002. Database on social violence in Indonesia 1990–2001. Jakarta, United Nations Support Facility for Indonesian Recovery.

Tahalele, Paul, and Thomas Santoso, eds. 1997. *Beginikah kemerdekaan kita?* Surabaya, Forum Komunikasi Kristiani Indonesia.

Tambiah, Stanley J. 1996. *Leveling crowds: Ethnonationalist conflicts and collective violence in South Asia*. Berkeley, University of California Press.

Taylor, Paul M. 2001. "Statement," testimonial presented to the United States Commission on International Religious Freedom. Hearings on religious persecution in Vietnam and Indonesia. 13 February.

Ternate Pos. 1999a. "Ambon bergolak, Sanana meradang." *Ternate Pos*. 26 January–1 February.

———. 1999b. "Ibukota Propinsi Maluku Utara?" *Ternate Pos*. 27 July–2 August.

———. 1999c. "Makian-Malifut, nasibmu kini." *Ternate Pos*. 18–23 August.

———. 2000a. "Bicaralah hanya dengan diam." *Ternate Pos*. 20–26 May.

———. 2000b. "'Hantu' RMS di Maluku Utara." *Ternate Pos*. 25-31 January.

———. 2000c. "Kasus pembantaian di desa Togoliua: Siti Hawa dibakar hidup-hidup." *Ternate Pos*. 18–24 January.

———. 2000d. "Pengakuan Yani Sabi, warga Togoliua: Dua hari menemani jenazah suami." *Ternate Pos*. 18–24 January.

———. 2000e. "'Perdamaian: Harga mati'." *Ternate Pos*. 24–30 October.

———. 2000f. "'Saya tak merekayasa insiden'." *Ternate Pos*. 20–26 May.

———. 2000g. "Setelah enam orang mati." *Ternate Pos*. 9–15 May.

Thalib, Ja'far Umar. 2000. "Menepis rekayasa fatwa seputar jihad di Maluku." *Salafy* 34: 6–10.

———. 2001. *Laskar Jihad Ahlus Sunnah wal Jama'ah: Mempelopori perlawanan terhadap kedurjanaan hegemoni Salibis-Zionis internasional di Indonesia*. Yogyakarta, Divisi Penerangan Forum Komunikasi Ahlus Sunnah wal Jama'ah.

Theidon, Kimberly. 2000. "How we learned to kill our brother?": Memory, morality and reconciliation in Peru. *Bulletin de l'Institut Français d'Études Andines* 29(3): 539–55.

———. 2003. Disarming the subject: Remembering war and imagining citizenship in Peru. *Cultural Critique* 54(1): 67–87.

Tindage, Ruddy. 2001. "Deklarasi damai Muslim-Kristen Maluku Utara." *Komunikasi* (May): 2–3.

———. 2006. *Damai yang sejati: Rekonsiliasi di Tobelo, kajian teologi dan komunikasi*. Jakarta, YAKOMA-PGI.

Tomagola, Tamrin Amal. 1999. Tragedi Maluku Utara. *Masyarakat Indonesia* 25(2): 289–302.

———. 2000a. "The Halmahera of North Moluccas." In *Political violence: Indonesia and India in comparative perspective*, edited by Olle Törnquist, 21-32. Oslo Centre for Development and the Environment, University of Oslo.

———. 2000b. "Kemelut di Jakarta, kematian di Maluku." *Tempo* 28(46): 18–20.

———. 2000c. "Krisis dan solusi tragedi Maluku Utara." *Detik.com.*

———. 2006. *Republik kapling.* Yogyakarta, Resist Book.

Trnka, Susanna. 2008. *State of suffering: Political violence and community survival in Fiji.* Ithaca, Cornell University Press.

Trouillot, Michel-Rolph. 1997. "Silencing the Past: Layers of meaning in the Haitian revolution." In *Between history and histories: The making of silences and commemorations,* edited by Gerald Sider and Gavin Smith, 31–61. Toronto, University of Toronto Press.

Ulaen, Alex J. 2003. *Nusa Utara: Dari lintasan niaga ke daerah perbatasan.* Jakarta, Pustaka Sinar Harapan.

Van der Veer, Peter. 1994. *Religious nationalism: Hindus and Muslims in India.* Berkeley, University of California Press.

Vel, Jacqueline A. C. 2001. Tribal battle in a remote island: Crisis and violence in Sumba (Eastern Indonesia). *Indonesia* 72 (October): 141–58.

Velthoen, Esther J. 1997. "'Wanderers, robbers and bad folk': The politics of violence, protection and trade in Eastern Sulawesi, 1750–1850." In *The last stand of Asian autonomies: Responses to modernity in the diverse states of Southeast Asia and Korea, 1750–1900,* edited by Anthony Reid, 367–88. New York, St. Martin's Press.

Verdery, Katherine. 1999. *The political lives of dead bodies: Reburial and postsocialist change.* New York, Columbia University Press.

Villiers, John. 1988. *Las Yslas de Esperar en Dios*: The Jesuit mission in Moro 1546–1571. *Modern Asian Studies* 22(3): 593–606.

Waileruny, Semuel. 2011. *Membongkar konspirasi di balik konflik Maluku; edisi revisi.* Jakarta, Yayasan Pustaka Obor Indonesia.

Warren, James Francis. 2002. *Iranun and Balangingi: Globalization, maritime raiding, and the birth of ethnicity.* Singapore, Singapore University Press.

Wertheim, Willem F. 1980. Moslems in Indonesia: Majority with minority mentality. Townsville, James Cook University of North Queensland, South East Asian Studies Committee.

Widjojo, Muridan S. 2009. *The revolt of Prince Nuku: Cross-cultural alliance-making in Maluku, c.1780–1810.* Boston, Brill.

Wiener, Margaret. 1999. "Making local history in New Order Bali: Public culture and the politics of the past." In *Staying local in the global village: Bali in the twentieth century,* edited by Raechelle Rubinstein and Linda H. Connor, 51–89. Honolulu, University of Hawai'i Press.

Willis, Avery T. 1977. *Indonesian revival: Why two million came to Christ.* South Pasadena, CA, William Carey Library.

Wilson, Chris. 2008. *Ethno-religious violence in Indonesia: From soil to God.* New York, Routledge.

Woodward, Mark. 1989. *Islam in Java: Normative piety and mysticism in the Sultanate of Yogyakarta.* Tucson, University of Arizona Press.

———. 2007. "Religious conflict and the globalization of knowledge in Indonesian history." In *Religion and conflict in South and Southeast Asia: Disrupting violence,* edited by Linell E. Cady and Sheldon W. Simon, 85–104. New York, Routledge.

———. 2010. Tropes of the Crusades in Indonesian Muslim discourse. *Contemporary Islam* 4(3): 311–30.

———. 2011. *Java, Indonesia and Islam*. New York, Springer.

Yanuarti, Sri, et al. 2003. *Konflik di Maluku Tengah: Penyebab, karakteristik, dan penyelesaian jangka panjang*. Jakarta, LIPI.

———. 2004. *Konflik Maluku Utara: Penyebab, karakteristik, dan penyelesaian jangka panjang*. Jakarta, LIPI.

Zarowsky, Christina. 2000. Trauma stories: Violence, emotion and politics in Somali Ethiopia. *Transcultural Psychiatry* 37(3): 383–402.

Zorbas, Eugenia. 2009. What does reconciliation after genocide mean? Public transcripts and hidden transcripts in post-genocide Rwanda. *Journal of Genocide Research* 11(1): 127–47.

Zubir, M. Goodwill, and Sudar Siandes, eds. n.d. *Potret gerakan Kristenisasi di Indonesia: Versi Da'i LDK Muhammadiyah*. Jakarta, Lembaga Dakwah Khusus, Pimpinan Pusat Muhammadiyah.

INDEX

Note: Page numbers in *italics* indicate illustrations.